THE TWENTY-FIFTH ANNIVERSARY OF VATICAN II
A LOOK BACK
AND A LOOK AHEAD

CONTRIBUTORS TO THIS VOLUME

Carl A. Anderson, J.D.
Dean
John Paul II Institute
Washington, D.C.

Benedict M. Ashley, O.P., Ph.D., S.T.M.
Professor of Philosophy and
Sacred Theology
John Paul II Institute
Washington, D.C.

Michael R. Cummings, Ph.D.
Associate Professor of Genetics
and Development
Department of Biological
Sciences
University of Illinois at Chicago

Patrick G. Derr, Ph.D.
Chair and Professor of Philosophy
Clark University
Worcester, Massachusetts

Avery Dulles, S.J., S.T.D.
Laurence J. McGinley Professor of
Theology
Fordham University

John Finnis, D.Phil.
Professor of Law and Legal
Philosophy
University of Oxford

Germain Grisez, Ph.D.
Harry J. Flynn Professor of
Christian Ethics
Mount Saint Mary's College and
Seminary
Emmitsburg, Maryland

John Haas, Ph.D.
John Cardinal Krol Professor of
Moral Theology
St. Charles Borromeo Seminary
Overbrook, Pennsylvania

John Harvey, O.S.F.S., S.T.D.
Founder of COURAGE
New York City

His Eminence
Bernard Cardinal Law
Archbishop of Boston

Alasdair MacIntyre
McMahon-Hank Professor of
Philosophy
University of Notre Dame

Albert S. Moraczewski, O.P., Ph.D., S.T.M.
Director, Pope John Center
Houston

David L. Schindler, Ph.D.
Editor, COMMUNIO, International
Catholic Review
Notre Dame

Marysia Weber, R.S.M., D.O.
Comprehensive Health Care
Corporation
Alma, Michigan

George Weigel
Ethics and Public Policy Center
Washington, D.C.

THE TWENTY-FIFTH ANNIVERSARY OF VATICAN II A LOOK BACK AND A LOOK AHEAD

Proceedings of
The Ninth Bishops' Workshop
Dallas, Texas

Russell E. Smith
Editor

THE POPE JOHN CENTER

Nihil Obstat: Rev. James A. O'Donohoe, J.C.D.

Imprimatur: Bernard Cardinal Law

The Nihil Obstat and Imprimatur are a declaration that a book or pamphlet is considered to be free from doctrinal or moral error. It is not implied that those who have granted the Nihil Obstat and Imprimatur agree with the contents, opinions or statements expressed.

Copyright 1990
by
The Pope John XXIII Medical-Moral
Research and Education Center
Braintree, Massachusetts 02184

Library of Congress Cataloging-in-Publication Data

The Twenty-Fifth anniversary of Vatican II, a look back and a look
   ahead : proceedings of the Ninth Bishops' Workshop, Dallas, Texas /
   Russell E. Smith editor.
      p. cm.
   "Proceedings of the Bishops' Workshop, February 5–9, 1990, Dallas,
   Texas"—T.p. verso.
   Includes bibliographical references and index.
   ISBN 0-935372-29-6 : $17.95
      1. Catholic Church—Doctrines—Congresses.   2. Christian ethics—
   Catholic authors—Congresses.   3. Vatican Council (2nd :
   1962–1965)—Congresses.   I. Smith, Russell E. (Russell Edward)
   II. Pope John XXIII Medical-Moral Research and Education Center.
   III. Workshop for Bishops of the United States and Canada (9th :
   1990 : Dallas, Tex.)   IV. Title: Look back and a look ahead.
   BX1751.2.T88   1990
   262'.52—dc20   90-20863
                                                                        CIP

Contents

ENDNOTE: A LOOK AHEAD

The Pope John Center presented its Ninth Workshop for Bishops from February 5–9, 1990. This gathering was again made possible through a generous grant from the Knights of Columbus. Several hundred bishops from the Canada, the United States of America, Mexico, the Caribbean and the Philippines gathered for a week of study, reflection and prayer.

The Pope John Center began these workshops in 1980. Workshops have occurred every year since, with the exceptions of 1982 and 1986. Each workshop concentrated on a specific topic or cluster of topics in the field of medical ethics. The lectures and plenary discussions of the workshops are published as proceedings in book form and are all still available from the Pope John Center. The titles are as follows:

New Technologies of Birth and Death (1980)

Human Sexuality and Personhood (1981) (now being revised for reprinting)

Technological Powers and the Person (1983)

Moral Theology Today: Certitudes and Doubts (1984) (with keynote address by Cardinal Ratzinger)

The Family Today and Tomorrow: The Church Addresses Her Future (1985)

Scarce Medical Resources and Justice (1987)

Reproductive Technologies, Marriage and the Church (1988) (a detailed examination of the then recently published *Instruction* on Respect for Human Life in its Origin and on the Dignity of Procreation [*Donum vitæ*])

Critical Issues in Contemporary Health Care (1989)

The title of the 1990 Bishops' Workshop is *The Twenty-fifth Anniversary of Vatican II: A Look Back and a Look Ahead.* The Second Vatican Council concluded on December 8, 1965. On that day, Paul VI declared: "The Second Vatican Ecumenical Council, assembled in the Holy Spirit and under the protection of the Blessed Virgin Mary, whom We have declared Mother of the Church, and of St. Joseph, her glorious spouse, and of the Apostles Sts. Peter and Paul, must be numbered without doubt among the greatest events of the Church." *(Papal Brief Declaring the Council Completed.)* The sixteen documents promulgated during the three year Ecumenical council affect every aspect of the Church's life. The conciliar renewal aimed not only to deepen the Church's understanding of the mysteries of Salvation but also to bring about a renaissance of holiness among all the members of the Church.

Holiness, conformity to the will of God in the example and grace of Christ, has a moral dimension. The dignity of personhood, the objective nature of the moral law and its normative immutability, and the public character of the Church's moral teaching are three pervasive themes in Vatican II's Pastoral Constitution, *Gaudium et spes.* These themes provided the structure for the 1990 Workshop.

His Eminence, Bernard Cardinal Law, the Archbishop of Boston and Pope John Center board member, presented the keynote address. In it, he looked back to *Gaudium et spes* relative to moral theology to see the work that has already taken place and also looked ahead to the future to outline the work yet to be done.

The first full day of the Workshop was dedicated to the Church's teaching on the human person. Philosophy Professor Patrick Derr and theologian Father Benedict Ashley, O.P., examined the historical development and contemporary usages of the concept "person," respectively. This was followed by genetics Professor Michael Cummings' talk on the definition of gene therapy and what its realistic possibilities will be by the year 2000. Father Albert Moraczewski, O.P., editor of the Center's monthly newsletter *Ethics and Medics,* followed this with a philosophical and theological consideration of whether there is a difference between a human being and a human person. He considered this in light of four medical situations in which this is an important concern: the beginning of life, particularly in early pregnancy; the end of life and the "total brain death" criterion for determining death; the persistent vegetative state; and the condition of profound mental retardation.

The question of exceptionless moral norms provided the context for the second full day of the Workshop. Professor of Christian Ethics, Germain Grisez, presented an overview of the arguments in support of the existence of exceptionless moral norms and a critique of the reasons advanced for the view that there are no such norms. Professor of Moral Theology, John Haas, followed this with a presentation of the Church's consistent teaching on the inviolability of innocent human life, based on profession of God, the "Lord and Giver of life," and as applied to the contemporary range of health care decisions from conception until death. Mayo Clinic trained psychiatrist Sister Marysia Weber, R.S.M., then examined the medical aspects of addiction. Moral theologian Father John Harvey, O.S.F.S., examined these medical facts of addictive behaviors in light of the moral teaching of the Church and offered advice about how pastoral ministers can best address these needs.

The final day of the Workshop was devoted to the relationship between "Christian" ethics and public policy. What are the incumbent responsibilities of the Church, of the Catholic faithful and Catholic politicians in the public moral debates of their pluralistic societies? Philosopher John Finnis discussed the complex relationship between faith and reason as sources of the moral doctrine of the Church. Philosopher Alasdair MacIntyre described the revival of classical moral theory, based on human reason and human action which derives from cultivation of moral character. This rediscovery and advocacy of the virtues was occasioned by the inadequacy of impoverished developments in moral theory, such as pragmatism, hedonism and consequentialism.

The dean of the Pope John Paul II Institute on Marriage and the Family, Carl Anderson, addressed the current debates about public policy. In a pluralistic society the Church has a particularly difficult role contributing to discussions and decisions on matters of public policy. She does this by means of integrating natural law principles and gospel values. The answer to the question of how much of the Church's moral doctrine derives from reason and how much from revelation largely determines what she can expect to contribute to public policy. This can be illustrated by examples taken from issues such as abortion, use of human fetuses for research and transplantation, and euthanasia.

The Workshop concluded with a panel discussion of Pastor Richard John Neuhaus's book, *The Catholic Moment: The Paradox of the Church in the Postmodern World* (Harper and Row, 1987.) The panel consisted of George Weigel of the Ethics and Public Policy Center in Washington, D.C., David Schindler, the editor of the English language edition of *Communio,* and world renowned ecclesiologist Father Avery Dulles, S.J. Each panelist discussed his views on if and how this might be "The Catholic Moment" for decisive Christian public involvement. Each considered the "signs of the times" and spoke about the Catholic Church's unique potential to contribute to the formation of culture and to proclaim human values in a secular humanist ambience.

The Pope John Center presents this volume of the Workshop proceedings for many reasons. Many symposia and conferences will be held this year in honor of the completion of the Second Vatican Council. The Pope John Center would like to contribute to the celebration of "one of the most significant events of the Church," to borrow Pope Paul VI's phrase. We present this collection of essays and discussions to those who are engaged in the pastoral and health care ministries of the Church. We hope that this volume finds its way to seminary libraries and houses of religious formation to assist those who must know and communicate the message of the Church. For the same reason, we offer this volume to all the Catholic faithful, and those beyond her borders who wish to know her teaching and understand its application. To all we say, *"Tolle, lege... fruere!"*

* * *

Many people contributed generously to the successful execution of the 1990 Workshop for Bishops. The planning, content and hospitality necessary for an international event of this magnitude depend on many hard-working, self-sacrificing individuals who obviously love the Church very much. We are very grateful to everyone who made this Workshop such a success.

We are very grateful to the Supreme Knight, Mr. Virgil C. Dechant, and to the Knights of Columbus for their generous sponsorship of this workshop. We are also very grateful to the faculty of this year's workshop, for their patience with the many deadlines and for their scholarly competence and presentations.

Special thanks go to the Most Reverend Thomas Tschoepe, Bishop of Dallas, for his gracious hospitality. Thanks also to the staff and seminarians of Holy Trinity Seminary at the University of Dallas for serving the Masses, singing, and acting as sacristans. In this regard, special thanks go to Father Thomas Cloherty for overseeing all the liturgical arrangements. We are also very grateful to the local councils of the Knights of Columbus and the Catholic Women's Guilds of the Diocese of Dallas for their kind assistance. Thanks also to the Spanish translators—Father Rudy Vela and his band from San Antonio and Forth Worth, and Sister M. Nieves, P. D. D. M., of the Sister Disciples of the Divine Master at the Liturgical Apostolate Center in Boston.

We are also grateful to the staff of the Doubletree Hotel at Lincoln Centre in Dallas for their graciousness and service. A very special word of thanks goes to the Nuns of the Poor Clare Federation of Mary Immaculate who prayed for the success and for the participants of the conference. Finally, we are deeply grateful to Mrs. Jeanne Burke and Mr. Donald Powers for their very hard work and diligent assistance from the beginning of this Workshop's conception to the moment this book was delivered to your hands.

The Reverend Russell E. Smith, S.T.D.

Editor

Feast of Blessed Fray Junípero Serra, O.F.M.
Boston, Massachusetts

To my brother Bishops
from North and Central America
The Caribbean and The Philippines

I greet you with great joy in the name of our Lord Jesus Christ. You have come from the widely scattered dioceses of Canada, the Caribbean, Central America, Mexico, the Philippines and the United States for the ninth Workshop organized by the Pope John XXIII Medical-Moral Research and Education Center. I join you once again this year in thanking the Knights of Columbus for their generous assistance in making possible these days of study and prayer.

The general theme of this year's gathering makes reference to the Holy Spirit's extraordinary gift to the Church that was the Second Vatican Council. Your reflections on "The Twenty-fifth Anniversary of Vatican II: A Look Back and a Look Ahead" offer you the opportunity to underline the past, present and future fruitfulness of the Council in the Church's life and mission. Truly, the Council constituted a great outpouring of the Holy Spirit upon the People of God. As I stated in the Encyclical Letter *Dominum et Vivificantem:* "Following the guidance of the Spirit of truth and bearing witness together with him, the Council has given a special confirmation of the presence of the Holy Spirit—the Counsellor. In a certain sense, the Council has made the Spirit newly 'present' in our difficult age. In the light of this conviction one grasps more clearly the great importance of all the initiatives aimed at implementing the Second Vatican Council, its teaching and its pastoral and ecumenical thrust" (No. 26).

Drawing from the richness of the conciliar teaching, your Workshop will focus on three specific themes of the Church's magisterium which deeply affect her mission: the dignity of the human person, the objective moral law, and the relationship between the Church and the world.

The Pastoral Constitution on the Church in the Modern World *Gaudium et spes* includes an entire chapter on the *dignity of the human person* (cf. Nos. 12–22). It teaches that man's inalienable dignity stems from the fact that he is created in the image of God, that he is capable of knowing and loving his Creator, and that he has received dominion over all other earthly creatures, which are to be responsibly used for the glory of God (cf. *ibid.,* 12). In a word, the human person is the one creature on earth that God willed for its own sake (cf. *ibid.,* 24).

These principles are the foundations of Christian anthropology, which, based on the Gospel, leads man to discover the full truth about himself, namely, his belonging to Christ. Everyone who is in Christ is raised to the status of a child of God, the object of divine condescension. This mystery of God's life-giving love for His children foreshadows and is the very source of our definitive glorification: 'the glory of God is the living man, yet man's life is the vision of God' (cf. St. Irenaeus, *Adversus haereses,* IV,20,7; cf. *Dominum et Vivificantem,* 59). Herein lies our greatest dignity and highest destiny.

Moreover, as your reflections will indicate, a constitutive factor of the human person's dignity as a creature redeemed by Christ is the capacity to know and observe the *objective moral law.* When speaking of the responsible transmission of life, the Council Fathers clearly taught that in making moral choices, "the morality of one's actions does not depend solely on the sincerity of the intention or the evaluation of motives, but it must be determined according to objective criteria drawn from the nature of the person and his acts" (*Gaudium et spes,* 51). In the heart of the human person is a law inscribed by God, a law which man "does not impose upon himself" (*ibid.,* 16; cf. also 51 and Rom 2:15–16). Thus, the person's innate dignity is safeguarded and affirmed through loving obedience to God's law, the rule of all moral activity.

Finally, your discussions will center on *the Church's relationship to the world*. In fact, the leaven of the Gospel enriches the world in so far as the Christian faithful bear effective witness in their lives and work to the truth about man's dignity and direct their actions according to the moral law. "In their pilgrimage to the heavenly city," the Council Fathers taught, "Christians are to seek and savor the things that are above. Yet this does not lessen, but increases the weight of their obligation to work with all people for the building up of a world that is more human. Indeed, the mystery of the Christian faith provides them with outstanding incentives and encouragement to fulfill this task with even greater energy" (*ibid.,* 57; cf. also 23–32, 40–45, 53–90).

Dear brothers, I wish to express my fraternal encouragement for your attention to the important themes of your meeting. May your discussions serve to renew your sense of pastoral responsibility, faced as you are by the profound confusion regarding fundamental principles of life and action affecting many people today. As man develops an ever greater knowledge and control of the world around him, he is often increasingly less able to understand himself and the purpose of his life. Your people look to the Church for wise and truthful guidance that will help them discover their human and Christian vocation and respond to it with confidence.

May the Holy Spirit inspire and enlighten you so that, as faithful and zealous pastors of the Church, you may explain the truths of faith and apply them with courage and compassion. May Mary, Seat of Wisdom and Mother of the Church, intercede for you in your service to her Divine Son and His Gospel. To all of you I willingly impart my Apostolic Blessing.

From the Vatican, January 20, 1990.

GREETINGS FROM THE KNIGHTS OF COLUMBUS

Virgil C. Dechant
Supreme Knight

It is my privilege, once again, to add a word of welcome to all of you on behalf of the officers and the Board of Directors of the Knights of Columbus, our one and a half million members and their families that represent the various countries in which we exist as well as my own personal welcome. In my travels, be it in the United States, Canada, Mexico, the Philippines, the Caribbean or parts of Central and South America, I often meet members of the hierarchy and invariably you comment on how much you derive spiritually, intellectually and socially from attending these workshops. One observation that is expressed frequently is that the information made available here by the expert presenters could not be had otherwise without hours and hours of reading, study and reflection. For this we, of course, owe a debt of gratitude to the Board and the staff of the Pope John XXIII Center.

As a lay order, the Knights of Columbus has always had as one of its basic principles, respect for the priesthood. Certainly, we strive at the international level to offer affirmation in a number of ways to the Holy Father, to our bishops and the Bishops' Conferences wherever we exist. We hope and trust that these initiatives provide example to our Knights at the state and local levels to go out and do likewise. And I'm sure that many of you can attest to the fact that our brothers are, indeed, doing that.

The theme of this workshop centering in as it does on the Second Vatican Council, is certainly apropos. Its emphasis on the meaning of personhood, on morality and ethics in society and in the area of health care and on the role of the Church in the future, focus in on many of the questions that confront you as bishops today. Surely, not all of the answers to current dilemmas will come shining through during this week, but we hope, at least, that some of the answers to the problems you face daily will be provided.

Please, also, allow me for a moment to call attention to the program of studies offered in Washington, D.C. by the Pope John Paul II Institute for Study on Marriage and the Family. This North American campus of the John Paul II Institute was founded with the blessing of the Holy Father and is sponsored and underwritten entirely by the Knights of Columbus. If you have in your diocese candidates for graduate degrees in these areas of study, please consider the Pope John Paul II Institute. I am happy to note, also, that several of its faculty members will be making presentations here at this workshop.

And, finally, Anne and I and my Knights of Columbus associates who are here extend our best wishes to each of you along with our prayers that the Holy Spirit will guide these deliberations and that Mary, the Mother of the Church, will watch over us all.

Thank you very much.

THE TWENTY-FIFTH ANNIVERSARY
OF VATICAN II
A LOOK BACK AND A LOOK AHEAD

**His Eminence
Bernard Cardinal Law
Archbishop of Boston**

As someone who has had contact with these Dallas workshops from the beginning, I know how absolutely indispensable is the support given by the Knights of Columbus, and I know how indefatigable is the work of the staff of the Pope John XXIII Center and all those who assist the staff in these workshops. I trust that it is not presumptuous to express to them the gratitude of us all.

We gather as bishops, year after year, to reflect upon the moral implications of bio-medical research and practice. It is

1

precisely our role as bishops which provides the context for my words this evening.

Twenty-five years ago the Second Vatican Council was concluded. Our ministry as bishops, if it is to be responsive to the spirit at work in our times, is a ministry which attempts to give faithful articulation, faithful expression to the teaching, to the spirit and, perhaps more importantly, to the spirituality of that singular ecclesial event.

When Pope Paul VI, who had been a participant in the Council's first session as a bishop, addressed the Council Fathers on the concluding day, December 7, 1965, he reminded them, and I quote: "The old story of the Samaritan has been the model of the spirituality of the Council. A feeling of boundless sympathy has permeated the whole of it. The attention of our Council has been absorbed by the discovery of human needs."

How apt it is for us to spend a few moments as we begin this year's workshop in considering the implication of the spirituality of the Good Samaritan for the whole Church and for us as bishops.

Before the event and in anticipation of what it might mean for the Church, Pope John XXIII spoke of opening a window so that the breath of the Holy Spirit might be more keenly felt within the Church. Surely we have experienced the fulfillment of his hope in the renewal of worship, in the commitment to the ecumenical movement and to inter-religious understanding and cooperation, in the more effective presence of the Church with those who suffer the deprivation of freedom, of food, or of shelter. Only last week the Holy Father raised his voice again on behalf of the continent of Africa reminding the wealthier and more powerful nations of the world of their unfulfilled responsibility to alleviate the poverty which haunts so many of our brothers and sisters throughout the globe, and particularly in Africa.

While Pope John XXIII caught in a phrase the hopes for the Council when he spoke of the opening of a window, it is a Lutheran Pastor, speaking more than twenty years after the event, who so well articulates the task of the Church in the light of the Council when he says: "John Paul has entered the modern world to help open the windows of the modern world to the worlds of which it is part." Pastor Neuhaus continues, "He (Pope John Paul II) is attempting to chart a Christian course that is not so much against modernity as it is beyond modernity. The only modernity to be discarded is the debased modernity of unbelief that results in a prideful and premature closure of the world against its promised destiny."

In addressing the opening session of the Council on October 11, 1962, John XXIII said:

> The solicitude of the Church in promoting and defending the truth derives from the fact that, according to the plan of God, 'who wishes that all men be saved and come to the knowledge of the truth' (1Tm 2:4) humanity cannot, without the help of the whole of revealed doctrine, attain a complete and secure unity of spirit, on which depends true peace and eternal well being.

Pope Paul VI in his closing address echoes this same theme when he says:

> We call upon those who term themselves modern human- ists, and who have renounced the transcendent value of the highest realities, to give the Council credit at least for one quality and to recognize our new type of humanism: we, too, in fact, we more than others, honor mankind . . . The Catholic religion and human life reaffirm their alli- ance with one another, the fact that they converge on one single human reality: the Catholic is for mankind; in a cer- tain sense it is the life of mankind. It is so by the ex- tremely precise and sublime interpretation that our religion gives of humanity (surely man by himself is a mys- tery to himself) and gives this interpretation in virtue of its knowledge of God: a knowledge of God is a prerequisite for a knowledge of man as he really is, in all his fullness; for proof of this let it suffice for now to recall the ardent expression of Catherine of Siena, 'in your nature, eternal God, I shall know my own.'

The theme of unity is central to the Council's work. This is a theme which is reflected in its magnificent treatment of the Church, of the Church's mission in the world, of ecumenism. It is a

3

theme that is evident in its teaching of divine revelation and the relation of scripture and tradition. It is the theme so evident in what Pope Paul VI called the spirituality of the Council, the spirituality of the Good Samaritan. The Council was called not to decide disputed doctrine or punish heretics, but to discover and reanimate the Church's mission to the world of our day, to heal the world's wounds.

All too often there are efforts to set one reading of the Council over against another. Not infrequently a false opposition is articulated between the ecclesiology of *Lumen gentium* and the ecclesiology of *Gaudium et spes*. How essential it is to be clear in our own minds as bishops that there is no opposition here. The Church of *Gaudium et spes* is the Church of *Lumen gentium*.

The Council addressed itself to the question of moral life in three of its great Constitutions, *Dei Verbum, Lumen gentium, Gaudium et spes*. There one sees expressed the following themes: the role of bishops as pastors in the Church; the nature of human moral action; the action of the Church as a believing community in and for the world.

I. A Look Back: The Second Vatican Council and Moral Teaching.

A. The Gospel is the source of every moral norm (*DV* 7). The role of the Church and her Pastors.

Dei Verbum clearly sets forth our role as bishops in transmitting the full and living Gospel to successive ages. Christ the Lord, in whom the entire revelation of the most high God is summed up (cf. 2Cor 1:20; 3:16—4:6) commanded the apostles to preach the Gospel, which had been promised beforehand by the prophets, and which he fulfilled in his own person and promulgated with his own lips. In preaching the Gospel, they were to communicate the gifts of God to all men. This Gospel was to be the source of all saving truth and moral discipline. This was faithfully done: it was done by the apostles who handed on, by the spoken word of their preaching, by the example they gave, by the institutions they established, what they themselves had received—whether from the lips of Christ, from his way of life and his works, or whether they had learned it at the prompting of the Holy Spirit; it was done by those apostles and other men associated with the apostles who, under the inspiration of the same Holy Spirit, committed the message of salvation to writing.

In order that the full and living Gospel might always be preserved in the Church the apostles left bishops as their successors. (*DV* 7).

The foundation of every moral norm, then, is the Gospel, the Good News of Salvation given in the person of Christ in whom the whole of God's saving action is united.

The moral life is presented directly within the context of the announcement of God's reign in Jesus by the Church through her pastors.

The Apostles, and bishops, have a central role in the proclamation of the Good News in Tradition and Scripture. Every moral norm must find its foundation in the action of the Church's pastors building up the Church according to the vision of Jesus' own words and actions and under the guidance of the Holy Spirit.

B. The objective moral order (*GS* 51).

As we look back at the Council to assist us today in our task of incarnating the spirituality of the Samaritan, the Council's teaching on the objective moral order is of critical importance. When we speak, in the Catholic tradition, of the objective moral order, we refer to the nature of the human person and human actions seen in the light of human destiny. We point to our inner unity between the act and its end, between acts, and between the acting human person and his or her ultimate destiny.

Addressing the question of moral decisions as regards married love and respect for human life, the Council texts emphasize the importance of seeing beyond the question of good intentions, to the question of how the decision to be made accords with the nature of human reality and the demands of authentic human action:

> When it is a question of harmonizing married love with the responsible transmission of life, it is not enough to take only the good intention and the evaluation of motives into account; the objective criteria must be used, criteria drawn from the nature of the human person and human action, criteria which respect the total meaning of mutual self-giving and human procreation in the context of true love... (*GS* 51).

Human nature is recognized in that unity of bodily and spiritual realities which make up the life of the individual. Moral life, then, is a service to this inner unity which is the constitution of the human person. The Council puts this clearly:

> Man, though made of body and soul, is a unity. Through his very bodily condition he sums up in himself the elements of the material world.... For by his power to know himself in the depths of his being he rises above the whole universe of mere objects. (*GS* 14).

The inner ability of man to know his true self and to recognize the law which God has inscribed in his very being, is the concept of conscience:

> Deep within his conscience man discovers a law which he has not laid upon himself, but which he must obey. Its voice ever calling him to love and to do what is good and to avoid evil, tells him inwardly at the right moment: do this, shun that. For man has in his heart a law inscribed by God. His dignity lies in observing this law, and by it he will be judged. (*GS* 16).

C. The infallibility of the *"Sensus Fidei"* of the People of God in moral matters (*LG* 12).

The Church as a community of believers in the world.

The third reference of the Council texts to the question of moral action underscores the role of the Church herself as a hierarchical community of believers, called to bring witness to the world concerning the inner life of faith:

> The holy people of God shares also in Christ's prophetic office: it spreads abroad a living witness to him, especially by a life of faith and love and by offering to God a sacrifice of praise, the fruit of lips praising his name (Heb 13:15). The whole body of the faithful who have an anointing that comes from the Holy One (cf. 1Jn 2:20, 27) cannot err in matters of belief. This characteristic is shown in the supernatural appreciation of the faith (*sensus fidei*) of the whole people, when, 'from the bishops to the last of the faithful' they manifest a universal consent in matters of faith and morals. (*LG* 12).

In this unanimity of belief the Church fulfills in an eminent way her role in the mission of salvation: "Since the Church, in Christ, is in the nature of sacrament—a sign and instrument, that is, of communion with God and of unity among all men ... " (*LG* 1)

It is especially in matters of faith and in questions regarding the moral life that the Church, as a community of believers, gives witness according to her inner nature as a communion drawn together by God's grace, to reveal to the world its own destiny, its calling to live in the unity of peace among all peoples by living in union with God.

II. Current issues.

A. The role of Scripture and Church tradition in the discovery of true moral norms.

In recent years, especially in regard to the questions and challenges arising within the medical field, there has been a growing tendency to miss the centrality of faith in assessing and responding to contemporary problems. On the one hand, there is the ever growing technical advancement often accompanied by an unfortunate tendency to reduce the human person to the status of an object, to lose sight of the total person and his or her spiritual destiny. On the other hand, it has become clear that ready answers to many of today's problems arising from the new scientific, medical, and technological capabilities which we have, with God's help, developed, are not usually found in the pages of the four Gospels.

Precisely with this in mind, one can see the importance of the living tradition of the Gospel, of the role of the Church, in her pastors, reflecting on our lives before God and in using that insight to assess and to evaluate the challenges which are placed before us today and in every age. Today, however, we experience a marginalization of the role of the teaching office of pastors within the Church, especially as regards questions of medical moral matters. Some see the Church as having nothing to say about these, "matters of fact"; others approach very complex and important questions with a superficial fideism "if God wanted man to fly . . . "; still others allow the Church to offer only a subsequent reflection or judgement on the goodness of new technologies and treatments, after the fact of their development and implementation.

Moral decisions should not be separated from the total vision of human life given to us in revelation, the truth about Christ, about man and about the world, as Pope John Paul II said in Puebla. Moral reasoning cannot be reduced to a calculus, (proportionalism), but must arise from within our life in Christ, a relational life which has its own dynamic. Morality must be at the service of man's inner unity. The best way to guarantee the primacy of man in medical moral decisions is the recognition of the living role of the Church and her pastors in proclaiming the Good News. It is in this living proclamation of Jesus' new life, that "every moral norm" finds its true foundation, because this Good News reveals the truth about man and his destiny in God.

B. The human reality: the natural moral law.

One of the grave problems which we face today is not only the loss of vision of revelation and of the central role of the Church's teaching office in the life of faith and in moral decisions, but the loss of the vision of the human person.

The contemporary mind forgets or fails to assess the goodness and prudence of proposed moral actions in light of the good of the whole human person, in all one's aspects, and in light of a destiny in God. This kind of assessment is what we mean by a reflection on the natural moral law. Far from the "law of nature" which can, at

8

times be brutal and destructive, the natural moral law refers to the whole of human reality, based on the nature of the human person and of human action (intellectual, emotional and motor); it is the full truth about man and his destiny as presented in the light of human reason, illumined by faith.

Today, there is a tendency to split the human person into discreet areas of interest, losing sight of the whole. There is a vain and damaging attempt to separate the bodily well-being of the person from spiritual well-being. In American culture this split is lived out as a division of "private" lives or concerns (subjective) from the "public" order (objective). The private is the creation of individual desire and the public the result of brokered convention, usually legislated by predominance of competing interests and adjudicated externally in the courts. The abortion tragedy as debated in the media and by politicians is a case in point.

The same tragic split is made manifest in the disintegration of married life, and of families, of the terrible destruction of drug abuse, and in the decline in sexual morality.

In so many ways, the heritage of the subject/ object dichotomy in modern philosophy has shown itself in our culture's self-understanding. What is so often missing is a vision of the unity of the human person, seen in light of his destiny in God and as reflected in the natural moral law. Without this vision, man comes to be treated as a means (exploited for economic gain; used for political predominance of power; object of experimentation; reduced to the role of consumer), rather than as an end.

How difficult it is to bring to bear in public debate that unified vision of the human person which the Church has to offer.

Moral action not only is to reflect that unity, but also, as pointed out so well by the Holy Father, moral action constitutes and strengthens that unity. The human person finds himself in the moment of moral action (John Paul II) more fundamentally than in thinking (Descartes) or in acts of desire (Freud), because in right moral action the split of subjective and objective is overcome, as the true good of the human person is "enacted" in a decision for the good and in the commitment to live out that decision in the circumstances of life.

It is the vocation of the Catholic to give witness to this total vision in the quality of one's own life. This is reflected in the

9

vocation of the lay person in the world: one is called to give concrete witness to the unity between the spiritual insight of that law which God writes on our hearts and the demands and challenges of one's daily life and duties. How immensely important is this in the world of medical research and practice today. If Catholic lay persons do not fulfill this vocation, then how can their respective fields of endeavor be brought into the service of the true good of humankind?

C. The lack of social consensus on important moral concerns.

Following the lack of a vision of the union of human life with God as revealed in the Good News of Jesus, following upon the subsequent difficulty in achieving a unified vision of the total good for the human person, the society of today finds it difficult to appreciate the common good as it is reflected in the life of the community. There is a lack of a common sense of the rightness of things and on the direction which our life has or should have. Rather than focus on the common good, public policy debate too easily degenerates into an arena of special interests competing one with another. Moral concerns are reduced to a consideration of "my values" as opposed to "theirs"; consensus on the recognition of the good is reduced to the affirmation of a false freedom formulated in aggressive terms: "who are you to impose your values on me!!!". An exaggerated sense of "tolerance" or "openness" is a thin gloss over the tragic failure to deal with the realities of our common humanity and of our common destiny in God. This leads to a false irenicism in which the pursuit of the full truth is left aside for the superficial agreement of the lowest common opinion. A radical relativism takes over in which it is denied that there are any common abiding goods, evils, norms, moral actions. Rather, the common life is reduced to a happenstance play of economic, social or political factors in constant change and competition with one another.

The result is a society enslaved to any number of partial goods, but not of true freedom and peace. No truly "public" discussion of moral matters takes place because no common ground for our community life is recognized, much less lived. Since man is by his essence a social reality, this state is an injustice to the human person. Religion and religious concerns as regards the moral dimensions of life, including medical moral questions, are marginalized to the private personal sphere as if what is at stake were just one's peculiar opinions about life.

This relativization of religious concerns returns us to the question with which we started, the determinative role of revelation and the role of the Church's teaching in moral matters.

III. A Look Ahead.

A. The Bishops as Teachers of the Faith.

The Council's attention to the theme of unity was one of its principal characteristics. It was a Council of and about the Church, that mystery of unity with one another and with God.

The bishop emerges in the Gospel and tradition as a servant of unity. He serves that unity in the local Church entrusted to his care and, together with the other bishops under the Holy Father, he serves that unity in the entire Church.

As moral teacher fulfilling the mission to preach Jesus' Good News in season and out, the bishop serves the union of each of the faithful with God. From the perspective of that original vocation to oneness of life with God, the vocation to holiness, the bishop as moral teacher is to serve, to build-up in the faithful a recognition of the unity of every aspect of life in one's calling to a union of life with God.

As leader of the Church, the bishop is called to build-up the communion of life which is the Church. In this way, the Church becomes a servant and promoter of the unity of the whole human family.

B. The Church as a moral teacher in an unbelieving world.

The moral teaching of the Church which the bishops minister is not an extrinsic command which is imposed over and against the vital flow and strivings of human life. Rather, it is a reflection on the truth about Christ, about man and about the world which reveals to the faithful the inner dynamism of their own lives, as received from God.

The moral teaching of the Church favors the unity of the human person and promotes a vision of the totality of human life by which the various aspects under question can be better judged and acted upon. The Church invites all to be conscientiously aware of the objective realities of human life and of human destiny in God, and to have the courage to act in accord with that truth.

C. The moral basis of universal solidarity and world peace. (*GS* 89, 78).

The Church is to be a servant of the unity of the entire human family. She does this by witnessing to the fundamental moral character of human life in each of her members. She does this by witnessing to and pointing out those abiding truths which are the common heritage of humankind because they are rooted in our nature and in the nature of human actions. She does this in turning from sin and in following the command of the Lord. The victory over sin and death which is God's word to the Church is the only word of salvation for the world as well. The peace and universal solidarity for which the world longs comes only through the word of Jesus and through the life of the Church in fulfilling her mission on Jesus' behalf. In the words of *Gaudium et spes*:

> The Church, in preaching the Gospel to all men and dispensing the treasures of grace in accordance with its divine mission, makes a contribution to the strengthening of peace over the whole world and helps to consolidate the foundations of brotherly communion among men and peoples. This it does by imparting the knowledge of the divine and natural law. (*GS* 89).

> Christ, the Word made flesh, the prince of peace, reconciled all men to God by the cross, and, restoring the unity of all in one people and one body, he abolished hatred in his own flesh, having been lifted up in his resurrection he poured forth the Spirit of love into the hearts of men. (*GS* 78).

The Church is a sacrament of universal solidarity because bishops as servants of ecclesial unity cooperate with the Spirit to fashion the Church in such a way as prefigures the future unity of all in God.

One of the characteristics of the Church should be its universal assent to the truths of faith and of moral life (*sensus fidei*). If, in fact, in our day we bishops are confronted with a Church and society in which incorrect and sometimes bitter divisions have arisen, this should not concern us only as a problem of external agreement or consent, something to do with the strategy of the Church in the public sphere. Rather, we have as a task the fostering of the common recognition of the truth: about Christ, about humankind and about God. This is significant for the inner health of the Church, as such, and remains an immense and pressing duty in our day. Our work must be more than the imposition of assent, however; it must be the winning over of minds and hearts by the strength of the truth which we are to speak in love (Eph 4:15). Without the inner unity of the Church in faith and morals, the hope of the world for its salvation grows dim.

The Fathers of the Extraordinary Synod of 1985 suggested that a catechism or compendium of all Catholic doctrine regarding both faith and morals be composed, a suggestion accepted by Pope John Paul II as responding "to a real need both of the universal Church and the particular Churches." This project certainly reflects a consciousness of our responsibility, as bishops, to the building up of the *sensus fidei.* We must not, at the peril of our own salvation, remain passive spectators as the *sensus fidei* is further eroded by an ersatz theology of dissent.

Conclusion.

We bishops do not gather here in Dallas as experts in medical matters, and we do not presume to function alone in deciding the moral questions which here arise.

At the same time, however, the bishop, as he serves the spiritual well-being of the faithful and of the Church community is not engaged in something at the "edge" of modern concerns. Rather, our task always enters into the very heart of what it means to be a human person in the world and before God, and so defines the framework, based on the Gospel and nourished by the living Tradition of the Church community, of every moral decision even the most complex and difficult.

As we recognize in faith, the wider community of the world depends on the work which is ours to do especially as ministers of the unity of the Church and as teachers in matters of faith and morals. In many ways, the moral sphere is the most challenging before us. Our success in promoting a vision of life among those engaged in the medical profession will define the ultimate goodness and correctness of what they do.

The wounds of today's world cannot be healed by medicine alone. They are wounds much deeper than the distress of dreaded diseases such as AIDS, or the fear of death itself, for they have to do with the unity of the human person within, and the unity of the human family.

The Church sees herself, then, as the Good Samaritan, bringing the best that she has to offer, in respect and deep compassion, to bind up and to heal the wounds of the world in this age and every age; she brings the Word of Life.

PART ONE

THE CHURCH'S TEACHING ON THE HUMAN PERSON

Chapter 2

THE HISTORICAL DEVELOPMENT OF THE VARIOUS CONCEPTS OF PERSONHOOD

Patrick Derr, Ph.D.

Introduction[1]

This essay will survey the history of the concept of the human person in Western thought and culture. The first part will survey some of the claims that philosophers have made about what it means to *be* a person. The second part will survey some of the claims that philosophers have made about which living beings should be *counted as* persons. The first question, about the *nature* of persons, is the *intensional* problem of personhood. The second question, about which living beings are to be *recognized* as persons, is the *extensional* problem of personhood.

Please notice that, in the following analysis, the term "human being" will be used to indicate that an entity is a living member of our species. Thus, the term "human being" will be used in a strictly biological sense. The term "person," on the other hand, will be used to indicate that an entity has a very special kind of moral status—that it deserves respect, for example, in the way that dogs or chickens do not. Here are some examples: Bishop Timothy Harrington is *both* a human being *and* a person. Sperm cells and gorillas are *neither* human beings *nor* persons. The Archangel Gabriel is *not* a human being but *is* a person. Fetuses *are* human beings but, according to a certain false ideology which now dominates North American law and medicine, they are *not* persons.

I: History of the Intension of the Concept of the Person

(A) The Mosaic Concept of the Person

The fundamental message of *Genesis* regarding the human person is that man is both an enfleshed creature of this world and a living image of the immaterial God. Thus we read:[2]

> Yahweh God fashioned man of dust from the soil.
> Then he breathed into his nostrils a breath of life,
> and thus man became a living being. [*Genesis* 2:7]

And:

> God created man in the image of himself,
> in the image of God he created him,
> male and female he created them. [*Genesis* 1:27]

The human person is not an angel or spirit, but a living body—a body which is made of this earth, which has a sexual identity, and which is good. Yet this body is alive, and human, and an image of the living God, only by virtue of a divine breath which is not from this world.

Genesis also calls attention to man's essentially social character. Thus we read, at *Genesis* 2:8, "It is not good for man to be alone."

18

That is the original view: the human person is a single, fleshy thing which has received from God a very special kind of life, which lives that life in community, and which is an image of the Lord.

(B) The Greek Concept of the Person

Plato offers a view of the person which is almost completely at odds with the original Mosaic view. For Plato, the person is essentially a mind or soul. The body is not only alien to our true being, it is an impediment, a burden which drags us away from our true good. Thus, in the *Phaedo*,[3] Plato refers to the body as "... an impediment which by its presence prevents the soul from attaining to truth and clear thinking." [66a] A little later in the same text, he writes:

> So long as we keep to the body and our soul is contaminated with this imperfection, there is no chance of our ever attaining satisfactorily to our object, which we assert to be truth. [66b]

> We are in fact convinced that if we are ever to have pure knowledge of anything, we must get rid of the body... [66d]

> ... so long as we are alive... [let us] avoid as much as we can all contact and association with the body, except when they are absolutely necessary, and instead of allowing ourselves to become infected with its nature, purify ourselves from it until God himself gives us deliverance. [67a]

Indeed, Plato writes:

> The philosopher's occupation consists precisely in freeing... the soul from the body. [67d]

In sum, for Plato, the person is some sort of disembodied ego. As for the body, it is a bad and contaminated thing, utterly different than our true being. Far from deserving respect or study, the body deserves to be despised in precisely the manner that a prisoner despises his prison. As we shall see, these Platonic themes have haunted Western cultures for more than two millennia, habitually predisposing it to every variety of Manichean error.

The greatest of the Greek philosophers, Aristotle, offers a view of the human person which is profoundly different from Plato's. In many ways, Aristotle's view is much nearer to *Genesis* than to the *Phaedo.* In *De Anima,* for example, Aristotle writes:[4]

> ... we can wholly dismiss as unnecessary the question whether the soul and the body are one: it is as meaningless as to ask whether the wax and the shape given to it by the stamp are one, or generally the matter of a thing and that of which it is the matter. [*De Anima,* Bk. II, Chpt. 1]

A little later, in the same text, Aristotle writes:

> As the pupil *plus* the power of sight constitutes the eye, so the soul *plus* the body constitutes the animal. [*De Anima,* Bk. II, Chpt. 1]

Far from adopting Plato's view of the soul as something opposed to and trapped within a hostile body, Aristotle describes the soul as "the essence of the whole living body." [*De Anima,* Bk. II, Chpt. 4]

In *De Anima,* as elsewhere, Aristotle is careful to point out that the soul—which is the form or essence of the whole human person—must never be confused with any particular power (such as sensation or thinking), although, of course, the soul is the *source* of such powers. [*De Anima,* Bk. II, Chpt. 2]

Finally, as *Genesis* has man created in intimate community, so does Aristotle emphasize the essentially social nature of the person. In the *Nichomachean Ethics* we read:

> For without friends no one would choose to live, though he had all other goods. [*Nicomachaen Ethics,* Bk. VIII, Chpt. 1]

> ... no one would choose the whole world on condition of being alone, since man is a political creature and one

20

whose nature is to live with others. [*Nicomachaen Ethics*, Bk. IX, Chpt. 9]

In the *Politics*, Aristotle observes that "... man is by nature a social animal." [*Politics*, Bk. I, Ch. 2] He continues:

> But he who is unable to live in society... must be either a beast or a god: he is no part of a state. A social instinct is implanted in all men by nature... [Politics, Bk. I, Chpt. 2]

In sum, according to Aristotle, the human person is a single fleshy being, which is essentially social. The human person can no more be divided into a body and a soul than the Pieta can be divided into a stone and a shape. All of these Aristotelian themes are confirmed and enriched by Saint Thomas.

(C) Medieval Concepts of the Person

As between Plato's vision of the person and Aristotle's vision of the person, there is no doubt that Aquinas sides with Aristotle. But Thomas also completes Aristotle, adding for the first time an adequate theological understanding of the soul and of the human person's immortal destiny with God. In *De Ente et Essentia* he stresses the person's unity:[5]

> That is why we say that man is a rational animal, and not that he is composed of animal and rational, as we say that he is composed of soul and body. We say that man is a being composed of soul and body as from two things there is constituted a third entity which is neither one of them: man indeed is neither soul nor body. [Chpt. Two, para. 9]

In the *Summa Theologica*,[6] Thomas emphasises these same points, and then moves beyond Aristotle by calling attention to the uniquely divine origins of the human soul. Referring to the soul as "the first principle of life in those things in our world which live" [Q. 75, a.I], he writes:

> Therefore, the soul, which is the first principle of life, is not a body, but the act of a body; just a heat, which is the principle of calefaction, is not a body, but an act of a body. [Q 75, a.I]

... it is clear that man is not only a soul, but something composed of soul and body. [Q. 75, a.IV]

For while the souls of brutes are produced by some power of the body, the human soul is produced by God. To signify this, it is written of other animals: "Let the earth bring forth the living soul" (*Gen.* i.24); while of man it is written (*Gen.* ii.7) that "He breathed into his face the breath of life." And so in the last chapter of *Ecclesiastes* (xii:7) it is concluded: "The dust returns into its earth from whence it was; and the spirit returns to God Who gave it." [Q 75, a.VI]

Speaking directly to the views of Plato, Aquinas writes:

If the soul, following the opinion of the Platonists, were united to the body merely as a mover, it would be right to say that some other bodies must intervene between the soul and body of man ... [But] all this is fictitious and ridiculous. [Q 76, a.VII]

But inasmuch as the soul is the form of the body, it does not have being apart from the being of the body ... [Q. 76, a.VII]

And finally, in the *Commentary on 1 Corinthians* [15], as if he could anticipate the very words which Descartes would use to revive Plato's errors, Aquinas exclaims:

Anima mea non est ego!
I am not my soul!

(D) Modern European Concepts of the Person

Descartes rejects the Aristotelian view of man in its entirety. For Descartes, as for Plato, man is no animal, but only an ego. Thus, in the *Meditations,* Descartes writes:[7]

But what is man? Shall I say a reasonable animal? Assuredly not! [*Med* II]

... thought is an attribute that belongs to me; it alone cannot be separated from me. I am, I exist, that is certain. But how often? Just when I think; for it might possibly be the case if I ceased entirely to think, that I should likewise cease altogether to exist. [*Med* II]

To speak accurately I am not more than a thing which thinks, that is to say a mind or a soul, or an understanding, or a reason... [*Med* II]

I am, however, a real thing and really exist; but what thing? I have answered: a thing which thinks. [*Med II*]

I am not the collection of members which we call the human body. [*Med* II]

And finally, in *Meditation* Six:

I know certainly that I exist, and... I rightly conclude that my essence consists solely in the fact that I am a thinking thing (or a substance whose whole essence or nature is to think). And although possibly (or rather certainly, as I shall say in a moment) I possess a body... it is certain that this I (that is to say, this soul by which I am what I am) is entirely and absolutely distinct from my body, and can exist without it. [*Med* VI]

Cartesian philosophy was supposed to have saved man from the new sciences. Instead, it dissolved man in a bath of sulfuric acid, leaving nothing behind but a ghost inside a machine.[8] Man's body was stripped of its humanity, and reduced to a blob of mechanistic dirt, not different in kind or in value or in dignity from any other little machine.[9] One's relation to one's body was not, finally, different than one's relation to one's coat or house or dog: one simply owned it—and, presumably, one could therefore use it or dispose of it as one pleased. Certainly, nothing could be learned about the human person, or about what was good for the human person, by studying the body.

Such a complete alienation of man from nature is wholly modern: it is impossible to conceive within the medieval systems of Saint Thomas or Saint Francis of Assissi. Yet this modern understanding of the human person, which alienates man from his body, must *a fortiori* alienate man from nature generally, and, indeed, even from other men.

2. Locke's Concept of the Person

The great English philosopher, John Locke, rejected Cartesian dualism—not because Descartes attributes *too little* to man when he reduces the person to a mind, but because, in Locke's view, Descartes attributes too *much* to the mind.

Locke categorically rejects innate ideas (such as 'God'), reduces sensation to an absolutely passive process, and reduces the mind's powers to such elementary operations as comparison and combination. The result, as regards our knowledge of the world, is skepticism.

The result, as regards our being, is the complete separation of "man" and "person". Locke defines "man" as simply a living organism characterized by a certain kind of biological organization—in other words, as one kind of animal among others. But these animals are not persons. A person, according to Locke, is:[10]

> a thinking, intelligent being, that has reason and reflection, and can consider itself as itself, the same thinking thing, in different times and places; which it does only by that consciousness which is inseparable from thinking and essential to it.... as far as this consciousness can be extended backwards to any past action or thought, so far reaches the identity of that person. [*Essay Concerning Human Understanding*, chpt. 27]

Persons are neither souls nor bodies, nor things composed of souls and bodies. They are simply continuous streams of rational consciousness. And where consciousness or reason is interrupted, there ends the person.

3. Hume's Concept of the Person

David Hume takes these Lockean themes to their logical conclusion, and reduces the human person to "*nothing* but a bundle or collection of different perceptions." Hume's analysis is simple enough:[11]

> I never can catch *myself* at any time without a perception, and never can observe any thing but the perception. When my perceptions are remov'd for any time, as by sound sleep; so long am I insensible of *myself,* and may truly be said not to exist. And were all my perceptions remov'd... I shou'd be entirely annihilated, nor do I conceive what is further requisite to make me a perfect nonentity. If any one upon serious and unprejudic'd reflexion, thinks he has a different notion of *himself,* I must confess I can reason no longer with him. [*Treatise of Human Nature,* Bk. I, Part IV, Sec.6]

> The mind is a kind of theatre, where several perceptions successively make their appearance... [But] The comparison of the theatre must not mislead us. They are the successive perceptions only, [and not the building] that constitute the mind. [*Treatise of Human Nature,* Bk. I, Part IV, Sec.6]

Thus, as Hume concludes:

> The identity, which we ascribe to the mind of man, is only a fictitious one. [*Treatise of Human Nature,*Bk. I, Part IV, Sec. 6]

And in this answer, we may fairly say, philosophical anthropology reaches its nadir. For what is left of the human person: no body, no mind, no soul, no substance, no identity, no self. Indeed, no person at all.

(E) Contemporary Concepts of the Person
In its *Pastoral Constitution on the Church in the Modern World,* Vatican II reaffirms the very themes emphasised five centuries ago by Aquinas. We read in the document:[12]

> Man, though composed of body and soul, is a unity.... He is obliged to regard his body as good and to hold it in

honor since God has created it and will raise it up on the last day.... When he recognizes in himself a spiritual and immortal soul, he [also]... grasps what is profoundly true. *Gaudium et spes,* ____§14.

By his innermost nature man is a social being; and if he does not enter into relations with others he can neither live nor develop his gifts. *Gaudium et spes,* ____§12.

Gaudium et spes is clearly continuous with the views of Aristotle and Aquinas.

(F) Summary & Analysis

The history of philosophical speculation about the intension or meaning of personhood—that is, about the nature of the human person—is really two very different histories.

There is one tradition which has its sources in the Torah and in Aristotle and in the Gospels. This tradition emphasizes the *unity* of the human person, and assigns fundamental importance to man's body—a body, however, which is unlike other bodies because it has as its form or 'principle of being' an immortal, rational soul. In this tradition, which understands the importance and special dignity of the human body, one can think clearly and correctly about such matters as sexuality and abortion. In this tradition, which also understands the essentially social character of the human person, one can speak meaningfully of 'solidarity', 'subsidiarity', and 'the common good.' Today, the *depth* and *power* of this philosophical tradition is nowhere more evident or more vital than in the writings of Pope John Paul II on the very topics of sexuality and solidarity.

There is a different tradition, which has as its sources Plato and various pagan religions. In this tradition, most thinkers, like Plato and Descartes, attempt to explain the unity of the human person by reducing man to a ghost—and thereby lose all appreciation of the body. Others, like Locke, distinguish between 'man' and 'person' by reducing man to a biological machine which is *not* a person—and then devising *ad hoc* notions of personhood in a futile effort to ground their political systems. A few, like Hume, abandon all hope of knowing anything about the body, or the mind, or the soul, or their relations, or, indeed, whether any of these are real at all.

II: History of the Extension of the Concept of the Person

We may now consider the history of the concept of the person *extensionally*—that is, by focusing on the answers which have been given to the question "Which entities ought to be counted as persons?" For our purposes (setting aside questions about apes and angels), we can reduce this question to the simpler form: "Which *human beings* ought to be recognized as persons?

There are two fundamentally different ways to answer this question. The first way, which has its sources in the Torah, may be called the Inclusivist Tradition. The second way, which has its sources in the threefold concupiscence, may be called the Exclusivist Tradition.

(A) The Mosaic or "Inclusivist" Tradition

Our question is, Which human beings are persons? The answer given by the Torah and the prophets is clear: *all* human life is precious to God; *no* innocent human being may be abused or killed with impunity. Thus the solemn warning to Noah and his sons after the flood:

> He who sheds man's blood, shall have his blood shed by
> man, for in the image of God man was made. [*Genesis* 9:6]

Precisely the same Inclusive answer is given by the *teaching* of Jesus—for example, by his repeated identification with the least and the lowly. But above all, it is given by *Incarnation* itself: for Jesus became man not by descending from the clouds in Imperial splendor, but by assuming the most humble and ordinary of human flesh.

In sum, the Mosaic and Christian traditions tell us that every living member of our species is a person made in the image of God. Moses, the prophets, the Messiah, and the Councils have made it unmistakably clear that it is not just a cultural elite, a religious elite, a white elite, a wealthy elite, or *any* elite whose members are to be recognized as persons. Rather, it is the entire human family.

In the history of our several American cultures, it is this Inclusivist Tradition—so deeply rooted in our Faith—that has been ever

27

working to enlarge the group of human beings who were recognized and respected as persons.

In the history of the United States, for example, it was the Inclusivist Tradition, with all its religious heritage, which insisted that the descendants of Black Africans were *persons,* and not—as our regressive and benighted Supreme Court insisted—chattel property. In the history of Mexico, this same Inclusivist Tradition is evident in the heroic efforts of Bishop Juan Zumaraga to protect the Indians and Blacks from being sold into slavery.

In season and out of season, the Inclusivist Tradition has insisted that *all* living members of our species—however colored, gendered, deformed, handicapped, poor, old, young, or small—all human beings are persons!

THAT is the Catholic answer to the question, "which members of the human species ought to be recognized as persons." And it is the correct answer.

(B) The Exclusivist Tradition

But it is not the only answer. And in the history of our several cultures, it is the answers given by a different and false tradition which have usually dominated. This tradition, the Exclusivist Tradition, is fundamentally committed to the claim that at least some human beings should be excluded from recognition as persons. The Exclusivist Tradition holds that *NOT* all human beings are persons, and that there are certain tests which human beings must pass before they can count as persons. By way of illustration, we may briefly review the criteria proposed by three contemporary philosophers.

According to Mary Anne Warren, the criteria which indicate whether or not a given human being is a *person* and has *rights* are these:[13]

"1. consciousness (of objects and events external and/or internal to the being), and in particular the capacity to feel pain;

"2. reasoning (the *developed* capacity to solve new and relatively complex problems);

"3. self-motivated activity (activity which is relatively independent of either genetic or direct external control);

"4. the capacity to communicate, by whatever means,
messages of an indefinite variety of types, that is, not just
with an indefinite number of possible contents, but on in-
definitely many possible topics;

"5. the presence of self-concepts, and self-awareness, either individual or racial, or both."

And if a human being flunks two or more of these tests (Warren
professes not to know exactly which combination of traits is sufficient for personhood), then he or she has the same moral status as
a snail or a dandelion.

According to Michael Tooley, a contemporary Australian philosopher, a living human being should be recognized as a person:[14]

" . . . only if it possesses the concept of a self as a continuing subject of experiences and other mental states, and believes that it is itself such a continuing entity."

This has the extremely unfortunate consequence of excluding
David Hume, who (as the passages from Hume *supra* show) most
certainly did not conceive of himself as the *subject* of experiences
or mental states (his "theatre"), but, rather, just as the states and
experiences (his "perceptions") alone.

According to Richard Brandt, a noted contemporary philosopher and a leading Utilitarian theorist, the only human beings who
should be recognized as persons are those:[15]

" . . . human beings at least eighteen years of age, with an
I.Q. at the time of at least 110, and not temporarily in a
psychotic or neurotic or even a highly emotional state of
mind."

On Brandt's view, there are *twelve* non-persons in the present author's home, since the then children are all too young and their
parents are, quite often indeed, highly emotional. Surely the claims

that individuals with I.Q. of 109 or age 17 are, by those very facts, not persons, is absurd on its face.

Indeed, were it not for the influence which bad philosophy has upon culture, one might regard these philosophical theories as comedy. But when one considers the influence of Exclusivism upon modern Western cultures, one can only regard them as tragedy.

Thus, according to the Ku Klux Klan's version of Exclusivism, human beings who happen to be Jews, or Blacks, or Indians, or Asians, or Catholics are not persons.

And thus, according to National Socialists in Nazi Germany, the *only* human beings who counted as persons were healthy, intelligent, able-bodied Aryans with 'proper' political views.

More recently, the Sureme Judicial Courts of the United States and Canada have adopted a version of Exclusivism which holds that preborn human beings are not persons, and may therefore be killed for any reason or for no reason.

(C) Exclusivism and Self-Interest

Even this cursory survey of the ways in which Exclusivist theories have been used to justify slavery, genocide, and abortion might move one to concur with Hegel's sad observation that the only thing mankind can learn from history is that mankind cannot learn from history. For the history of the Exclusivist Tradition offers a lesson so clear and so evident that no culture, indeed no person of good will, should fail to see it. The lesson is this: *NO COMMUNITY—however advanced, however cultured, however moral—NO COMMUNITY has ever drawn an excluding line between 'mere human beings' and 'real persons' which was ANYTHING but a reflection of its own transient SELF-INTEREST.*

Thus, it was no accident that the founders of this nation excluded the African slave upon whom half the economy depended; it was no accident that Pharaoh excluded the Israelite; it was no accident that the Scandinavian settlers in the American midwest excluded the Indian whose land they coveted; it was no accident that Jonah tried to exclude the Ninehvite; it was no accident that Chief Justice Taney excluded Dred Scott; and it was no accident that Hitler excluded the Jew.

And just so, it is no accident that in time of war, normal, decent people can only kill 'Gooks, 'Huns,' and 'Krauts'—not real

30

persons. First the enemy must be depersonalized; then he can be killed. That is why, today, in all the best hospitals in the U.S. and Canada, doctors and nurses starve little 'vegetables'—not handicapped babies. First, one must depersonalize; then one can kill.

(D) Two Arguments for the Inclusivist Tradition

Roman Catholics *believe*—indeed, Roman Catholics *know*—that the Inclusivist Tradition is correct. Unfortunately, the great majority of contemporary Roman Catholics live in cultures which do not share this belief, and which instead subscribe to some version or other of the Exclusive Tradition.

By way of conclusion, then, it may be opportune to consider two simple, compelling, and non-theological arguments which demonstrate that the Inclusivist view of personhood ought to be adopted by all men of good will. The first argument is rather more "humanistic"; the second rather more "scientific".

2. The Humanistic Argument

Exclusivists draw a line between the human beings who *are* persons and the human beings who are *not* persons. Inclusivists do not draw such a line. Now, surely it is clear that the scholars and politicians who adopt Exclusivism today are not wiser, not morally better, and not more liberated from their own history and their own self-interest than were Pharaoh, Thomas Jefferson, Roger Taney, George Custer, or the Prophet Jonah. Accordingly, if, like those earlier exclusivists, today's exclusivists choose to draw a line betwen the 'mere human beings' who *aren't* persons and the 'special' human beings who *are* persons, one can reasonably expect that they will not draw a *better* line than Jefferson, Taney, or the prophet Jonah. They will simply draw a *different* line, a line that reflects *their* history and *their* self-interest. In retrospect, as history shows, it is all too clear that *every single line that has ever been drawn between 'mere human beings' and 'real persons' has been wrong*—and not *just* wrong, but *horribly, hideously, catastrophically* and *undeniably* wrong. Every version of exclusivism that has preceded our own time has been clearly and utterly wrong.

What then of the new versions of exclusivism? Can any person of good will really believe that todays politicians and scholars are the first people in human history who are so wise, so morally pure,

31

and so free of any self-interest, that they and they alone, unlike all who went before them, will finally figure out which 'mere human beings' can really be bought and sold and tortured and killed because they aren't real persons? No. No person of good will can choose to believe that the several contemporary Western cultures are the first communities in human history whose Exclusivisms (which, after all, are not even mutually consistent!) will *not* turn out—like *every* Exclusivism before—to be hideously, catastrophically wrong.

2. The "Scientific" Argument

That was the *first* argument for Inclusivism and against Exclusivism. There is a stronger one.

The problem of adjudicating the dispute between Exclusivism and Inclusivism can be understood as a problem of rational theory preference. There are two theories about personhood and the building of human communities, and there is a body of cultural evidence which extends backward for approximately six thousand years.

For six thousand years, the Exclusivist Tradition has offered various predictions about which human beings could be tortured, killed, or enslaved because they weren't really persons and didn't deserve to be respected or protected. And for six thousand years, whether it was depersonalizing women or Jews or Indians or Africans, the Exclusivist Tradition has been *wrong*—obviously, utterly, and unmistakably wrong.

For the same six thousand years, the Inclusivist Tradition has insisted that *all* human beings are persons and deserve to be respected and protected. And for six thousand years, whether it was defending women or Jews or Indians or Africans, the Inclusivist Tradition has always been right—obviously, utterly, and unmistakably right.

So there are two theories and there is a large body of tragic and bloody evidence. The evidence shows that Exclusivism has never been right, and that Inclusivism has never been wrong. Can one rationally choose to accept as true a theory that has always been wrong and to reject a competing theory that has always been right? No. On the basis of the evidence, one cannot *rationally* choose Exclusivism, and one cannot *rationally* reject Inclusivism.

So: Moses, and the prophets and Christ and all the Councils are correct, and it doesn't need theology to prove it; it only needs a little reason, a bit of history, and a modicum of good will. *EVERY* human being—however handicapped, however racially categorized, however ill, however gendered, however retarded, however economically disadvantaged, however old or however young— EVERY living member of our species is a person, and deserves our respect and protection.

In conclusion, what we can say about the Catholic view of the human person is this: the Torah announced it, Christ perfected it, and all the data of reason and history confirm it.

Notes

1. Earlier drafts of this essay benefitted considerably from the criticisms of my colleague, Michael Pakaluk.

2. The scriptural quotations used below are from *The Jerusalem Bible,* Doubleday & Company (Garden City. N.Y., 1966).

3. All quotations from the *Phaedo* are taken from *The Phaedo,* translated by Hugh Tredennick, in *The Collected Dialogues of Plato,* Edited by Edith Hamilton and Huntington Cairns, Princeton University Press (Princeton, New Jersey: 1963).

4. All quotations from the Aristotle are taken from *The Basic Works of Aristotle,* edited by Richard McKeon; *De Anima* translated by J. A. Smith; *Ethica Nocomachea* translated by W. D. Ross; *Politica* translated by Benjamin Jowett; Random House (New York: 1941).

5. Saint Thomas Aquinas, *On Being and Essence,* translated by Armand Maurer, C.S.B., Second Revised Edition, The Pontifical Institute of Mediaeval Studies (Toronto: 1968).

6. All quotations from the *Summa Theologica* are taken from *The Basic Works of Saint Thomas Aquinas,* edited by Anton C. Pegis, Random House (New York: 1945).

7. All quotations from the *Meditations* are from *The Philosophical Works of Descartes,* Volume One, Translated and Edited by Elizabeth S. Haldane and G. R. T. Ross, Cambridge University Press (Cambridge: 1969).

8. Descartes would have been profoundly disappointed by this assessment, for it was clearly his *hope* to give an adequate account of the unity of the human person which, notwithstanding his profound mind/body dualism, would involve the body. Thus, in the second to last paragraph of the *Meditations,* he writes:
> "From this it is quite clear that, notwithstanding the supreme goodness of God, the nature of man, inasmuch as it is composed of mind and body, cannot be otherwise than sometimes a source of deception." [*Med.* VI]

But even this *ad hoc* effort to reconnect mind and body reveals Descarte's profound Platonism: for insofar as the body is involved in the nature of the human person, it is the subverter of truth and the source of error!

9. Indeed, as Descartes explains at length in *Part V* of the *Discourse on Method* [in Haldane & Ross (eds.), *op. cit.*], it is only by virtue of language and rationality that we could

33

ever be certain that any given human body was not an automaton "which bore a resemblance to our body and imitated our actions as far as it was morally possible to do so" but which possessed no consciousness or soul. Except insofar as it is *used* by a mind or soul, the human body is no different than an animal body. And about animals, according to Descartes [*idem.*], we can be sure "that they have no reason at all, and that it is nature which acts in them according to the disposition of their organs, just as a clock, which is only composed of wheels and weights is able to tell the hours."

10. The quotations from Locke below are from *Locke's Essays: An Essay concerning Human Understanding and A Treatise on the Conduct of the Understanding,* (Philadelphia: 1852).

11. The quotations from Hume below are taken from David Hume, *A Treatise of Human Nature,* Edited by L. A. Selby-Bigge, Oxford University Press (Oxford: 1888).

12. Following the Daughters of Saint Paul edition.

13. Mary Anne Warren, "On the Moral and Legal Status of Abortion," in *The Problem of Abortion,* edited by Joel Feinberg, Wadsworth Publishing Company (Belmont, CA: 1984), pages 111–2.

14. Michael Tooley, "Abortion and Infanticide," in *The Rights and Wrongs of Abortion,* edited by Marshall Cohen *et alia,* Princeton University Press (Princeton, NJ: 1974) page 59.

15. R. B. Brandt, "The Morality of Abortion," in *Abortion: Pro and Con,* edited by Robert L. Perkins, Schenkman (Cambridge, MA: 1974), page 161.

Chapter 3

CONTEMPORARY UNDERSTANDING OF PERSONHOOD

The Reverend Benedict M. Ashley, O.P., Ph.D.

Classicist and Historicist World-Views

Every contemporary world-view has its own understanding of the human person—Christian, Judaic or Islamic; Hindu, Buddhist, or Confucian; Marxist or Humanist—each subdivided into a spectrum from fundamentalist to liberal. A superficial scan of this vast array of images of the human person would be unprofitable. The differences in understanding the human person between Catholic theologians today, although considerable, seem to me less significant than their common conviction that the "classicist world-view" of the person needs to be revised in accordance with modern "historical mindedness."[1] Therefore, I will concentrate on this area of current agreement.

35

The leading systematic theologians of the Vatican II period—Karl Rahner, Edward Schillebeeckx, Hans Urs Von Balthasar, Yves Congar, Hans Kung—were all marked by their "historical mindedness,"[2] and most younger theologians have followed in their paths, though they sometimes lack the grounding in the classicist world-view possessed by most of these masters. Since none have better described the difference between these two views of the human person than Bernard Lonergan, I will quote him in full from his well-known essay, "The Transition from a Classicist World-View to Historical-Mindedness."[3]

One can apprend man abstractly through a definition that applied *omni et soli* and through properties verifiable in every man. In this fashion one knows man as such; and man as such, precisely because he is an abstraction, also is unchanging. It follows in the first place, that on this view one is never going to arrive at any exigence for changing forms, structures, methods, for all change occurs in the concrete, and on this view the concrete is always omitted. It follows . . . , that this exclusion of changing forms, structures, methods, is not theological; it is grounded simply upon a certain conception of scientific or philosophic method; that conception is no longer the only conception or the commonly received conception; and I think our Scripture scholars would agree that its abstractness, and the omissions due to abstraction, have no foundation in the revealed word of God.

On the other hand, one can apprehend mankind as a concrete aggregate developing over time, where the locus of development, and so to speak, the synthetic bond is the emergence, expansion, differentiation, dialectic of meaning and of meaningful performance. On this view intentionality, meaning, is a constitutive component of human living; moreover, this component is not fixed, static, immutable, but shifting, developing, going astray, capable of redemption; on this view there is in the historicity, which results from human nature, an exigence for changing forms, structures, methods; and it is on this level and through this medium of changing meaning that the Church's witness is given to it.

If we look at the human person with this historical-mindedness characteristic of contemporary theology, what are the chief features that stand out? It seems to me that there are five on which most theologians would agree. I will also indicate in a sentence or two what a classicist theologian might have to say about each. Why assume that what Lonergan calls the "transition" from one world-view to another has finished the dialogue between them?

Subjectivity of the Human Person

The historicist world-view seems to have originated in the so-called "Copernican revolution" in philosophy initiated by Descartes and brought to its climax by Immanuel Kant, often spoken of as "the turn to the subject,"[4] in response to the value-free objectivity claimed by natural science in its remarkable progress after Galileo. In a mechanistic Newtonian world human persons refused to be machines or mere objects, and became aware of their existence as subjects, feeling, thinking their own thoughts, making their own choices.

This *subjectivity* of the human person is not the same as "subjectivism." Rather it is a term for our humanity in its difference from all other beings in our visible world. Among the objects that make up the world, only we persons are "subjects," that is, self-conscious and free. Consequently, we can not be defined as being this or that as objects are, since we are responsible for making ourselves whatever we become by our own choices. Therefore, to speak of human "nature" is to risk reducing the person to an object, of losing precisely what makes us persons.

Hence, many contemporary theologians prefer to make use not of the classicial philosophies of being which began by an analysis of the objects of knowledge but of the post-Kantian "critical philosophies" which begin with an analysis of the subjective conditions of knowledge and the phenomena of experience. The question of objectivity and real existence is dealt with only subsequently.

Thus, for example, in the theology of Karl Rahner, the human subject is analyzed in depth by a method of "transcendental deduction" *a priori* to concrete experience and then "correlated" with that experience.[5] In the method of Lonergan, on the other hand, one begins with concrete experience, but fixes attention not on the content of that experience but on the process of inquiry by which the subject can fully appropriate that experience as its own;[6] while in Schillebeeckx's later thought subject and object are "inextricably intertwined" yet the phenomenological viewpont remains dominant.[7]

What would a classicist say to all this? Certainly what makes us more than animal is our intelligence and through intelligence we are self-conscious, but do we first of all and with fundamental certitude know ourselves as subjects? Or are we first aware of the objective world and secondly and reflexively that we are knowers of that world? Yet no doubt modern culture emphasizes this reflexive awareness. I believe this is why so many people in our culture find the Church's pro-life arguments against abortion cast in the terms of classical theology unpersuasive. They grant that persons have rights, but persons are subjects; and therefore pregnant women possessed of subjective feelings and interests have rights. But the fetus is only potentially a subject since it is yet not self-conscious and lacks feelings and interests. Is it so obvious then that it is a person? Consequently, Catholic theologians who are pro-life today have to labor strenuously to show that by beginning with understanding of the person, rather than denying as Kant did that we can know the noumenal self.

Historicity of the Human Person

The second feature of this contemporary understanding is the "historicity" of the human person. The classicist world-view included human history, but it did not appreciate the historical consciousness of the human person. Human persons are fundamentally marked by historicity, because their existence as they actually experience it cannot be separated from its historical context. Sartre said, "Man has no nature, but a history."[8] but it would be better to say that our nature is our liability to be shaped by and our capacity to shape history.

38

We are, in Heidegger's term "thrown into" a world we did not make. We are defined by our relations to the objects and persons of our world, yet we are responsible by our free decisions for creating ourselves and for remaking the world into which the next generation will be born. We are, therefore, not simply persons, but persons of our time, inescapably modern or post-modern.

This does not mean that we are confined to the limits of the present. It is the very essence of our historicity than we remember the past and anxiously anticipate the future. Yet past and future are known to us and have significance only in terms of the present. Consequently, this recognition of human historicity does not imply an acceptance of "historicism," the notion that we can stand outside our present and view the march of history with a neutral eye. No, our historicity requires us to use the past to build the future not to try impossibly to relive it. We must, therefore, cease trying to define ourselves as persons by some timeless abstraction called "human nature."

This theological emphasis on historicity became very evident in Vatican II where for the first time an ecumenical council was primarily concerned not with orthodoxy, which was hardly in question, but relevance and communication. Therefore, today Catholic theology and Biblical scholarship is above all marked by a historical consciousness just as scholastic theology was marked by a metaphysical consciousness. Hence, also the traditionalist reaction against the Council, since for traditionalists the very function of theology is to help the Church transcend the variations of history, which may be inevitable, but which they see as erosive of orthodoxy.[9] The historically-minded, on the contrary, see the Council as accepting a view of the human person according to which orthodoxy can be maintained only at the price of rethinking the faith in every generation and through every cultural change.

Relationality of the Human Person

A third characteristic of the person for the historically-minded is its *relationality*.[10] Objects may be conceived in isolation, but the human person exists only in relation to a world with which it is constantly dealing and especially to other persons through whom it comes to recognize its own personality. Our self-consciousness cannot be a Cartesian ego, although it was Descartes who first made "the turn to the subject." *Cogito,* but I think always of myself in relation to a world which manifests itself in me and relation to other subjects with whom I communicate. Since this network of relations is a society with a particular historical culture, it seems difficult to avoid a certain cultural relativism in our view of Christian life. How can we separate a "natural law" from the culture in which that law is actually lived? While today we would be horrified at the burning of heretics at the stake, yet in the social context of the Middle Ages, the greatest and most saintly theologians not only did not deplore but advocated this horrid deed.

The linkage of subjectivity and relationality explains why "modern man" (and woman) is at once intensely *individualistic* and intensely *socializing.*[11] As subjects human persons must be free of all external coercion to take possession of their own lives, but these lives can have meaning only in involvement in the reconstruction of social reality. We see this exemplified often in the modern intelligentsia who demand total freedom of personal expression, yet are constantly propagandizing for the restructuring of all traditional institutions according to their own ideals. Note that modernist "conservatives" are just as caught up in this paradox as are modernist "liberals." The modernist conservative is a libertarian as regards private life, but a social activist in his or her determination to apply the "magic of the market" to rendering society economically efficient in the manner of Social Darwinism.

This relationality of the human person, while often resulting in pressures to conform, also puts a premium on the personal in the sense of the idiosyncratic. We make ourselves interesting and important by becoming obviously unique. We have to have something to offer that others lack in the free market of living. Hence we are no longer so much interested in what is common to all human beings, but rather in the variety of persons. We feed on confessional autobiographies and personal "profiles" which reveal the most intimate details of personal lives in order to achieve recognition in the confusion of human names and faces.

Consequently, the notion of universal moral norms, whether of a natural or a divine law, seems irrelevant to the actual lives of persons, each of which is unique and lived in unique circumstances. Moral good or evil is not to be found in the conformity to some general rule usually inapplicable, but in the effort or neglect to construct a life rich in human values. In this perspective it is easier to see why the "main-stream" moral theologians of today, having opted for the paradigm shift to modernity, find a moral methodology of proportionate reason so much more realistic and personalistic than the classical moral method.[12]

Language and the Human Person

Since social relations are maintained by communication and communication is through language, and language expresses meanings, a fourth emphasis of the historically-minded is on the human person as the *creator of meaning through language*. As subjects we think and choose, but this is possible only through symbols of some sort, through a language, which is not natural, instinctive, or universal to humankind, but a human invention, differing from culture to culture and from age to age, that is, through our historicity. Not only do we, in our relationality and for the sake of our relations, create languages, but through languages we create meaning. In even a deeper way, as Heidegger and Ricoeur have emphasized, language once created creates us, because we are born into a culture whose symbols largely determine how the world appears to us.

From this arises the great concern today for *hermeneutics* and *semiotics* that is the problem of translation and interpretation of symbolic expressions whether verbal or non-verbal.[13] To think about the human person as religious, necessarily requires that we understand the symbols that speak to faith, that reveal God to us, whether in the liturgy, the Scriptures, or the preached Word and the teaching of the Church and its tradition. But as history changes and the network of social relations change and individuals in their subjectivity receive the Word in terms of their own varied and changing experience, the old symbols lose their meaning or take on false meanings, unless they are somehow renewed. This is why the very nature of the human person makes it necessary for contemporary theology to rethink and re-express classical theology, and why it becomes so frustrated if it lacks the freedom for this task.

The post-modernists have pushed this theme of human linguisticality to the extreme of "deconstructionism" which amounts to a denial that communications between human persons can ever succeed, because nobody says what they really mean, and, even if they tried to be wholly honest, would run up against the barrier that the other would be interested only in what he agreed with, namely, what he already thought himself.[14] This pessimism need not be accepted as final, but it is a striking way of recalling the Biblical account of the Tower of Babel and pointing out that only the Penecostal miracle of tongues can hope to overcome this consequence of our sinful condition. Pluralism is a fact, but it should not make us give up our ecumenical efforts at communication.

Liberation of the Human Person

The fifth mark of the modern understanding of the person is the emphasis on the *need of persons to liberate themselves.*[15] Persons exist always in a power struggle to be free of control by others or to gain control over others. "Truth" is a function of ideologies used as weapons in this struggle. We are not just subjects as self-conscious, but we are either "subjects" of domination by others, or we are subjectors. The freedom of the self-conscious subject is an illusion, if we suppose that we are free to live our own lives without a struggle to attain that freedom against the oppression of the powers that be.

Modern theology has more and more carried on a self-criticism of the elitist tendencies of modernity, with the result that one of the features of post-modernity is the emphasis on political theology, on liberation theology, and feminist theology. The hermeneutic of today is a "hermeneutic of suspicion" and deconstruction which seeks to uncover in all the documents of the past and the institutions of the present the hidden agenda of the struggle for power. This demands the abandonment of classical ideas of scholarly objectivity and neutrality, and requires conversion and commitment. But this "conversion" is not merely the conversion in faith and morals of traditionalism, nor even the "conversion" of understanding urged by Bernard Lonergan, but an option for one side or the other in the power struggle. Vatican II's "preferential option for the poor" is understood in this sense, and the "poor" or the "oppressed" become the side with which one has identified, while one's opponents are by definition the "oppressors." Theology thus is no longer merely a study but a *praxis* which formulates the concerns of the oppressed and motivates their efforts to break their bondage and this bondage is not just personal sin but rather sinful social structures.

An Historical-Minded Evaluation

I have tried to describe the chief points of emphasis which are being developed by contemporary theology in its efforts to revise the classical view of human nature. That these features of the human person are of great significance, were often neglected in pre-Vatican II theology, ought to be taken into account by all theologians today, and especially by the Church in teaching and preaching, who can deny?

A serious question is raised, however, by statements like the following one of Lonergan:[16]

> ... the old foundations [of theology] will no longer do. In saying this I do not mean that they are no longer true, for they are true now as they ever were. I mean they are no longer appropriate... One type of foundations suits a theology that aims at being deductive, static, abstract, universal, equally applicable to all places and to all times. A quite different foundation is needed when theology turns from the deductivism to an empirical approach, from the static to the dynamic, from the abstract to the concrete, from the universal to the historical totality of particulars, from invariable rules to intelligent adjustment and adaptation.

In taking this stand for a new foundation for theology, Lonergan was not unaware of the risks and warned "our disengagement from classicism and our involvement in modernity must be open-eyed, critical, coherent, sure-footed."[17] Certainly theologians like Lonergan, Rahner, and Schillebeeckx made great efforts to show that they were not disloyal to the work of Aquinas, but were engaged in a work of what Heidegger called "retrieval," an effort to maintain a dialogue with the classical past in which new questions were raised for St. Thomas that he in his historical context had never thought of asking. Yet Lonergan was certainly correct when he said that contemporary theologians generally conceive modern theology as a "paradigm shift" from what they perceive as classical theology, especially that of Aquinas. As Lonergan put it, this does not mean they deny the truth of Aquinas' theology of the human person, but they have simply lost interest in it. The consequence is that, unlike Lonergan, Rahner, and Schillebeeckx, they no longer feel any special obligation to relate their understanding of the human person to the classical view (often in the form of a caricature) except by way of contrast.

But is it possible to treat of human historicity, subjectivity, relationality, etc. without grounding these characteristics in a metaphysical and a theologically dogmatic understanding of human nature as it transcends cultural relativity? And was not this precisely the foundation firmly laid by classical theology? The great theologians of Vatican II, for all their talk of new foundations, in fact worked very hard to show that the "turn of the subject" which they took in one way or another ultimately led back to an affirmation of this metaphysical and dogmatic tradition and confirmed it. The question, therefore, is whether in fact their adoption of this "turn to the subject," for all the stimulation to fresh thinking about the human person it has produced, really opens a path to the future, or is it now proving a dead end?[18]

Perhaps, the mistake of much Vatican II theology has been not to be historical-minded enough about the wisdom of making this turn to the subject. Common to the period of theology just preceding Vatican II was the feeling that official Thomism, for all its merits, had become a serious obstacle to dialogue with "the modern mind." Rahner sought to surmount this barrier by transcendentalizing Thomism and historicizing it with help from Heidegger. Lonergan took another path of finding in Thomism a way to metaphysics through cognitional theory. Schillebeeckx sought a way out in a theory of religious experience. What was common to all was the turn to the subject and an effort to find something of Kant's *a priori* foundation for knowledge even

44

in Aquinas. What was lacking I believe, was a critical exploration of the historical situation in which European thought turned to the subject.

When we look at the research that has been done of this question in the last thirty years, different possiblities open up. The modern mind is polarized between the objectivity of modern science and the subjectivity of modern philosophy and theology. Was this split, which we are now struggling to overcome, historically inevitable? Was it made necessary by a dialectic intrinsic to the nature of human self-understanding? That seems to be the hidden assumption of our theologians which leads them to conclude that the Church must accept this situation and make the best of it. Or was this polarization due rather to strictly historical factors which we must recognize but which do not of themselves tell us what attitude to take toward it.

I believe the second explanation is the better, and I suggest the historical hypothesis that the turn to the subject was due to a previous wrong turn taken by the natural sciences in the seventeenth and eighteenth centuries when the teleological approach to nature was abandoned for mechanism.[19] Because the remarkable subsequent development of science was, mistakenly, attributed to this turn, it became and still is a dogma of science that our world and consequently human nature are without intrinsic purpose. Consequently the objective scientific picture of the world is value-free, and silent both about the world's Creator and the relation of humanity to its Creator.

If we were to ask further why science took this disastrous turn to mechanism, I suggest a second historical hypothesis, that this interpretation of natural science in an anti-teleological way served the ideological interests of the intellectual elites of the Enlightenment whose concern was to promote humanism as a substitute for Christianity. Furthermore, the Enlightenment was the result, and we can very well say the divine punishment, on the Church for its negligences that led to the Reformation schisms and the subsequent religious wars. The European intelligensia, disillusioned with a fratricidal and fanatic Christianity, turned to a religion of humanity whose hope was in the power of a science and technology unrestricted by any divine purposes for nature and for man.

If these historical hypotheses can be substantiated, and I have given evidence for them elsewhere,[20] then what is needed in theology today is not an effort to understand ourselves by starting with questions posed in the perspectives of Humanism, for that is what the turn to the subject really was, but from the perspectives of our own Christian tradition, whose formulation as the classical world-view, although certainly not final, was essentially sound. Of course, this does not exempt us from showing how on this solid foundation, all the truth to be found in modern science and in modern philosophy with its emphasis on historicity, subjectivity, etc., can be consistently integrated. Vatican II, I believe, called us to that task. We must be grateful to the theologians who contributed to this decision by the Council, but Vatican II did not, I repeat, did not declare that these theologians had demonstrated the right way to accomplish that task. Rather the Council affirmed the solid foundations already laid in the metaphysical and dogmatic achievements of its classic tradition as the grounds for future progress.[21]

Notes

1. Bernard J. F. Lonergan, S.J., "The Transition from a Classicist World-View to Historical Mindedness" in *A Second Collection,* ed. by W. F. J. Ryan, S.J. and B. J. Tyrell, S.J. (Philadelphia: The Westminister Press, 1974), p. 1–9.

2. For the anthropologies of these theologians see the following: Karl Rahner, *Hearers of the Word,* translated by Michael Richards (Herder and Herder, 1969) with discussion by Louis Roberts, *The Achievement of Karl Rahner,* (New York: Herder and Herder, 1967); Bernard J. F. Lonergan, SJ, with discussion by David Tracy, *The Achievement of Bernard Lonergan* (St. Louis: Herder and Herder, 1970); Edward Schillebeeckx, *Christ: The Experience of Jesus as Lord,* translated by John Bowden (New York: Seabury-Crossroad, 1980). Chapter 2, p. 731–743, treats question "What is Humanity?" and is a good summary of current understanding according to which there can be no "universal human nature" but only "anthropological constants" such as: (1) Relationship to human corporeality, nature and the ecological environment; (2) Involvement with other persons; (3) Connection with social and institutional structures; (4) Conditioning by time and space; (5) Mutual relationship of theory and practice; (6) Religious and 'para-religious' consciousness of man (utopianism, What future does he want?); (7) Irreducible synthesis of these six dimensions. But no specific norms can be deduced from these constants. For Hans Urs von Balthasar, see *A Theological Anthropology* (New York: Sheed and Ward, 1968, republished as *Man in History,* 1982) with discussion by Louis Roberts, *The Theological Aesthetics of Hans Urs Von Balthasar* (Washington, DC: Catholic University of America, 1987); for Hans Kung see his *On Being a Christian* (Garden City, NY: Doubleday, 1976) pp. 249–273 with discussion by Catherine Mowry LeCugna, *The Theological Methodology of Hans Kung* (Chica, CA: Scholars' Press, 1982).

Yves Congar's point of view can be gathered from his little work, still untranslated, *Esprit de l'homme, esprit de Dieu* (Paris: Editions du Cerf, 1983).

3. Reference in note 1 above, p. 5 f.

4. Turn to the subject

5. Cf. Ann Carr, *The Theological Method of Karl Rahner* (Missoula, Montana: Scholars Press for The American Academy of Religion, Dissertation Series, no. 19, directed by David Tracy, 1977.)

6. A concise summary of Lonergan's conception of method is found in the first chapter of his *Method in Theology* (New York: Herder and Herder, 1972) pp. 3–26. For his conception of subjectivity see his essay "The Subject" in *Second Collection* (note 1 above) pp. 69–86.

7. Cf. Schreiter, Robert J., C.PP.S. and Mary Catherine Hilkert, O.P., eds., *The Praxis of Christian Experience: An Introduction to the Theology of Edward Schillebeeckx* (San Francisco: Harper and Row, 1989). Chapter 1–2 of *Christ* explain his idea of "experience" as "inextricable intertwining" of the subjective and objective in the encounter with reality. Religious experiences are ones in which point to something which transcends experience.

8. Yet see Thomas C. Anderson, *The Foundation and Structure of Sartrean Ethics* (Lawrence, KS: The Regents Press of Kansas, 1979) who shows (pp. 57–60) that even for Sartre's ethics there is teleology and the concept of certain universal human needs which must be satisifed.

9. *Being and Time* (New York: Harper and Row, 1962) I, 5, p. 174, German edition p. 135.

10. See Remy C. Kwant, *The Phenomenology of Social Existence* (Pittsburgh, PA: Duquesne University Press, 1965) for a discussion of human relationality from a phenomenological perspective.

11. This paradox is well illustrated by Wade Clark Roof and William McKinney in their study, *American Mainline Religion* (New Brunswick: Rutgers University Press, 1987) which hypothesizes that the main reason for the high rate of Church affiliation in the U.S.A. (compared with most European countries) along with an extreme pluralism of belief is the need Americans feel for some kind of community support in a culture that is extremely individualistic (they quote Thomas Jefferson's famous remark, "I am my own sect.")

12. For a survey of the controversy (favorable to the proportionalism) see Bernard Hoose, *Proportionalism: The American Debate and its European Roots* (Washington, DC: Georgetown University Press, 1987). For a criticism of the system see Germain Grisez, *The Way of the Lord Jesus*, vol. 1, *Christian Moral Principles* (Chicago: Franciscan Herald Press, 1983) Chapter 6, pp. 141–172 with extensive bibliographical references.

13. For an introduction to the current state of these disciplines see Richard E. Palmer, *Hermeneutics: Interpretation Theory in Schleiermacher, Dilthey, Heidegger, and Gadamer* (Evanston, IL: Northwestern University Press, 1969) and John Deely, *Introducing Semiotics* (Bloomington, IND: University of Indiana Press, 1982).

14. For a discussion of these recent developments see David Ray Griffith, William A. Beardslee and Joe Holland, *Varieties of Postmodern Theology* (Albany: State University of New York Press, 1989), especially Griffin, p. 32–40.

15. *Ibid.* Griffin, pp. 81–94 and 129–148.

16. "Theology in its New Context" in *A Second Collection* (note 1 above) p. 63 f.

17. Lonergan's whole emphasis is on the "self-appropriation" of our knowledge. For him "objectivity" is achieved by a disciplined awareness of our subjective processes in knowing. Is it not rather that we test the validity of our knowing processes by their success in letting objects "speak for themselves"? On the contrary, Heidegger (although he never wholly freed his thought from phenomenological idealism) in his second phase came to

stress the contemplative passivity of human knowledge and to attribute the "forgetfullness of Being" to the tendency of western man to manipulate reality rather than to let it reveal itself.

18. See Fergus Kerr, *Theology After Wittgenstein* (Oxford: Blackwell, 1986) pp. 7–16 and on Hans Kung, pp. 15–16 and David Braine, *The Reality of Time and the Existence of God* (New York: Oxford University Press, 1988) pp. 232–236 and 250–1 for rather severe criticisms of Rahner from the viewpoint of analytic philosophy.

19. This is the argument of my *Theologies of the Body: Humanist and Christian* (St. Louis: Pope John Center, 1985).

20. *Ibid.*

21. On this continued recommendation of Aquinas as a "preferential exemplar: for Catholic theology see the letter of Paul VI, *Lumen Ecclesiae, The Pope Speaks,* 19 (4:1975) 287–307 in which he especially praises Aquinas' "cognitive and ontological realism" and the addresses of John Paul II, "Perennial Philosophy of St. Thomas for the Youth of Our Times", Nov. 17, 1979, *Osservatore Romano* (English edition), Dec 17, 1979, p. 6–8, and "Method and Doctrine of St. Thomas in Dialogue with Modern Culture", Sept. 13, 1980. *Osservatore Romano* Oct. 20, 1980, p. 9–11. In the first of these addresses (n. 9) John Paul II states his own understanding of the human person. "We are indebted to St. Thomas for a precise and ever valid definition of that which constitutes man's essential greatness: 'he has charge of himself' (*ipse est sibi providens*; cf. *Contra Gentiles* III, 81). Man is master of himself, he can make provision for himself and form projects toward fulfilling his destiny. This fact, however, taken by itself, does not settle the question of man's greatness, nor does it guarantee that he will be able, by himself, to reach the full perfection of personality. The only decisive factor here is that man should let himself be guided in his actions, by the *truth*; and truth is not made by man; he can only discover it in the nature that is given to him along with existence. It is God who, as Creator, calls reality in being, and, as revealer, shows it forth ever more fully in Jesus Christ and in his Church. The Second Vatican Council, when it speaks of this self-providence of man 'in so far as it involves knowing what is true' (*sub ratione veri*) as a 'kingly ministry' (*munus regale*), goes to the heart of this intuition. This is the teaching which I set out to call to mind and bring up to date in the Encyclical *Redemptor Hominis,* by drawing attention to man as 'the primary and fundamental way for the Church.' " (n. 14)

Chapter 4

PASTORAL CONCERN
THE CHURCH'S TEACHING ON THE
HUMAN PERSON

MODERATOR: First of all, I would ask if Dr. Derr or Father Ashley would want to comment on the presentation that either one of you made.

FATHER ASHLEY: I think the two papers agreed on a very essential point, and that is locating a big difficulty in theology due to the influence of Descartes and a little later of Kant and their dualistic conception of the human person. We both brought that out.

DR. DERR: I would say the same thing in a different way. If the turn to the subject is to be defined by what happened in Modern European philosophy then the turn to the subject must inevitably end in losing the subject.

MODERATOR: Frightening.

BISHOP: This is addressed to Dr. Derr. From the "Inclusivist" perspective that you elaborated and that we would all identify with: would you see that as resolving the question of the person-hood of the fetus? Would you also pursue a little bit more the question of ensoulment.

DR. DERR: First, personhood. The inclusivist perspective resolves the moral question definitively and it resolves the political question, in the public domain, definitively too. I take it that a person of good will really cannot deny that every past effort to carve out some part of of the human family as not 'personal,' and as not possessed of dignity and not deserving protection was a horrific failure. *Every effort to depersonalize some fraction of the living members of our species has been a catastrophe.* I think that is undeniable. It is also undeniable that every effort to do so has been transparently correct at the time in the context of when it was done. For example, it seemed self-evidently correct to most ministers in New England that blacks weren't persons in 1830.

Now, today, some say that the fetus is not a person. But I do not believe that any grounds can be adduced which make the exclusivist claim today better or more rational than any exclusivist claim in the past. We have an intellectual tradition which has produced the worst catastrophes in human history: It's exclusivism. It has *never* been right. And yet, once again, we're asked to believe it is true.

I think one can say that history shows that exclusivism is utterly false. It's impossible to accept the claim that there are any members of our species who are not persons. The fact that the unborn seem like a different case is, I think, only a comment on the sad state of historical education today.

Every case in the past seemed like a different case. It seemed obvious to slavers that depersonalizing blacks was very different than depersonalizing English serfs two centuries before. Each culture finds its own version of exclusivism to be unique and plausible and the really correct one. And they're always wrong.

So our culture is doing it again. And it's wrong. And I think if we can overcome the sort of prejudice about our own self interests, people of good will should be able to grant that it is as wrong as it has always been in the past. There's reason to set the fetus aside as being a different case.

Now about ensoulment. For me that's a more difficult question because I'm not a theologian; I can only blunder around as an amateur. But Aristotle and Aquinas define the soul as the form or the essence of the whole human person, and we know now (having five hundred years more biology than Thomas had) that the whole human person *is* present, developmentally, at the moment of conception. After conception there are no changes anywhere in the developmental sequence which are plausible "ensoulment" times. So I think that today, given what the biological sciences have told us, it's utterly implausible to say that the soul would not be present at conception.

The person who will develop is present at conception and I think that means the soul is present at conception. You can't have a human body without a human soul as far as I know unless the body is dead and the embryo is not dead.

BISHOP: If somebody says to one of us, you say that you cannot destroy this embryo because it's a person, if they were to say to us, "What is a person?", how would we answer them? Would we say it's a rational animal, it's a center of responsibility or it's an image of God or in some simple language, how do we answer that question?

FATHER ASHLEY: Well, I think I would say: ask persons when they thought they began to be. And all I think, unless they are really very ideological, will grant that they began to be in their mothers' wombs. That same person, that same being was there before each of us was born.

Ordinary language shows that. We all say that. That you were "born" means you were there before you were born. So it's pretty hard for people when they stop to think about it not to admit that the unborn child is just that. That each of us was once an unborn child.

Now the question at exactly what point that came about is somewhat more difficult and people argue about it but ordinarily, certainly, people would say it was when their mothers became pregnant. But what was "implanted" in the womb except this organism that already existed so that you began even before you were implanted in the womb? Thus you finally end up with the moment of conception.

I think we ought to talk in terms of the continuity of the individual that because people in their ordinary life know that they existed before they were born.

BISHOP: You say that *this* is a person. What does that mean? I don't think it's a question of the time.

FATHER ASHLEY: I really don't know how we got to talking about "person" as something different from an individual human being. That seems to me an artificial distinction that has just come about very recently because of this controversy.

BISHOP: Well, then your definition would be a human individual.

FATHER ASHLEY: Yes.

BISHOP: A person is a human individual?

FATHER ASHLEY: Yes. I don't see any difference at all—in the ordinary usage, between a human being and a human person.

DR. DERR: I agree with that. Perhaps as a pedagogical or pastoral matter, you'd have to try to figure out what the intellectual vocabulary of your interlocutor was. If you were talking to someone who conceives of moral discourse in terms of "rights, rights, and rights," which is a common way for people to think today, then I suppose to be understood by them you might have to say what you mean by person, among other things, is an entity that has rights in the way that rocks don't have rights and trees don't have rights.

If you were talking to someone who's utilitarian and wants to boil every moral question down to consequences (what are the consequences?) then to be understood, you might want to say something like, "when I say that a pre-born child is a person what I mean is that it is one of the things whose welfare has to be considered. We have to consider the welfare of this being like we consider the welfare of ourselves."

If you're talking to my neighbor who's a taxicab driver, the most effective phrase might be the simplest. You might say, to him, that by person you mean a member of the human family.

BISHOP: I seek clarification on the matter being discussed now, "animation."

St. Thomas, following Aristotle, defended delayed animation, a progression from the vegetative life, then a corruption occurs and the sensate life takes over and there's also a corruption and then afterward the *vita intellectiva* takes place or the *anima intellectiva.* Of course, St. Thomas did not say when these things occur, but following his principle, that the material be disposed for its

52

proportionate form, the conclusion of many philosophers is that of delayed animation.

That's my first request for clarification.

The second has something to do with the correlation between the use of the term "human life" and "person."

I understand that some secular thinkers distinguish between these two.

And I also understood from Dr. Derr that the traditional inclusivistic approach is that every human life is a person. I don't know if I understood you correctly. My difficulty here is a text that I recall from my school days on the *Commentary on the Nichomachean Ethics.* I don't exactly remember the place, but he says something like this: Some change could occur, could happen that would hinder entirely the mind's happiness by hindering a virtuous life all together. And he gives an example: Sickness that is caused by insanity, madness.

Since happiness consists in living humanely—I think that's what he said—or according to *recta ratio,* reason, consequently, a person who is afflicted with madness cannot be happy anymore. And in this sense he concluded, consequently, in the sense of living humanely, this person, afflicted with madness, is all together to be considered or equivalent to death.

FATHER ASHLEY: On that first point—there are many people now who don't cite St. Thomas on anything else except this question of delayed hominization! One has to go a little further than the fact (which you correctly state) that St. Thomas says that you couldn't have the human soul in matter unless the matter was first properly disposed. You then have to ask, what do you mean by "properly disposed"? As I understand St. Thomas' position (which is just that of Aristotle) the matter is properly disposed for the spiritual soul when the primary organ which unifies the operation of the whole organism is present. Consequently, Aquinas and Aristotle thought that the primary organ is the heart. Therefore, when the heart appears even in a rudimentary form in the fetus, they concluded that at that point the infusion of the spiritual soul could occur, but not before.

Now, I think that is biologically sound. The unity of an organism depends on a system within the organism and that system depends on some primary organ. We know in the adult human being that primary organ is the brain. We say that when you have brain death, the person is dead and the soul cannot be present any longer because the brain is no longer living.

Some people, therefore, say that in modern biology we have to argue that as soon as a rudimentary brain appears in the embryo then the spiritual soul has been infused. And that's correct as far as it goes.

But we also have to ask further, "before the brain appears, before a rudimentary brain appears, is there some "pre-brain," some primary organ that accounts for the unity of the total organism and the fact that it is self-developing? And, of course, there is. At the very beginning there is the nucleus, the fertilized zygote which contains the genetic information necessary for the development of the whole organism.

Others argue that there is a period after the first cell division when you simply have a cluster of cells and, therefore, not an individual. And that this situation lasts until twinning can no longer occur. During the period in which twinning can take place the embryo (or "pre-embryo" as they call it) is just a group of cells.

Well, that's biologically false. From the very first cell division there is already a certain organization within the blastula phase and then the gastrula phase of the developing organism. One pole of the organism is determined to become the head eventually, and the other pole to become the tail of the organism. So that according to modern biology, at all times, the organism has a primary organ. Otherwise, you wouldn't have a single unified organism which is developing according to a definite program.

So, according to the principal of St. Thomas, when a primary organ exists which is specifically human in character and which can produce the whole human organism, at that moment you have the infusing of the human soul. That takes place at the moment of conception, i.e., of fertilization.

DR. DERR: I'd perhaps add something about the terms. I would distinguish between human life and a human being. I think a human being is a member of a species whether born or unborn, adult, child, what have you. There is a general sense in which we might say that cells falling off of our tongue have human life. That is, they're alive and they're derived from something human. But they're not members of our species. They're simply pieces or parts.

54

Germ cells are human. We can tell that they're not germ cells from any other species. But they're not human beings.

So I think there is a broader category of things that are human in some sense or other and which are alive and, therefore, which we might say have human life that are not human beings and not persons. The phrase 'human life,' I think, is sometimes used in public debate deliberately to confuse the issue when people try to say, "well, you're not making any distinction between adults and sperm cells or hair follicles" and that's false. I think, as Father Ashley has pointed out, we can make very good, reasonable biological distinctions between whole organisms at whatever stage of their development and pieces and parts of those organisms.

FATHER ASHLEY: As to the other text, I would think that when St. Thomas says that a person is "as good as dead," he's talking "morally" in the sense that this person has no possibility of further perfecting his or her life. But it doesn't mean that he or she is ontologically no longer a person. At least that's the way I would interpret the text.

BISHOP: On Page 81 of *Critical Issues in Contemporary Health Care* and I'd like to hear both of you comment, just if you would indulge me. How would you respond to the vision of this particular doctor who has a vision of the human person which I think is pretty common today.

"I think I've given my own philosophy which can be stated this way: You and I are equipped with this unbelievably creative instrument, the thinking, sensing, realizing, feeling and, above all, giving and living brain. But if you reduce my brain to the level of that possessed by a bird which is what the autonomic system is, then I think my essential humanity will have departed my residual body." From your perspective, given the history of the development of the human person, where does this fit in and how would you respond to it.

DR. DERR: Can I answer this one first? I'm going to guess that that's either Fred Plum or Ronald Cranford because I've heard both of them say that in court. Is that a good guess or a bad guess?

BISHOP: Fred Plum.

DR. DERR: First of all, I think it would be important to distinguish an ontological question from the range of moral questions about how this sort of impairment might influence our decision-making about medical care. But in the developmental history of the whole organism called a human being, it sometimes happens at some stage in life that we suffer severe neurological impairment. What we have then I think is an impaired human person and maybe in some cases it's not appropriate to treat impaired human persons quite as aggressively as we would treat other human persons. But we're still making a decision about the human person: The persistently vegetative patient or the severely neurologically impaired chronic patient that Plum wants to depersonalize is still, I believe, a person. And we still have a duty to care about their welfare and to worry about how we treat them and whether and when we let them die. They have not sunk to the moral status of a slug or a bird as he would imply. They will be a person until they die.

FATHER ASHLEY: I would agree with that and I would say— following the line of argument I've already given about the primary organ of the body—if the primary organ was so injured that all you have left are certain kinds of reflex actions, you might possibly make a case that the person is already dead. And perhaps some day we will know enough about the brain to be able to say which part of the brain is really the primary organ in which case we could refine our definition of death.

But at present I think it's pretty well agreed that we don't know enough about the brain to make any kind of distinction of that sort. So that unless the brain is totally dead, we still have a person—we have a person because the primary organ is still essentially intact. It can scarcely function but it is still functioning at least minimally so it's still alive and we have to assume that such a person is a living person.

BISHOP: A queston for Dr. Derr. This question may be more for the Supreme Court than for you. As I understand them, the Supreme Court, the media and the proponents of the exclusivist tradition all hold that the fetus is not a person or, as we have just said, a human being.

Now, if not a person or a human being, what is it? What's left? Do any of them have a term or an identification of what a fetus is if not a human person or a human being?

DR. DERR: Yes. Yes, I've learned this term debating ACLU people. And you already know the word: it is "potential." The name applied to the pre-born child is "a potential person," where "potential" is not used in any metaphysically coherent sense which Father Ashley could explain. But when a Supreme Court Justice says that the pre-born child is only a potential person, he *means* that it absolutely isn't a person.

The kind of language analysis that Father Ashley mentioned earlier can be used to show the incoherence of calling a pre-born child a potential person. Here is how you can do it if we call a block of marble a potential copy of The Pieta, what we *mean* in normal English is that it absolutely, positively, definitely isn't a copy of The Pieta (which begs the question that's suppposed to be argued!), and, in addition, that it will never become a copy of The Pieta unless something quite extraordinary is done to it by an external agent (which is absolute nonsense when applied to the developing human person, since something tragic and destructive must be done to the pre-born child in order to prevent its full development!).

So popular culture does have a magic word, which it uses to name the human fetus, the word "potential" but the way they use that word is not the way it's ever been used in any coherent philosophy. They're using it in a way that's simply nonsense.

BISHOP: Just four short comments and the last two are questions, if I could.

On the matter of hominization, I just wonder what Father Ashley thinks the impact would be on the possible philosopical requirements of a certain development of the matter in order to have a human substantial form since we accept as matters of faith that the Incarnation took place at the moment of conception of Jesus and it's a defined dogma of faith that we have an Immaculate Conception which meant there had to be a soul. Now, that wouldn't have to mean that everybody got a soul the same way but it certaily would indicate that it's not impossible to have a human soul in forming the material of a single right from the very beginning.

I mention it because that argument was being used for delayed hominization by some theologians back fifteen or twenty years ago and I don't think that it's reconcilable with either the Third Council of Nicea or the Incarnation or with Pius IX with regard to the Immaculate Conception.

Second, on hominization, that whole argument, as you pointed out very well disappeared when Gregor Mendel came along and started genetics and indicated that we have all that we need for the full development of a child in the one cell. And it seems to me, as you said, people not only cite St. Thomas only in that one instance but they also bury Mendel when they wouldn't do it to any other scientist at the time.

The two points on questions, one of them in a sense was just raised. Dr. Derr, the three current ideas of person that you gave are all ones that seem most people would characterize as pretty far out. Most of the people, ordinary people, Planned Parenthood even and doctors, I think, would not demand that much although maybe there are more of them now. What do you think is the average ordinary idea of what they would require of a person or is it just birth? You indicated that it's potential which means not a person but at some point it reaches personhood. Do you think that there's a consensus outside on what does constitute a person at the present time?

And the last thing I'd like to hear a little bit more comment on establishing the personhood of an unborn child or the matter of the personhood of somebody who was terminally unconscious because it seems to be those are the two critical areas for us now.

DR. DERR: Well, your first two points were observations with which I agree. I grant that the theories of exclusivism which I read to you sound far out to many, ordinary, decent people. But they're not far out in contemporary philosophical literature. The criteria that are being adduced for personhood by philosophers, theologians, geneticists, and self-styled ethicists are indeed far out. Now, do people in medicine have more common sense? That's not really clear to me. I'm inclined to believe, on the evidence, that all the professions are equally corrupt and equally confused.

Doctors aren't any worse than philosophers or theologians, but they're not any better either. Many pediatricians truly believe that retarded infants are not persons. There's a vast body of attitudinal research which shows that most physicians now believe that severely handicapped children are not persons.

As a nation, we have just put in charge of the scientific task of mapping the human gene, a man who is notorious for his habitually repeated view that no human being should be counted as a person until they're three days or a week or two weeks old and their parents have decided to accept them. That's Professor Watson's view and he has made no secret of it. It does not seem to bother anyone in government or the National Science Foundation on the National Institutes of Health, does it?

I grant that the views I have quoted seem far out. If you were less gentle, you might have said they're revolting. But they are in fact current and popular and, apparently, they don't upset people very much. We're in bad days with regard to personhood.

Now, about your other question: I'm not aware of any consensus answer. What binds the exclusivist tradition together is that they know who they want to get rid of. They're not sure what real people have in common. They can't be sure what real people have in common because they've splintered the person. They don't have anything left to give a coherent answer about.

FATHER ASHLEY: Your remarks about the Immaculate Conception are very interesting because I do think that that's one of the reasons that Christians came very quickly to see that abortion was wrong because of the text in Luke about John the Baptist leaping in the mother's womb. Such texts certainly influenced Christian thinking about the status of the unborn child. And that's one of the reasons that St. Thomas had difficulty about the Immaculate Conception of Mary because he didn't know how to fit it in with what he thought was the scientific conclusion about the time of ensoulment. He also had to explain the conception of Jesus by a special miracle anticipating the normal time of ensoulment. By this miracle the Holy Spirit immediately disposed the matter of Jesus' body so that the human soul could be infused at conception. So science has now helped theology out of some of its puzzles! It's much easier to deal with that kind of question when the scientific mistakes are removed.

The point that's most argued right now regarding immediate animation is the twinning case. That's being widely used and there are all kinds of articles coming out in one way or the other trying to prove that we do not have a human being until the twinning period is over. The mistake, of course, is to try to say that the embryo (or as they now call it, the pre-embryo) is just a mass of cells, and this is biologically just not true. We need to get the biologists to state the facts very clearly and then we need to give a consistent philosophical and theological analysis of the facts.

BISHOP: On this same topic, I think that St. Thomas Aquinas used the philosophical definition of Boethius for the person. An individual substance of a rational nature.

Now suppose that for a moment that between conception and the moment of the end of twinning, (some say about fourteen or fifteen days) suppose that could have one and after this two and after this one organism again. The possibility of twinning followed by fusion is a bit embarrassing. There's a period in differentiation which makes, I think, things difficult to evaluate.

Secondly, I would just like to refer to your own speech, Father Ashley, which I found very interesting. You say that one of the tasks of the Church would be to try to root historical minded views in a more classicist view, the one had for many centuries.

But could we not say also that history and our relational language are also something objective and that as classicists we should try to know what kind of objectivity there is in this historical minded view?

FATHER ASHLEY: I quite agree that it is objectively true that we are historical beings just as truly as we're thinking beings. But the question remains whether or not in understanding the human person we should begin with what is common to all human beings and then ask about what are the things that are individual and peculiar to each and understand these peculiarities in the context of what is common, or whether we should leave out that commonality and simply deal with what is peculiar, individual and conditioned. It seems to me that the first way is the better way. We should begin with trying to figure out what is human nature as something common to all human beings. That's what we're discussing here when we're trying to decide who is a human person. When we take that way then what we find out about the human person is that all human persons are social, they all speak, they all change, they're all part of history.

But when we come down to talking about Chinamen and Jews and Blacks and people of different race, that's a very important consideration. But these differences make sense only in terms of the fact that they're, first and foremost, all human.

BISHOP: But at least from the pedagogical point of view, should we not consider the possibility of doing what I just indicated because if we try today to stretch it from philosophical or metaphysical point of view, the nature of human person and so on, maybe we won't be understood, we won't be heard.

FATHER ASHLEY: Well, there is a difference between the rhetorical and the apologetic question—the problem of making ourselves understood and the question of what is true or not. I think it's disastrous to mix those things together because we end up then by forgetting what is true in order to be persuasive.

DR. DERR: Amen. Let me, please, comment on the issue of twinning because much is being made of it and I really think it's a red herring. It is alleged that an embryo very early in its development cannot be a person because possibly it might divide and become twins and surely it would be incoherent to say that it was two persons in one. Well, I think the second premise of that argument is false. I think it's *not* incoherent to say that a zygote destined to be two individuals has in it two principals of being, two forms or two acts. There are two persons acting. And one of the first and most dramatic acts will be to separate from each other.

Parenthetically, I think it's important to remember that numerical individuation (being one or two things) is a different problem from identification. Dollars ordinarily are individuated and identifiable. For example, in your pocket, there's one, two, three, four and so on. But many dollars in the modern economy are individuated and yet not identifiable. For example, when ten thousand dollars is wired across the ocean into an active corporate account and then, ten months and a thousand transactions later, ten thousand dollars are withdrawn, it doesn't even make sense to ask whether it's the *"same"* dollars that were withdrawn. Electronic dollars aren't identifiable even though, of course, they *are* individuated. So being able to know whether we have one or two persons in the zygote is a different problem than being able to make sense of the claim that there could be two persons in the zygote. The 'knowing' and the 'being,' like individuation and identification, are different problems.

Now, the second case that you raised is a little bit more puzzling, a little bit more troubling. It's the hypothetical case of a zygote which might divide and then recombine. This phenomenon has never been documented for humans but if it did occur, we would be on good ground if we chose to say that we have one principal of being which is acting, for a brief period of time, in two pieces of matter, and that it will act in a unified way in the future. That is just what we say, in a less dramatic way, about persons who have lost limbs in industrial accidents and then have them reattached: the accident victim's body is in two pieces for however long it takes to get into surgery. But even before the surgery, there is only one person, albeit parts of the person's past and future body are temporarily separated from each other. So, in my view the twinning phenomena do not cause metaphysical chaos for our view of the person.

BISHOP: Father Ashley, do any modern Catholic theologians in adapting to the historical mind approach say or teach that the fetus is not a human person?

FATHER ASHLEY: I think this is what's involved in a good deal of the current discussion. For example, there's my friend Dr. Tristram Englehart who is a medical ethicist. He's not exactly a theologian but he's a Catholic and teaches I believe at Baylor Medical School in Houston and is widely influential in this country. He has maintained in publications the position that personhood is essentially subjective in the sense I mentioned. For him a person must be an actually thinking, willing being. Consequently, he says the child who cannot yet enter into human relationships is not really a person but is only considered a person. Our society, he argues has reasonably agreed to consider small children persons but we have not agreed to consider the fetus a person because the fetus is not yet able to enter into human relationships.

I think the point I was trying to stress in my paper is that the reason that so many people in our society cannot see that the fetus is a human being is because for them person means the self-conscious subject. That's the way they define a person. Consequently, in the conflict of rights between a mother and her unborn child, it is only the mother who is certainly a person, while the fetus is not a person because it can't yet think and feel. Hence, our position seems monstrous to such people because they say, "Here you're valuing this woman who can think and feel and with whom I can sympathize less than this lump of flesh which has no interior feeling or thought?"

In my opinion, the error behind that attitude is that modern culture defines person merely in terms of subjectivity and not of the ontological characteristics of the person. But this position cannot be applied consistently. If you really press it, it leads to a lot of moral dilemmas, yet that's what many pro-choice proponents are holding on to. And so until we can shift people's thinking from this notion of person merely as subject to the notion of person as a whole entity which is both objective and subjective, we won't get anywhere in the abortion debate.

Chapter 5

GENE THERAPY: ACTUALITIES AND POSSIBILITIES

Michael R. Cummings, Ph.D.

INTRODUCTION

Conservative estimates of the impact of genetic disease on human populations indicate that world wide, some 53 of every 1,000 live born individuals will exhibit a genetic disorder before the age of 25 (Baird, P., *et al.,* 1988). This figure includes disorders caused by single genes, chromosome abnormalities, and cases involving the interaction of genetic and environmental factors. Because genetic disease affects some 5% of the population, it is a significant factor in public health. In the discussion to follow, it is important to remember that genetic disorders are a unique type of human disease. In cases of infectious disease, *e.g.,* tuberculosis, treatment can be directed at the agent responsible for the condition through medication or vaccination. The current large-scale effort to find an effective treatment for AIDS is an example of the commitment to this philosophy of treatment.

In the case of genetic disease, however, the only available therapies involve the routine treatment of symptoms rather than the root cause of the condition, and in most cases, the results are unsatisfactory. For example, individuals afflicted with hemophilia, a genetic disorder associated with uncontrolled bleeding, must undergo repeated transfusions to provide the clotting factors they are unable to produce. At best, the protection provided by this treatment is intermittent, and as a by product, has exposed almost all hemophiliacs treated in this way to the HIV virus associated with AIDS. The urgent need to provide effective therapy for inherited disease has given rise to the idea of treating these conditions by directly altering the defective gene in affected individuals. This approach is embodied in the concept of gene therapy.

For our purposes, we can define gene therapy as the deliberate alteration of genetic information within a human being, with the intention of correcting a genetic disorder. While the term gene therapy has only recently achieved widespread usage, and is often perceived as a new concept, early attempts at gene therapy in humans were first reported over two decades ago, and the concept in many ways is a logical extension of therapies developed over 50 years ago.

In assessing the present status of gene therapy, and in discussing its potential applications and developments, we will first review the development of current therapies used in treating genetic disorders, and discuss the possible types of gene therapy. To understand how this therapy works, we will then discuss its biological basis and the technology that makes it possible, and update the clinical experiments now underway in human gene transfer. In addition, we will consider how this technology can be used in clinical applications, and preview the genetic diseases that may be candidates for gene therapy. Finally, we will discuss some of the societal implications that must be considered as gene therapy develops into a clinical tool for the treatment of inherited disorders.

BACKGROUND TO GENE THERAPY

Gene Product Therapy

Product replacement is a form of therapy in which normal quantities of an absent or defective gene product are supplied to the affected individual. The first genetic disease to be treated in this manner was diabetes. Diabetes is caused by the absence of a gene product, the protein insulin. Insulin was first extracted in pure form from livestock in 1922, and has been used in the treatment of diabetes for over 60 years. Recently, the human insulin gene itself has been isolated and inserted into bacterial cells using recombinant DNA technology, and human insulin produced by bacterial cells is now available for therapeutic use.

Genetic disorders caused by a lack of human growth hormone can be successfully treated by product replacement using growth hormone extracted from the pituitary glands of cadavers. Recently, the human growth hormone gene has also been isolated and employed to produce commercial quantities of the growth hormone protein in recombinant bacteria. A limited number of other genetic disorders can also be treated by product replacement, including hemophilia, the bleeding disorder mentioned previously. There are three conditions necessary for use of product replacement in treating genetic disease. First, the gene and/or the gene product associated with the disease must be known; second, this product must be available or extractable from some source, and third, some information about its mode of action must be known to allow its clinical use. Unfortunately, only a small number of genetic disorders meet these conditions, and product therapy has achieved only limited use. The main problem is that in many genetic disorders, the gene product is unknown, effectively preventing the use of product therapy.

Organ Transplantation

The use of organ transplants to treat genetic disorders is a form of therapy in which an entire set of genetic information is transferred to the affected individual through cells of the transplanted organ. In this case, the nature of the defective gene and its product may be unknown. Polycystic kidney disease is an inherited disorder that affects about 1 in 1000 individuals, and a significant fraction of those patients receiving kidney dialysis are victims of this disease. Transplantation of an immunologically matched kidney is an effective form of treatment for this disease, even though the mutant gene, its gene product and its mode of action are completely unknown. As with product replacement, there are several preconditions for this type of therapy. The focus of the genetic disorder must lie within a single organ or tissue, and the affected organ must be transplantable. Recent advances in organ transplants, including new methods for matching donors and recipients, new drugs to suppress transplant rejection, and the development of hybrid organs, called neo-organs, will undoubtedly increase the use of this treatment.

Viewed in its historical context then, gene therapy is not necessarily a dramatic or new innovation, but instead, is an extension and refinement of past and present therapeutic strategies for treatment of genetic disorders. In this case, the refinement being developed under the rubric of gene therapy consists of transferring a single gene and its control elements to a target tissue instead of providing either an intermittent supply of the gene product, or an entire set of genetic information as in organ transplants.

GENE THERAPY

Somatic Therapy vs. Germ Line Therapy

Before we begin a discussion of the biological basis of gene therapy and the steps involved in the process, we should clarify the types of gene therapy that are possible. There are four types of gene therapy: somatic cell therapy, germ cell therapy, enhancement therapy and eugenic therapy (Nichols, 1988). Our discussion will center on the first two types, somatic therapy and germ cell therapy. Although the technologies in these two forms of therapy are somewhat similar, the ethical, moral and societal implications of these two types of gene transfer are quite different. Somatic cell gene therapy involves the transfer of a gene to an individual for therapeutic purposes, but the transferred information will not be inherited by the patient's offspring. Germ line therapy, on the other hand, involves transfer of genetic information that will be inherited by the patient's progeny.

Somatic therapy, by its nature, can be performed on individuals at many stages of development, including adulthood. In addition, the therapy can be attempted at successive stages of development such as infancy, childhood, adolescence or adulthood, and if necessary, can be repeated a number of times within any developmental stage until successful. In some genetic disorders with onset in adulthood such as Huntington's disease, treatment by somatic therapy would be possible while the individual is still pre-symptomatic. Although somatic therapy might be used to successfully cure a condition in a given individual, it would not prevent the same genetic defect from being inherited by offspring of the patient. Further, somatic cell therapy might be difficult to use in cases where the genetic disorder affects a number of tissues or organs, or where the disorder manifests itself prenatally.

Germ cell therapy can take two forms: insertion of genes into gametes before fertilization, or transfer of genes into newly fertilized eggs or early stage embryos. By its nature, this form of therapy is restricted to germ cells of the parental generation, or a single stage of the recipient's development. In gamete therapy, a normal gene would be transferred into the sperm or eggs of an adult affected with or carrying a genetic disorder, in effect correcting the defect in the progeny before conception. In zygote therapy, genetic information is transferred into the newly fertilized egg or into the cells of an embryo within a few hours after fertilization. In either form of germ line therapy, all cells of the resulting individual would be altered, making it unnecessary to target specific tissues or organs. In addition, the transferred genetic information would be inherited by all offspring of the recipient, preventing the disorder in future generations.

Biomedical Prerequisites for Gene Therapy

Current research efforts are directed at the development of techniques for human somatic cell therapy, that is, the transfer of genetic information that will not be passed on to future generations. The technology of germ line therapy is well advanced, and was first used in animals a decade ago. It is currently being used in both research laboratories and commercial applications to improve agricultural livestock. The use of germ line therapy is not currently a research goal for human gene therapy, but will be discussed in a subsequent section.

Several prerequisites must be met before either somatic or germ line gene therapy can be used to treat a specific heritable disorder (Weatherall, 1989). First, the gene associated with the disorder must be known. This entails not only knowledge of its pattern of inheritance and its location on one of the twenty-three human chromosomes, but also its size, molecular organization and the adjacent regulatory regions must be well characterized, and the gene cloned using recombinant DNA techniques. Second, the appropriate target cells must be identified and available for transfer. Third, a safe and efficient method for introducing the gene into the target cells must be developed. Fourth, the expression and activity of the transferred gene must be controlled. Each of these prerequisites represents a formidable research task, and in many cases, will be different for each genetic disorder to be treated. To illustrate just the difficulties of scale that must be faced in repairing a genetic defect by gene therapy, imagine the planet earth has been transformed to the microscopic size of a human cell. On that scale, the chromosome containing the defective gene would correspond to one of the smaller countries of the world, and the defective gene itself would be about the size of a small city or town in that country. The chemical components of the gene, the nucleotides in a DNA molecule, would correspond to individual dwellings in the town.

With these biological prerequisites in mind, let us then review the possible strategies that can be adopted to facilitate gene therapy as a clinical procedure.

Strategies of Gene Transfer
The overall strategy for gene therapy can be stated rather simply. A normal copy of a gene is to be inserted into the cells of an individual with an inherited genetic disorder. The normal copy of the gene will be expressed, to provide the function missing in the genetic disorder, correcting the underlying biochemical defect, and in turn, the clinical symptoms of the genetic disease. Gene therapy can employ any of several experimental strategies (Friedmann, 1989). A defective gene already present in a cell can be

supplemented by insertion of a normal copy, or a defective gene may be removed and replaced with a normal copy, or alternately, a new gene may be inserted where no copy currently exists. Over the past 7–10 years, several methods have been developed to alter or replace the expression of mutant genes by the introduction of normal genes. Based on work in a number of experimental systems, it appears likely that the strategy of gene supplementation will be employed in early trials of human gene therapy.

Genes can be transferred into human cells by several techniques. While many of these are suitable for research purposes, they have limitations or deficiencies that make them unsuitable for clinical use in human gene therapy. Two methods of transfer, direct injection into single cells using micromanipulation and the use of viruses to transfer genetic information are potentially useful for gene therapy. Microinjection is of limited value in somatic therapy, since each of millions of cells in the target tissue would have to be injected individually, but this method can be used in germ cell therapy, where a single fertilized egg would be the recipient. For somatic therapy, it appears that genetically altered viruses from a family known as human retroviruses will be employed to transfer genetic information. During its life cycle, the genetic information of the retrovirus is transferred to human cells during the process of viral infection. This information becomes integrated into one of the human chromosomes, and is passed to all cells that arise from the infected cells (Nichols, 1988; Kohne, *et al.,* 1989).

For use in gene therapy, the genetic information of retroviruses must be altered through the use of recombinant DNA techniques to remove one or more viral genes and replace them with the human gene to be transferred for therapeutic purposes. These genetically engineered viruses carrying human genes as passengers will be used to infect human target cells. When the human gene is inserted into a chromosome along with the viral DNA and activated, it will produce a therapeutic amount of a normal gene product. Even though not all cells of the body have been altered, it is hoped that enough of the gene product will be synthesized to correct the genetic disorder. Tests in animals, including mice, monkeys and dogs, have shown that retroviruses carrying mammalian genes can be efficiently transferred to host cells, and that transferred genes are expressed.

70

The choice of which cells will receive the transferred gene is also an important issue (Kohn, *et al.,* 1989). The target cells must be accessible, able to be manipulated *in vitro* and reintroduced into the patient. In order for gene therapy to be effective over the long term, the target cells should also be long-lived or actively dividing. Two tissues are leading candidates as targets for gene therapy: liver and bone marrow. Work using bone marrow has advanced the farthest, and early trials in gene therapy will most likely employ this tissue. A discussion of other target tissues is largely beyond the scope of this review.

In summary, then, somatic gene therapy will most likely be directed at a genetic disorder with its locus of action in bone marrow, using a retrovirus to carry the human gene to be transferred, in an attempt to supplement or correct a defective gene. Although no clinical trials employing any form of gene therapy are currently underway, other experiments in human gene transfer have started, and with minimum alterations in protocol, will serve as the basis for the first attempts at somatic gene therapy. Because this work is a direct precursor to gene therapy, it is considered below.

Current Experiments in Human Gene Transfer

On May 22, 1989 scientists at the National Institutes of Health in Bethesda, Maryland began experiments that involved the transfer of genetically altered cells into humans. While this work is not designed to replace a defective gene, success in these experiments will allow gene therapy trials to proceed. In the work at Bethesda, genetically altered white blood cells known as tumor infiltrating cells (TIL cells) were transferred into patients with advanced cases of melanoma, a fatal form of skin cancer. In the body, TIL cells seek out and infiltrate tumors, destroying cancer cells. In these experiments, TIL cells were isolated from melanoma tumors surgically removed from the patients. *In vitro,* the cells were infected with a modified retrovirus carrying a bacterial passenger gene. The treated TIL cells were then injected into the melanoma patients to monitor the pattern of migration and survival of the marked TIL cells. If the present experiments with TIL cells and melanoma patients go as expected, trials on human gene therapy are expected to follow in a short time, perhaps in the next few months. In gene therapy experiments, the bacterial gene inserted into the retrovirus will be replaced by a normal human gene designed to correct a genetic disorder, and the target tissue will be different.

PROSPECTS AND POTENTIAL APPLICATIONS OF SOMATIC GENE THERAPY

The choice of genetic disorders that can be considered for treatment by gene therapy is of necessity limited by the resources and knowledge currently available. The probable choice of bone marrow as the target tissue for initial attempts at gene therapy narrows the list of candidate disorders to those whose primary mode of action is in the marrow cells, or the white blood cells (lymphocytes) derived from marrow (Kantoff, *et al.,* 1988). It may also be possible to consider genetic disorders involving some general aspect of metabolism that might be corrected by gene action involving bone marrow cells. The obvious candidates for gene therapy, then, are genetic disorders for which bone marrow transplantation is currently used or which might benefit from gene action in bone marrow cells. Some of these are listed in Table 1.

Of the disorders listed, it appears that the leading candidate for somatic gene therapy is severe combined immunodeficiency disease (SCID) associated with adenosine deaminase deficiency. This is a rare genetic disorder in which the affected individual has

TABLE 1

CANDIDATE DISEASES FOR SOMATIC GENE THERAPY

Genetic Disorder	Current Treatment
sickle cell anemia	transfusion
adenosine deaminase deficiency (SCID)	bone marrow transplant
alpha^1-antitrypsin deficiency	none
hemophilia	product replacement
thalassemia (alpha and beta)	transfusion
purine nucleotide phosphorylase deficiency	none
Fanconi's anemia	bone marrow transplant
Lesch-Nyhan disease	drug therapy
adrenoleukodystrophy	bone marrow transplant

no functional immune system, and succumbs to infections that would be trivial in unaffected individuals. The case of the 'boy in a bubble' who lived in an artificial, sterile environment for 15 years is an example of an individual with SCID. This disorder is caused by a mutation in a single, well characterized gene that has been recovered and studied using recombinant DNA techniques. In addition, experiments with animal systems mentioned previously have indicated that there is a high probability of success in correcting this condition.

Possible Limitations to Gene Transfer

As in any new technique to be implemented clinically, there are a number of actual and potential limitations to the use of gene therapy.

First, at least in its initial stages, there is only a very limited number of genetic disorders that can be treated using gene therapy, and since most of the disorders are relatively rare, there will only be a small numbers of individuals who can benefit from this treatment. Along these lines, the observation that there are more people working on gene therapy for SCID than there are patients in the world population is probably true.

Secondly, there is not yet enough evidence that the treatment will work well enough to benefit the patient.

These two limitations will probably be self-correcting, as the techniques of gene therapy come into widespread use. In addition, it seems likely that the relationship between risk and benefit will become resolved. There are however, a number of potential limitations and abuses of gene therapy that still need to be considered:

The effects of gene therapy itself and its potential side effects, may not be reversible or treatable.

There is potential for deliberate misuse of gene therapy on the part of individuals seeking treatment in the absence of a genetic disorder. Implantation of growth hormone genes to augment height is an example. This use of gene therapy has been termed gene enhancement.

In spite of the monumental efforts to develop gene therapy, in the long run, it may not be any safer, cheaper or more effective than alternate methods. Consenting patients or their custodians may not be well informed about the potential risks and benefits of the therapy.

PROSPECTS FOR GERM LINE GENE THERAPY

Although human gene therapy will probably begin with the treatment of single gene defects in somatic tissue to correct biochemical disorders, the possible use of this technology to alter the genetic constitution of future generations through germ cell therapy cannot be ignored. Although there are no current plans to employ germ line therapy, arguments for this type of treatment will probably become stronger once somatic cell therapy is in place. Consequently, it is important to review developments that affect the implementation of germ line therapy.

Diagnosis of Preimplantation Embryos and Gametes

Using a relatively new technique of molecular biology, known as PCR (polymerase chain reaction) analysis, several groups have recently succeeded in performing genetic analysis on single cells removed from 6–10 cell human embryos (Buster and Carson, 1989; Handyside, *et al.,* 1989). This experimental type of fetal research seeks to determine whether the embryo carries a defective gene that would result in a disorder such as muscular dystrophy, Tay-Sachs disease, hemophilia, cystic fibrosis or a number of other disorders. The embryos continue to develop *in vitro* after such treatment, but operated embryos have not been implanted *in utero* to determine whether normal development would proceed. As methods of gene transfer develop, it can be expected that genetic disorders in early embryos might be repaired using gene therapy. As mentioned earlier, techniques of gene transfer by microinjection currently used in animal husbandry could be employed on such human embryos.

More recently, PCR analysis has been used on developing human oocytes to determine if they carry a defective gene (Verlinsky, *et al.,* 1989). In this technique, oocytes are recovered by uterine lavage and an accompanying sister cell, the polar body, has been recovered by microdissection and used in genetic diagnosis. The genetic state of the oocyte can then be determined by inference. Such sorting of oocytes prior to *in vitro* fertilization could be employed to prevent transmission of x-linked genetic traits; selection of gametes bearing normal genes would represent an indirect form of germ cell gene therapy.

The current evidence from research on laboratory animals and livestock is that germ line gene therapy, like somatic cell therapy, is limited technically by the inability to control the expression of the transferred gene (Pursel, *et al.,* 1989). Its application to humans, will, in turn depend on more research to achieve proper control over the amount of gene product expressed, the time of its expression, and the tissues in which expression takes place.

IMPLICATIONS FOR SOCIETY

After an extended period of anticipation, gene therapy seems ready to emerge as a method of treatment for genetic disorders. Most of this delay can be attributed to the stringent requirements and difficulties inherent in each step of the processes necessary to accomplish this technical tour de force. In many ways, somatic gene therapy represents an extension of strategies that have been employed for decades in the treatment of genetic diseases, and there is currently little debate about the need or the ethics of this form of gene therapy.

The role of somatic gene therapy as form of treatment has been carefully examined and accepted by a number of scientific and medical organizations, ecclesiastical bodies and public policy analysts who have participated in the formulation of policy and the system of oversight that will accompany the use of this procedure (Roberts, 1989). Included in this array of individuals and institutions is His Holiness, Pope John Paul II, who took note of gene therapy in his address to the 35th General Assembly of the World Medical Association.

The role of germ line gene therapy, on the other hand, is less well defined, and much more problematic (Fowler, *et al.,* 1989). However, as somatic cell therapy becomes commonplace, arguments for germ line therapy will undoubtedly be advanced. For example, many single gene disorders that will be amenable to gene therapy have serious developmental effects early in embryogenesis, and treatment at any time after birth would have no impact. Treatment of these conditions in early stages of development, *i.e.,* in the zygote or early embryo, would be necessary to ensure that therapy would be effective. Thus, for these conditions, the only form of effective gene therapy would be germ line therapy. The side effect of this treatment would be a permanent alteration of the genetic information transmitted to offspring. A second argument in favor of germ line gene therapy is that of efficiency. Instead of correcting a genetic disorder in each generation of a family by somatic therapy, germ line therapy would permanently correct the problem for all future members of the family line.

The approach to germ line therapy needs to be carefully considered as it raises many ethical, legal and even constitutional issues, including how such therapy would affect the notion of personhood and humanity. Should we, for example, permanently introduce animal or plant genes into the genetic heritage of humans if they prove more effective in treating disorders than the corresponding human genes? Can individuals affected with a genetic disorder claim an ethical right to germ line therapy to prevent defective offspring? Or conversely, can an individual refuse such treatment when to do so would impose a burden of a potentially lethal genetic disorder on one's offspring?

Issues relating to the ethics of germ line gene therapy need to be met and clearly articulated now. This discussion should not be deflected by the claim that germ line therapy is not currently a goal of research or clinical application. The development of somatic cell therapy has been accompanied by an exemplary public discussion of the ethical and moral dimensions of this treatment, and the emergence of a general consensus about its use. This is the time for a similar discussion of germ line therapy.

On the fringes of this whole argument is the specter of intervention by gene therapy to produce individuals with enhanced athletic or intellectual abilities (gene enhancement therapy), or the use by the state to modify or alter human characters such as behavior as a form of eugenic therapy. While these arguments may seem somewhat far-fetched, please remember that earlier in this century, genetics was also a powerful force in both science and society. In this country, genetics was coupled with the doctrine of biological determinism and used to pass restrictive immigration laws, involuntary sterilization laws, and marriage laws. Genetics also played an important role in the social programs of the Third Reich. Although the technology has changed, and we regard ourselves as more sophisticated than those living half a century ago, the human potential for hubris and pleonexia or smugness remains. Let us, therefore, welcome treatments like gene therapy that can relieve the burden of genetic disorders with open arms, but also with open eyes.

References

Baird, P. A., Anderson, T. W., Newcombe, H. B., and Lowry, R. B. 1988. Genetic disorders in children and young adults: a population study. Am. J. Hum. Genet. 42: 677–693.

Buster, J. E. and Carson, S. A. 1989. Genetic diagnosis of the preimplantation embryo. Am. J. Med. Genet. 34: 211–216.

Fowler, G., Juengst, E. and Zimmerman, B. 1989. Germ line gene therapy and the clinical ethos of medical genetics. Theoret. Med. 10: 151–165.

Friedmann, T. 1989. Progress toward human gene therapy. Science 244: 1275–1281.

Handyside, A. H., Pattinson, J. K., Penketh, R. J. A., Delhanty, J. D. A., Winston, R. M. L. and Tuddenham, E. G. D. 1989. Biopsy of human preimplantation embryos and sexing by DNA amplification. Lancet i: 347–349.

Kantoff, P. W., Freeman, S. M., and Anderson, W. F. 1988. Prospects for gene therapy for immunodeficiency diseases. Ann. Rev. Immunol. 6: 581–594.

Kohn, D. B., Anderson, W. F., and Blaese, R. M. 1989. Gene therapy for genetic diseases. Cancer Investig. 7: 179–192.

Nichols, E. K. 1988. *Human Gene Therapy.* Cambridge Mass: Harvard University Press. 251 pp.

Pursel, V. G., Pinkert, C. A., Miller, K. F., Bolt, D. J., Campbell, R. G., Palmiter, R. D., Brinster, R. L., and Hammer, R. E. 1989. Genetic engineering of livestock. Science 244: 1281–1288.

Roberts, L. 1989. Ethical questions haunt new genetic technologies. Science 243: 1134–35.

Verlinsky, Y., et al, 1989. Genetic analysis of polar body DNA: a new approach to preimplantation genetic diagnosis. Am. J. Hum. Genet. 45: A272 (abstract).

Weatherall, D. J. 1989. Gene therapy: getting there slowly. Brit. Med. J. 1298: 691–693.

Chapter 6

PERSONHOOD; ENTRY AND EXIT

The Reverend Albert S. Moraczewski, O.P., Ph.D.

Vatican Council II celebrated the mystery of the human person, it asserted the dignity of persons, and noted humankind's restless urge for increasing mastery over the world. Its Pastoral Constitution on the Church in the Modern World, *Gaudium et Spes* states:

> Believers and unbelievers agree almost unanimously that all things on earth should be ordained to man as to their center and summit (*Gaudium et spes* #12, p. 913).

In particular, we are concerned here with issues of the impact of biomedical technology on human persons and human society. The pivotal issue in all of medical ethics is the nature and origin of the

78

human person. What sort of a being is the human person, when does it begin to exist, and when does it cease to exist—if it does—are to be considered briefly in this paper. Included in the discussion will be a very brief consideration of the persistent vegetative state, brain death, and profound mental retardation as they relate to existence of a human person.

THE HUMAN PERSON:
AN ENIGMA WRAPPED IN A RIDDLE

Two earlier papers at this workshop have presented a historical development of the concept of person (Patrick G. Derr, "An Analysis of the History of the Concept of the Human Person," in this volume, p. 15) and current views and usage of the term (Benedict M. Ashley, O.P., "Contemporary Understandings of Personhood," in this volume, p. 35) Here, I will focus more on the ontogenesis of the adult human person in order to appreciate the entry and exit of the human person in the temporal world. In particular, I will review critically the major objections raised against the human zygote and early embryo being human persons.

Reflecting the words of the Psalmist, *Gaudium et spes* asks the question:

> But what is man? He has put forward, and continues to put forward, many views about himself, views that are divergent and even contradictory. Often he either sets himself up as the absolute measure of all things, or debases himself to the point of despair. Hence his doubt and his anguish (*Gaudium et spes* #12, p. 913).

Without ignoring what has been said previously by the preceeding speakers, I want to develop a concept of the human person which I will use in this paper.

The human person is one of those common realities which like time—as St. Augustine so aptly noted—everyone knows what it is until asked to define it. Are the terms "human person", "human being", and "human life" synonymous? One could distinguish them by saying that the "human person" refers to a human individual as the subject of rights and responsibilities. The second term, "human being" could simply refer to a member of the species *Homo sapiens sapiens.* "Human life" could designate an organism which manifests certain basic characteristics associated with a human genome, i.e., set of human genes, or to life as it exists in a part of a human organism. But all refer to the same objective reality albeit under different formalities.

The attribution of personhood to human beings, as some would insist, is not arbitrary. Since *agere sequitur esse,* the person primarily will be revealed by decisions and acts, and these in turn will shape and fashion the person. But it should not be overlooked that the most basic and revealing act of what a living thing is, is precisely what it becomes in its mature stage. A caterpillar does not fully reveal its nature until it becomes a butterfly or moth. A caterpillar is one developmental stage (larvae) of the same creature that later manifests itself as a butterfly of moth. Among living beings the earlier stages of development may, in outward appearance, be very different than the mature stage. Yet it is one and the same individual who has traversed various stages to reach maturity.

Yet an exclusive biopsychological comparative analysis of what humans and other primates *do* is necessary but not sufficient to specify what is a person. Used in isolation the methods of modern anthropology, biology, and psychology preclude an analysis of the data that would yield an answer. Bound by a methodology which limits itself to what is measurable and material, modern science logically excludes a *priori* the possibility of finding a non-material principle as a radical explanation of what is observed. Dedicated to a reductionism which seeks ultimate explanation at the level of neurons, genes, molecules and atomic and subatomic structures, and their respective activities, modern biology and psychology are blinded to the existence and operation of a spiritual soul and therefore unable to identify and explain the human person in its most basic being and operation.

The human person is an enigma straddling two worlds. The human person is neither the body or soul taken separately but both taken together, not united as *two things* but fused as two *principles* to form the one being. In that bonding *Gaudium et spes* sees part of the human glory:

Man, though made of body and soul, is a unity. Through his very bodily condition he sums up in himself the elements of the material world. Through him they are thus brought to their highest perfection and can raise their voice in praise freely given to the Creator. For this reason man may not despise his bodily life (*Gaudium et spes* #14, pp 914–915).

Although in part material, measurable and tangible, the human person has a non-material, a spiritual principle by which it transcends the limitations of matter. Because the human soul of itself is not extended in space it is non-commensurable. As the ancients said, "the soul is totally in the whole body and totally in each part." the "size" of the soul cannot be measured by the size of the body it informs. Whether in the fully mature adult human body or in the zygote or in the embryo, the soul has the same "size"—and same inherent dignity, albeit not the same perfection. *That* is acquired gradually over time.

The human person shapes itself; it is a microcosm but one which determines the sort of a person it will be. All other creatures are limited by their materiality to be what they are. Their potential as a species and as individuals is strictly limited. But a human person is not so limited: though the body does place limits of various kinds, the human person through technology partially transcends many of these limitations. Examples include: telescopes and microscopes to go beyond the normal limits of our vision; telephones, and radio to extend the power of our voices; autos, trains, boats, planes, and space vehicles to give us "seven league boots" which pushes our range and rate of local movement far beyond where our legs will take us; computers to assist and extend various intellectual and artistic skills. We should also include the numerous medical and surgical procedures which aid and augment the body's natural healing powers.

Yet it is not these technological accomplishments which primarily reflect the human person's transcendance. Rather, it is love and the *moral* decisions an individual makes. We become what we love. Our free decisions and consequent actions shape us. Human freedom means that there is no universal inner coercion which determines our choices. God's infinite power rather than destroying that inner freedom guarantees it in its basic being in its operation. (see St. Thomas, *Summa Theologiae,* I, 83; Sr. Terese Auer, *The Apparent Antinomy of Divine Causality and Human Free Choice,* unpublished doctoral dissertation, Houston, University of St. Thomas, 1989).

ENTRY

In the midst of this splendiferous human reality stands the riddle of origin and destiny. While many people will agree to the greatness and the accomplishments of humans and human society, many have great difficulty in attributing such nobility to the earliest beginnings (and terminal stages) of individual human life. Representative of many, Professor Clifford Grobstein asks in his recent book, *Science and the Unborn:*

> Can a single cell be a human being, a person, an entity endowed with unalienable right to life, liberty, and the pursuit of happiness? (Clifford Grobstein, *Science and The Unborn,* New York; Basic Books, 1988, p. 5).

His answer is no. His basic reason is that although the human zygote is undoubtedly human to its core, it has not yet achieved adequate unity and uniqueness as an individual. But what makes an individual, individual? In an article, Clifford Grobstein ("Biological Characteristics of the Preembryo" in *In Vitro Fertilization and Other Assisted Reproduction,* eds. Howard W. Jones, Jr. and Charlotte Schroeder, *Annals of the New Academy of Science,* Vol. 541, 1988, pp. 346–8) distinguishes the genetic individual from developmental individual ("oneness" or "singleness"). He refuses to recognize the preembryo as a true individual as is the actual embryo (the first visible sign of which is the primitive streak, (see, *ibid.*) However, if the "preembryo" were not an individual *in the sense* of being an organism, it would not arrive at being an embryo. Considerable directed organizational activity is going on before it becomes what Grobstein calls the "actual embryo." The normal (usual) process does not involve twinning or recombination. Differentiation does not make the individual; that is one stage in the individual's development. If there were not a direction (telos) from the beginning of individual life, the result of cell division would be just a clump of cells and not an organism, not an embryo. Our analysis will show that the human zygote is fully individuated and unique organism, and, indeed, can be perceived as a person once the terms of the judgement are understood.

One empirical way to approach the issue as to when does a human person begin is to commence with the mature adult when there is no doubt that the individual is a human person, and then, to reverse the developmental chronology. The objective is to determine whether there is a point in the development of the human being where we could assert—if we can—that a human individual is not a human person.

If we, then, go backwards in time and follow in reverse order the developmental sequence of human person starting with mature adults, we note that after a certain point the younger the individual the less clearly *adult* human characteristics are exhibited. The young adult, the adolescent and the prepuberty child increasingly show fewer of the developed mental and physical skills which are found in the mature adult. The three-year old child and the infant may be able to speak but cannot write although can scribble and copy figures. Part of the explanation is neurological in that certain neurons and neuronal networks are not yet complete in their structure and connections. Hence, the necessary motor skills are not yet available to the person. The new-born child, while recognizably human in form and configuration, does not act as the adult human, adolescent, or prepuberty child. Except for a few philosophers, most adults would not seriously deny that a new born human child is a person. Such a neonate is no less a person although clearly at an early stage in the long development process by which the powers of the individual are gradually actualized.

Although the conscious and competent *adult* human manifests characteristics which are uniquely associated with humans, the *actual* presence and exercise, here and now, of these adult activities in an individual are *not* required for us to denominate the individual as a person. The sleeping or anesthetized adult is indubitably a person even if at the moment is not actually exhibiting the essential and basic characteristics of an adult human person. Only the impediment of sleep or anesthesia prevents the individual from speaking, writing, reasoning, willing, and so forth. The ten-year old is considered a person as well as the one-year old who cannot as yet read or write poetry, prose, or anything else of this sort.

Continuing the reverse chronology through the time of birth in the development of the human being, we enter the relative darkness of intrauterine life. In this nine-month period there takes place an amazing process of growth and development. Starting from just before birth and tracking backwards in time, we note that the individual human being gradually looks externally less and less as a human being until it cannot be distinguished from a clump of cells or indeed a single cell at the very beginning (except, of course, by microscopic analysis of the chromosomes).

The cell—the zygote—resulting from a union of the two half sets of chromosomes (from oocyte and sperm) is the first step in the formation of an *adult* human person. Again, Professor Grobstein:

> In roughly nine calendar months a single human cell, the zygote produced at conception, or fertilization, multiples in cell number, becomes cohesive, reorders, grows further, differentiates, and forms a multiplicity of functioning parts. Throughout this orderly and as-yet only incompletely comprehended process, the developing entity *maintains its initial endowment of individuality* [emphasis added] and elaborates it into a human infant composed of billions of cells that are organized into one of the most intricate entities known to science (Grobstein, *ibid,* p 4).

At the initial step of fertilization which is identifiable and non-repeatable for this individual, the entity is an organism: it is one being, living and belongs to a definite species—*Homo sapiens sapiens.* It will *not* develop into a member of another species—dolphin, chimpanzee, or cat. Because of disease or injury or death, this organism may not become a human adult or infant, it may die *in utero,* at birth or afterwards. Although it may be born with mild or severe mental or physical handicaps, nonetheless, it is human. As the Vatican Congregation for the Doctrine of the Faith noted:

The human being must be respected—as a person—from the very first instant of his existence (*Instruction on Respect for Human Life in its Origin and on The Dignity of Procreation,* Congregation for the Doctrine of the Faith, February 22, 1987, #I,1).*

But would such handicaps, especially profound mental retardation, situate an individual outside the society of human *persons?* Some years ago Joseph Fletcher provided a 20-proposition profile of humanhood. One such proposition states that if the individual had an IQ below 40 he was questionably a person, below 20, definitely not a person (Joseph Fletcher, "Indicators of Humanhood: A Tentative Profile of Man", *The Hastings Center Report,* Nov. 1972, pp. 1–4). For comparison, the American Association on Mental Deficiency considers a person to be mentally retarded if they have an IQ below about 70. It defines mental retardation as:

... significantly subaverage general mental functioning resulting in or associated with concurrent impairments in adaptive behavior and manifested during the developmental period (H. I. Kaplan and B. J. Sadock, *Comprehensive Textbook of Psychiatry,* Vol. 2, Fifth Edition: Baltimore: Williams & Wilkins, 1988, p. 1729).

Severe mental retardation is represented by an IQ between 20–40, while below 20 is considered *profound* retardation. These latter two categories together represent about 4 to 6% of all mentally retarded persons. Yet these are not considered non-persons by the Association; it would not agree with Fletcher's exclusion principle. In all cases, as a living member of the human species, the profoundly handicapped individual is a human person. Because of the biological deficits he is not able—like the sleeping or anesthetized person—to manifest the characteristic human physical and mental skills. Nonetheless, such an individual is no less a human person than a fully mature adult. Also, because of the severe damage to, or gross underdevelopment of the brain, the profoundly handicapped person will never be able to *become* an *adult* human person. Yet given a human and humane environment where persons interact with smiles, stroking and gentle words on a daily basis, profoundly retarded individuals will maximize their potential and react with some human awareness as a very young baby does with smiles and sounds of pleasure—even a few words as "Mama" or "Dada".

As we have seen the human person results from the ontological union of body and soul, of matter and spirit. Hence, the critical point of a person's entry into this world is precisely the instant the spiritual soul—the immaterial principle—is infused into the matter. But is this point in time ascertainable? The Congregation for the Doctrine of the Faith states:

> This declaration expressedly leaves aside the question of the moment which the spiritual soul is infused. There is not a unanimous tradition on this point and authors are yet in disagreement (*Declaration on Procured Abortion,* Nov. 18, 1974, footnote 19).

In addition, the *Declaration* stated that this moment cannot be decided by science (*ibid.*) for it is a philosophical problem since the issue involves a non-material component (the spiritual soul) which as such is not directly a subject of empirical science and its current methodologies.

But this does not mean that science is totally silent on the subject. It can provide, and indeed has provided, important data regarding the fertilization and the development of the embryo. Earlier hesitations, based supposedly on St. Thomas, to accepting completed fertilization as the moment of entry of a person into the world was based on the totally inadequate biological knowledge available at the time of St. Thomas (see Benedict Ashley in an *Ethical Evaluation of Fetal Experimentation,* eds., McCarthy and Moraczewski, St. Louis, Pope John Center, 1976, pp. 113–133). Removal of that hesitation can be based on modern biological knowledge of the process of fertilization and of the human zygote's genetic and cellular structure which uniquely possesses from the beginning the power to develop, unless impeded by disease or injury or death, into an adult human person. Zygotes and embryos are organisms because they possess a primary organizer or integrating center by which the activities of the various cells are integrated into a functional unity so that development takes place in an orderly and timely fashion and not merely as clumps of cells.

By philosophical analysis of these new data one can come to a reasoned and reasonable conclusion, namely, that at the beginning, when the half-sets chromosomes from each parent functionally united to form the full set of human chromosomes necessary to integrate and direct the subsequent development of the new organism, *that* is the moment when the new human person enters the temporal world.

> From the time that the ovum is fertilized, a new life is begun which is neither that of the father nor of the mother; it is rather the life of a new human being with his own growth. It would never be made human if it were not already human (*Declaration on Procured Abortion*).

Science has shown this organism is already a complex being with the necessary inner dynamism to allow its specific development to an adult. All it now needs is the appropriate interactive environment not only for nourishment and shelter but also for chemical factors necessary for continued growth and differentiation. At the very beginning it is unified, it is a member of the human species. It is a living, developing organism that will proceed through a number of stages in a smooth, continuous manner. This organism is driven from within, absorbing nutrients and other factors from the maternal blood stream and directing its own progressive development to one goal—the adult human person.

It may be difficult to imagine that first cell of the developing human embryo *radically* has all the essential power of the adult: to build cities, write poetry, compose symphonies, worship God and receive a share of Divine grace! All that is required is time and the appropriate psychosocial environment for the organism to develop so that those powers can be exercised through the appropriate bodily organs.

OBJECTIONS

A variety of objections have been raised to the notion that the human *person* begins at the time the new human zygote first appears. Most of these objections focus on the assertion that the zygote does not exhibit substantial unity and individuality which is requisite in order for the zygote (or very young embryo) to be a person. Several reasons in support of that assertion have been cited in the literature (see, for example, Carlos A. Bedate and Robert C. Cefalo, "The Zygote: to Be or not to Be a Person," *The Journal of Medicine and Philosophy,* 14: 641–645, 1989; Thomas J. Bole, III, "Metaphysical Accounts of the Zygote as a Person and the Veto Power of Facts," *op. cit.,* 14: 647–653, 1989, J. D. Biggers, "Generation of the Human Life Cycle," in *Abortion and the Status of the Fetus,* W. B. Bonderson *et al,* Dordrecht: D. Reidel Publ. Co., 1983/ 84, pp. 31–53). The following are representative objections:

1. The formation of identical twins (monozygotic twins) from the zygote or embryo;
2. The formation of hydatidiform moles as a result of fertilization;
3. The recombination or fusion of what was originally two separate embryos to form a single embryo;
4. The requirement of extra-zygotic factors for the proper development of the zygote and embryo;
5. The essential continuity of life such that there is no break in the continuum of human life from one generation to the next.

Although these objections have varying degrees of persuaveness, they need each to be considered. By way of anticipation and in brief, none are convincing on close examination of the facts and logic: the thesis stands—a human being is a person from the moment the new human individual is present, that is, from the zygotic stage onwards.

I will consider the objections in order:

1. The objection is well stated by Grobstein:
   So far as is known, the cells of the inner cell mass of the early blastocyst are little different in developmental capability from the zygote. Each can contribute to any part of the embryo, and separation of the mass into two

parts can still yield two or more embryos. It is only when the later-stage blastocyst has penetrated and implanted in the uterine wall that properties of the inner cell mass change and it becomes committed to the production of a single individual.

The stage of commitment to developmental individuality is often referred to as primary embryonic organization—the beginning of formation of the embryo proper. In the process, the inner cell mass is transformed into an embryo—a rudiment capable of building a single complete multicellular individual. In this sense, primary organization lays down the basic structure of a single organism. It is represented in the three main body axes: head and tail, left and right, back and front.

This first sign that primary organization is underway is the appearance of what is called the primitive streak (see *ibid.,* figure 4, page 27).

There are various ways in which identical twins can be formed: (separation at the 2-cell stage; splitting of the inner mass into two separate groups; splitting at a later stage but before appearance of the primitive streak (see T. W. Sadler, *Langman's Medical Embrology,* fifth edition, Baltimore: Williams and Wilkins, 1985, pp. 102–105). Nonetheless, the fundamental question is the same and concerns the presence of two distinct embryos (and persons) where before there was only one. Three speculative responses may be suggested:

a) There never was a single embryo (or person) in the first place. For reasons, unknown at this time, what was thought to be one zygote after fertilization was actually two because of some unspecified factor influencing the fertilization process. But this explanation is not likely since there is no adequate evidence to support it. One may adduce the fact that twinning occurs in families; that points to a possible genetic influence (more below) in the earliest phases of the fertilization process.

b) The initial zygote was one individual but during the first cell division the two daughter cells lost (or, never established) the necessary physical communication link which would make them one organism. There is evidence of such intercellular communication early on:

> Thus, we shall see that cells of the embryo establish communication among themselves and create a microenvironment. They adhere to one another, interact with certain extracellular elements, and show limited mobility before implantation" (Patracea Calarco-Gillam, "Cell-cell Interaction in Mammalian Preimplantation Development" in Leon Browder Developmental Biology, Vol. 2, *The Cellular Basis of Morphogenesis,* 1986, p. 330).

As a consequence one daughter retained the original soul, and the other received another soul since it was still apt matter. The primary organizer's role here is critical. It is the physical instrument of the soul for integrating the cell's activities and making it an organism. After the first cleavage of the zygote, the daughter cell (blastomere) which has the primary organizer is the one which retains the original soul should the two cells lose effective communication-contact. It is similar say, to an adult human being, who loses an arm or leg, or even has a hemicorporectomy (where the lower part of the trunk and legs are surgically removed), the remaining portion which retains the brain (the primary integrating center for a more developed human organism) is the original person. However, because the removed arms, legs, etc are no longer totipotential they cannot receive another spiritual soul. They do not constitute another human person. But in the case of the very early embryo the outcome is different; because the other cell is still apt matter it cell receives a soul. It is still totipotential and the cell's primary organizer becomes effective. The primary organizer is probably the nucleus. For whatever reason one of the two nuclei (at the two-cell stage) is dominant. The two cells are therefore two separate individuals albeit in close embrace due to be enveloped by a common *zona pellucida.* Full physical separation takes place a few days later.

   c) Another possibility—but less likely, I believe—is that the original being died as a result of the failure to form or retain the union of the two cells. But since each cell is still totipotential at this point, then each is suitable matter to receive a new human unifying principle, a soul. Each becomes a new human being, a new human person.

It should be noted that at the beginning stages the "adhesive bond" and communication between the cells are rather weak. But experimental evidence shows that as the organism develops, certain cell-to-cell bonds become increasingly strong.

> After fertilization, the zygote progresses by a series of five cleavages to blastocyst stage... During the 8-cell stage, a process termed compaction ensues, which is characterized by increasing adhesion between blastomeres and a general rounding of the embryo. After the development of tight junctions between the external cells of the morula (approximately the 16-cell stage), the embryo accumulates fluid in the intercellular space and blastulates at approximately the 32-cell stage. (Calarco-Gillam, *ibid.*)

Thus, if the physical unity of cells, due to some inherent genetic influence or external injurious factor, would be lost, these early cell groupings would not remain bonded and become separated. Even if this separation of cells would come a few days later in development—until about the 14th day beyond which evidence indicates no twinning takes place—the principle is the same: either one group of cells retains the original soul and the other gets a new one, or initial individual cell dies because of the physical division and both receive new soul since each group has retained totipotentiality. (The same problem and solution applies proportionately whether the initial unifying principle is a vegetative, sensitive, intellectual soul.)

The formation of identical twins should not be the primary basis for deciding the individuality of the zygote and early embryo. In over 99% of human births, one individual is born. Identical twins occur in about one out of 320 births. Nonetheless, as an exception, the fact of twinning needs to be considered, and whether in fact, it presents a insuperable objection to the individuality, the unity and the uniqueness status, of the zygote and blastocyst stage of human development. If so, then the original explanation needs to be modified.

The fact that the original cell (zygote) (indeed any bacteria or protozoan cell) becomes two at mitosis does not mean that the original was not truly an individual. This means the splitting of one individual into two new individuals, as such, does not deny the true individuality of the original, its unity and uniqueness. Planaria, a free-swimming flat worm, can be split in half longitutionally and form two new individuals. It is multicellular and regeneration of the two halves occurs in the adult stage as well. One multicellular individual can become two when split in two by human intervention.

But another question. Are the two daughter cells new and different individual from the original? The answer depends on whether the cell is protozoan or metazoan, i.e., a multicellular organism. In the former the daughter cells are two individuals, in the latter case the daughter cells, generally, constitute one individual, the same one which gave rise to two cells. As divisions continue, the one and same individual acquires more cells which also begin to differentiate, specialize, to become the various tissues and eventually organs of the one original individual. If twinning takes place at a later stage—in blastocyst stage—where there is already positional differences of the cells, e.g., outside and inside (the trophoblast and embryoblast), the initial or original individuality is not *ipso facto* negated. We have little data as to what brings about this splitting at a later stage of early embryonic development; so, we must argue with incomplete information. Presumably the intercellular bridges, gap junctions, or whatever communication link which unites these early cells breaks down so that *reciprocal communication between the two groups is broken*. Since at this early developmental stage each group of cells—as shown by subsequent development—is capable of forming a total new individual, the separation results in twins.

An additional factor may be relevant as previously mentioned. Twinning is familial, that is, families with one set of twins are more likely to have others than those families who do not. There is a genetic component to twinning which means that there is tendency, rooted in the genome of one or both parents to the formation of twins. Hence, in particular cases of identical twinning there is present from the beginning a genetically influenced factor which initiates a biological train of events leading to formation of twins.

Apparently, twinning does not occur (at least successfully) after the primitive streak appears (about 14 days after fertilization). One explanation is that the cells have begun to differentiate—they have lost their totipotentiality—and are not capable of forming two embryos each undergoing individual development.

But the problem arises for us because how can one human person become two, with the understanding that a spiritual soul (the human soul) is non-material, not extended in space, and hence cannot be cut in twain? If the one body—represented by two cells up to about 60 cells—is one person, what occurs when the cells of the inner cell mass—the embryoblast—of the blastocyst subdivides into two distinct groups? The soul does not divide. One cell or small totipotent group of cells containing the primary integrating center could retain the original soul and be the original person, while the other group also being totipotential would receive a new soul and activate a new primary integrating center for that embryo because it is capable of developing into a distinct human dividual. The unitary and unique status of the initial zygote and early blastocyst would thus be preserved.

One can grant that personal individuality is progressive. A combination of genetic, extrogenomic factors, and postnatal psychosocial influences and experience gradually interactively shape the individual. At each moment during development and indeed until death the effect of extrapersonal factors will be determined by the actual condition of the person (*Quidquid recipitur per modum recipientis recipitur*). But all this development is subsequent to the establishment of the individual from the very beginning. Less than 1% of born children are identical twins. These would be exceptions to the rule of one oocyte, one sperm, one child. The exception should not be *the basis* for an explanation of embryogenesis, nor, of course, should it be ignored. A consistent, reasonable explanation for the fact of identical twinning has been proposed.

A basic principle is that there cannot be *two principles* of life and unity in one and the same individual. One cell, one soul. But let me suggest that because of some genetic factor operative in the fertilization process and early cleavages, there is a lack of continuity between the two resulting cells; this would require *two* principles of life and unity, two souls. Because of the encasing *zona pellucida,* the two might not be able to physically separate until a later date. Thus, it would appear that the embryoblast underwent subsequent subdivision when already it was two individuals in close proximity. This explanation would seem to require that fertilization be considered to end at metaphase. As the chromosomes separate and the cell divides, in the case of identical twins, the two daughter cells each acquire a distinct soul (principle of life and unity). Hence, twinning has already begun even though the physical separation may only become manifest later.

2. A second objection has to do with the existence of hydatidiform moles which result from defective fertilization. These occur in two major syndromes: complete (CHM) or partial (PHM). The former is the result of the fertilization of an "empty oocyte (ovum)." The oocyte lacks chromosomes. As a result of fertilization, the zygote (and embryo) has the male chromosomes. The zygote thus formed lacks the apt matter (since it lacks the biological capacity for proper development) for receiving a human soul and consequentially is not a human person (see Aron E. Szulman, "Clinicopatholic Features of Partial Hydatidiform Mole," *The Journal of Reproductive Medicine 32* (9) pp. 640–643, 1987).

The partial hydatidiform moles are a different situation. They result from an abnormal fertilization where two spermatazoa (or a single one with an abnormal set of chromosomes, i.e., double the number) penetrate an apparently normal oocyte. This results in a zygote with 69 instead of the normal 46 chromosomes. While the clinical picture can vary, for our purpose here one would have to question whether a zygote, embryo, or fetus with 69 chromosomes constitutes apt matter for the reception of a human soul. Most of these fetuses die before 9 weeks of intrauterine development (see Szulman, *ibid.*).

This is not a question about a normal zygote or embryo subsequently *becoming* a hydatidiform mole (complete or partial). Rather from the outset there is a profound biological abnormality which, most likely in the case of the CHM, results in a being which is not a person. In any event, the existence of CHM or PHM does not present a convincing argument against the normal zygote, embryo, or fetus being a human person. I grant that in particular cases it may be difficult to make such a determination because of the present lack of information regarding the absolute minimum requirement for substantial unity and personhood and whether it is verified in a particular case.

3. The fusion of early embryos—if it does take place in humans—can be explained by the fact that one embryo dies (for reasons unknown at present). Perhaps one cell (or small group) dies because its primary organizer fails to function (well enough) and the organism dies as an organism but the individual cells survive. Because of close physical proximity, the surviving embryo annexes the surviving cells which become part of its body even if the genetic makeup is different and results in an individual with cells of two different genetic constitutions (this is called mosaicism).

4. A fourth objection cited is that the genome does not possess all the required information for the production of the adult person. At all stages of human development (indeed of all living things) outside factors are required for the completion or perfection of the individual. For example, a new born child not only *needs* nutrients but also eventually must be *taught* the human skills of speech, writing, etc. Similarly, a zygote, embryo and fetus need and are influenced by exogenous factors. For example, between the third and the eighth week of fetal development the developing embryo is very sensitive to environmental toxins. The "thalidomide babies" without arms or legs are memorable but infamous examples.

The fact that the developing zygote and embryo needs factors outside of the information strictly contained in the genome does not argue against its initial and continued substantial unity. To say that a zygote embryo are unique individuals does *not* require that all their future characteristics be predetermined at the earliest states. There are contigent events that occur during development, e.g., nutritional status of the mother, environmental substances (teratogens), hypoxic incidents, physical accidents to mother, and events associated with birth, which can and do have a marked impact on the physical and mental status of the born individual. What is required, and what is present, is the substantial unity of the individual which perdures to adulthood and death. Thus substantial unity required by personhood does not mean that *all* future features—structural and behavioral—of the individual is fixed by the genome. A number of characteristics associated with a person result from environmental interactions. A process called "induction" is operative, apparently, in higher animals including humans, whereby certain embryonic cells influence the development of adjacent centers. While the interaction as such may not be encoded in the genome, the *capacity* to influence and be influenced is, even if such additional factors requisite for the proper development of the zygote, embryo, and fetus are not genomic in origin. In the early embryo, spatial position is important; for example, the *outer* cells of the blastocyst become the placenta and membranes, where the inner cells become the embryo proper. The fundamental organizing drive is inherent and dominant since the organism normally terminates in an *adult* member of the human species (and no other) unless impeded by disease, disorder, or accident.

5. There is no question that human life originates from human life and in that sense there is a continuum. Human parents generate, through egg and sperm, human children. But there is an *individual discontinuity:* The child is neither father or mother, nor both. The child is a distinct individual sharing the same nature as the parents but is a distinct member of the human species. That individuating discontinuity takes place at the completion of fertilization: a new human individual person commences to exist.

Whatever a person may be, it is not limited down to the actual manifestation of the characteristics which are found in the adult stage. The person, then, is understood to be the dynamic substrate, the animated foundation, from which the human characteristics are developed. Better still, the person is the being of the human species who has the inborn capacity or potentiality to acquire and develop—unless impeded by disease or injury—those skills such as speech, writing, thinking, willing freely, questioning and finding explanations for the wonders the world presents. In brief, a person is created by God in His image and is a self-determining being, self-acting and self-perfecting being whose absolute beginning is at the time in which fertilization has been completed and who, by the grace of God, is called to share the Divine life for eternity.

EXIT

Once the human person begins existence in the temporal world, how does it exit? Death seems to be the way. Death of the person refers to the irreversible termination of the living, acting individual in this life (see Pope John Paul II, "Determining the Moment When Death Occurs," *Origins*, Vol. 19, No. 32, January 11, 1990, pp. 523–525). The ordinary signs involve permanent cessation of heart beat and respiration. The permanent loss of consciousness, lack of reflexes, lack of response to various stimuli, electrocortical silence of the brain, and absence of blood flow through the brain 15–20 minutes, also indicate death of the person if certain caveats such the absence of certain drugs as barbiturates and phenothizines, and the body has not been cooled as by being in ice water.

These latter and other related criteria refer to what is termed as "brain death." More accurately, one should refer to them as brain-related criteria for the determination of death. There are *not* two deaths: death and brain death. Rather, there are *two sets of criteria*, two ways of determining the death of a human person. Since 1968 there have been a variety of brain-related criteria for death, differing largely in the specific technological details of how the irreversible total non-functioning of the brain was to be determined (see "A Definition of Irreversible Coma," *Journal of the American Medical Association*, Vol. 205, No. 6, August 5, 1968, pp. 85–88; Peter McL. Black, "Guidelines for the Diagnosis of Brain Death," in A. H. Rapper and S. F. Kennedy, eds., *Neurological and Neurosurgical Intensive Care*, Second Edition, Aspen Publication, 1988, pp. 323–334; Daniel Wikler and Alan J. Weisbard, "Appropriate Confusion over 'Brain Death'," *Journal of the American Medical Association*, Vol. 261, No. 15, April 21, 1989, pp. 2246; Albert S. Moraczewski and J. Stuart Shawatter, *Determination of Death*, St. Louis: The Catholic Health Association of the USA, 1982).

More recently an increasingly intense discussion is swirling around the issue as to whether neo-cortical brain death is sufficient. This is the part of the brain, the outer mantle of the brain, which is necessary to carry out cognitive and voluntary act. Up to the present the medical brain-related standard for death is death of the entire brain including the brain stem where the control center for respiration is located. If this center is destroyed, spontaneous respiration ceases and a mechanical respirator is required to supply oxygen to the lungs.

"Neo-cortical death" refers to the destruction or permanent non-functioning of the cortex, that part of the brain necessary for the higher cognitive and affective functions of the person. It has been argued that neo-cortical death without destruction of the lower brain centers is sufficient basis for declaring a person to be dead (see, Richard M. Zaner, editor, *Death: Beyond Whole Brain Criteria*, Dordrecht; Kluwer Acdaemic Publication, 1988). By such criteria a person could be breathing spontaneously and the cardio-vascular system functioning properly, and yet be declared dead. Although the person would be permanently unconscious and totally unable—as far as human observers are concerned—to carry out any human acts, integrated human life at a physiological level would continue. Some might be tempted to say here that there is present human life but not the life of a human person. This is not correct.

From the view presented in paper, if an organism possesses human life it is also a human person. I believe that according to our present state of knowledge, it is more correct to consider the entire brain as the primary material integrating center of the developed human person. Hence, it is more secure to require death of the whole brain so that it is evident that there is no longer present an integrating center, no longer an organism and therefore no longer a human person.

A neurological condition which has become increasingly common given our means of keeping persons alive who have been seriously injured is that of the persistent vegetative state (PVS). It is a form of eyes-open permanent unconsciousness in which the patient has periods of wakefulness and physiological sleep/wake cycles, but at no time is the patient aware of him or herself or the environment. Neurologically, being awake but unaware is the result of a functioning brain stem and a total loss of cerebral cortical functioning. (see American Academy of Neurology's statement in *Neurology*, 39:125–26, 1989).

Is a human individual in this condition described above (PVS) a living person? By the criteria discussed earlier regarding what constitutes a person, the answer would have to be "yes." The individual is an organism and a member of the human species. Hence, such an individual is a person albeit not able to function at a cognitive or affective level and is in a permanent state of unconsciousness without reasonable hope of recovery. Brain damage has placed a severe limitation on the ability of the person to act in the temporal world. Even at the most basic level of life such a person has to be aided by other persons by supplying artificial nutrition and hydration in order to live.

While these brain-related criteria are more evident and applicable to the human adult, the irreversible loss of truly integrated activity by the individual at any stage of development marks the end of temporal life. In that situation, there is no organism. If the organism under consideration is human, then the absence of an integrating center also indicates the absence of a human *person.* A human *organism* (that is, a substantial whole and not a part) with essentially a full set of adequately functional chromosomes *is* a human person. Just as the formation of a human organism marked the beginning of a human person, so, too, the destruction of the same organism signals the exit of a human person from this spatiotemporal world.

Philosophically, one can argue that the human soul, being a spiritual principle, has no parts into which it can disintegrate. Hence, since presumably the soul is not annihilated at death it continues in existence (singing, I suppose, "I ain't got no body"). But since the soul, of itself, it not a person, then strictly speaking, the complete person as such ceases to exist. Only faith can tell us that this same human person (which exists in some incomplete form as the soul) perdures into a transtemporal world and will be resurrected in the absolute future when body and soul are reunited.

The exit of a person, then, is not simply the reverse of the entry. The spiritual soul did not exist prior to its infusion into a body. To be sure, the phrase "infusion into a body" evokes the image of some pre-existing spirit being transferred from some heavenly storage depot and being placed into a container, the body. To state in words the creative activity of God is impossible. We can say simply that God creates *ex nihilo* the human spirit at the time and place when and where there is suitable matter. "Suitable matter" refers to structured matter which has the *capability of developing* the kind of material structures and function through and in which the human soul can carry out its functions. But in the earlier stages of human development the soul's functions are primarily directing the growth and differentiation of the cells in an orderly and timely fashion. As development proceeds, especially after birth the soul's function becomes more complex involving sensory, motor, and intellectual activities. The developed human brain and body is the necessary material subservient structures. The extremely complex structure of the brain with over 10 billion neurons and over 10 trillion connections provides the material substrate for the soul's highest cognitive and volitional functions. The body with hands and vocal apparatus, as well as the complex supporting system, is also part of the goal of development.

The reverse process—the cessation of the human organism's existence—involves not the return of the human spirit to non-existence but a change in its relationship to this specific matter. The body is no longer unified by the spirit. The spiritual soul continues in existence but the nature of that existence is largely unknown.

Death of a human person, then, is not its annihilation. Since self-identity of the human person is linked to its memory, those memories must somehow be recorded and stored, as it were, in the soul. Whatever role the body, especially the senses and the central nervous system, had in the original acquisition, storage, and retrieval of memories, that is lost as the body corrupts after death. Hence, it would seem that the soul is a *person* (albeit an incomplete one since it has no body) for it must have retained in some form the memories which constitute a person's identity in order for there to be real continuity from a temporal past to a transcendent future. The soul also retains a metaphysical relationship to the body. This means when matter and soul are reunited at the Resurrection, the two principles will constitute the same person who existed in the temporal world.

While death of a person marks a change in the relationship of the soul to the body, the *reason* for that change is that the material structures can no longer "support" a spiritual soul. The material is no longer disposed *for that stage of development* to receive or maintain a spiritual principle. This is so because the physical integrating center which is essential for constituting an organism is severely and permanently damaged or destroyed. Starting with the nucleus of a single cell to the brain of an adult person, the material integrating center is proportionate in size and complexity to the stage of development. The more complex is the whole organism, the more complex must be the integrating center. The irreversible destruction of this center's integrating function, marks the end of the organism's existence as an organism and the end of that human person in this world.

CONCLUSION

The nature of a human person is reflected by what it uniquely does. By an exercise of self-determination, of intelligence and freedom, humans interactively have shaped their identity. With increasing effectiveness, human persons, singly and collectively, have controlled and modified their environment. The society of human persons, by a gift of God, was made to share dominion over the world in which it exists.

Being a creature of matter and spirit, the human person is a microcosm of the created universe. The human person has an absolute beginning (at the formation of the zygote) but no absolute termination. At death there is a transition, the nature of which is not clear since revelation is relatively silent. However, the promise of Jesus, underscored by His Resurrection and Ascension, and by the Assumption of the Blessed Virgin Mary, teach that human persons will ultimately be reconstituted and exist as individual persons in a transcendental world to share " ... forever a life that is divine and free from all decay" (*Gaudium et spes* #17, p. 917).

By the grace of God the human person is invited to sit and banquet at the family table of the Holy Trinity. This creature of dust and God's breath of life (see Genesis 2:7), frail and fallen, but raised and rewarded, is called to share—body, and spirit—the glory of God (see Romans 8:18–21).

Notes
*In that statement "his existence" clearly does not refer to the male gender but is to be taken in the generic sense precisely as refering to a human entity. Yet it is not clear whether the *Instruction,* aware of the earlier document's (Declaration on Euthanasia—1974) cautionary statement (footnote #19) about the debate regarding the precise moment of the soul's infusion, is stating that the respect is due "as *if* the individual were a person" or because the human being *is* a person.

Chapter 7

PASTORAL CONCERNS
GENETICS AND PERSONHOOD

FATHER MORACZEWSKI: Dr. Cummings' presentation was an excellent summary of the status of gene therapy. I think most of you would have picked up the fact there are a number of ethical questions that need to be investigated. I thank Dr. Cummings for saying we need to work on these right away before the process gets too far. So I hope we will be entering into a careful ethical review of many aspects of gene therapy and all that it implies.

DR. CUMMINGS: I have one comment to offer on the process of twinning. Some studies have shown that parts of the twinning process or that a substantial fraction of twinning might be genetically controlled. The process is not entirely random. There are genes which may influence the twinning process. Twins run in families, for example. That seems to be a well known empirical observation.

BISHOP: You mentioned that the conception of the human being is a process taking six or seven days. Are we justified in talking about the moment of conception then? And if so, when is that moment?

FATHER MORACZEWSKI: I believe what I said was that the fertilization process is extended over time. When it is completed, *that* can be considered the moment of conception; a new individual human organism if now present. The subsequent development is development of the organism, but it's already an organism, already a human person. So the process that I referred to is the fertilization *process.* The sperm approaches the egg, disperses the outer layer of cells (corona radiata), penetrates through the protective barrier (zona pellucida) and having entered the oocyte, liberates its chromosomes to intermingle with the chromosomes of the oocyte. When that process comes to a point where there is a new integrating center we now have a new individual.

BISHOP: Father Moraczewski, could you apply your theory to the question of the anencephalic baby? How would the "exit" of a person fit in with this or how you would explain that to someone?

FATHER MORACZEWSKI: Several points need to be made regarding the question of the anencephalic child: first, the condition of anencephaly is a spectrum, a range of defects involving the brain and skull. The amount of functioning brain tissue left will vary from one child to another and, ordinarily, the individual may come to term. If the child is born he or she may live only a few hours or a few days, so that in a certain sense it's born dying. But the principle is this: The anencephalic child is an organism, there is a primary integrating center, and at this point of our understanding for the sake of simplicity, the brain may be considered such a center. Although the whole brain in an anencephalic child is not present, usually there still is a functioning brain stem so that the child is able to breath spontaneously. From what we currently know, we would have to say that she or he is an individual human organism and, therefore, a human person. The person remains until death and that event may occur just before birth or right after birth. But we need to understand that anencephaly is a range of conditions all involving a defect during development but not enough to change our understanding that it is a human organism and, therefore, a human person but one with a very short life.

BISHOP: Dr. Cummings, you went rather rapidly over those areas of gene therapy where there's an ethical dimension to be viewed or to be studied. Would it be possible for you to repeat the ethical issues involved concerning gene therapy? Are there studies by theologians at the present time concerning those particular questions that you bring forth?

DR. CUMMINGS: Well, the two aspects of gene therapy that I talked about were somatic and germ cell gene therapy. The aspect of somatic gene therapy has already received a very thorough ethical review and it appears that meeting the normal criteria for medical treatment there appears to be little controversy about the application of somatic cell gene therapy as a medical technique.

The problem arises when you consider the approach of germ cell gene therapy. In the latter case, you're talking about introducing a genetic change into an individual that will be inherited by all the offspring of that individual so you are, in effect, changing the genetic makeup not only of the individual being treated but offspring of that individual and the progeny of that individual.

Germ cell gene therapy in scientific terms is always described as not being currently a goal of gene therapy research or effort or clinical trials and, in fact, that's true. But there is a separate body of technology available for germ cell therapy that has been developed in livestock and animal studies.

I think that somatic cell therapy will advance rather rapidly if for no other reason than the argument from efficiency, that it is faster, it's neater and it's better in a technical sense as a therapeutic strategy.

I have reviewed the literature on gene therapy and, specifically, germ cell therapy all the way back to 1980 and I've been unable by computer search to find much information that's been generated about the theological and ethical issues relating to germ cell therapy. That's why I wanted to bring that to the attention of this group because I think it's a topic that needs to be thoroughly explored and questioned and answered now before this technology is upon us.

FATHER MORACZEWSKI: I would add, one of the problems, of course, is working with the isolated human embryo.

In other words, if in order to do gene therapy with a germ cell line, you'd have to isolate in some way the cells involved and that presents certain problems. That is one area that investigation has begun, theological investigation has been done but it's just begun.

It needs a lot more review to understand all of the biological parameters as well as the ethical ones. But one area of concern is the isolating the individual *in vitro.*

BISHOP: Dr. Cummings, the presentation was very clear but I think your starting point was already well beyond my information on this. The first of them is where is gene therapy applied? When you apply therapy, are you changing every cell in the human body and if you do that, do you do it by injecting one cell and then it automatically spreads to everything else?

DR. CUMMINGS: Well, that's where the division between somatic cell therapy and germ cell therapy really comes into play. In somatic therapy, the idea is to insert a single gene or a number of genes into a single target tissue or into a specific organ or tissue like bone marrow and hope that the bone marrow cells when re-implanted will produce a normal gene product. So only those re-implanted cells in the body would be altered. That would be an example of somatic cell therapy. I also mentioned liver as a tissue in which this might work. Liver has an enormous capacity to regenerate and so you can take out a piece of the liver, dissociate those cells and transfer genes into those cells, allow the liver to grow *in vitro.* The cells will gradually reaggregate or reassociate and this cell mass is introduced into the liver where it will attach and regenerate. So gene therapy wouldn't even be the whole liver. It would only be those cells that would be genetically altered.

The idea behind somatic therapy is that while the rest of the cells of the body may carry a defective gene, treated cells would have a normal gene and, hopefully, would produce enough the gene product to correct the defect.

When you do germ cell therapy, you're effecting this change at a very early stage of development, say, in the fertilized egg when you have only a single cell. And if you do this by microinjection into the single cell, then all cells derived from that cell (which would be every cell in the body) would carry this altered gene. So in somatic cell therapy, the goal is to genetically alter a limited number of cells that would produce enough gene products to correct the defect. In germ cell therapy, the idea would be to change the genetic constitution of every cell in the body, including the cells that are going to form the sperm and egg for the next generation.

BISHOP: Does nature want some people not to reproduce or want their children not to live very long so that strains that are weak are not going to wind up being perpetrated? I suppose for most of us there's a difference between accepting genetic defects and doing experimentation that may create new genetic situations.

DR. CUMMINGS: Well, there are two parts to that answer. One is that by creating genetically altered individuals we are in effect allowing the survival of individuals who might not normally survive, but we do that with other medical forms of treatment as well. In this case, however, what we are doing gradually is increasing what's called "genetic load." That is, increasing the number of individuals in a population who carry a defective gene. There are problems related to this. For example, every child born in the United States is tested for a metabolic disease known as PKU which is a genetic condition that occurs in about 1 in 40,000 individuals. If a newborn is identified as having PKU, they are put on a special diet for seven to fourteen years that allows them to develop normally. These dietary programs have been put into effect only in the last twenty years or so. Individuals who carry this genetic defect are now reaching childbearing age. When females who carry this genetic defect are having children, they are back on a normal diet and they have high levels of a particular substance in their blood which crosses the placenta and damages the brain development of their children no matter whether their child is genetically normal or not because the mother is genetically defective. Similar kinds of problems may arise in gene therapy as well.

But the second part of the answer is that as we discussed increasing the genetic load of a population, we're doing it very slowly so there's no reason to suspect that we as a species are breeding ourselves back down to the level of protozoa or something.

BISHOP: Dr. Cummings, relative to the enhancement therapy that you spoke about, we had a question about steroids. We didn't know whether those affect genes like this dietary thing that you were talking about a moment ago, whether any of that is transmitted to the offspring or what the effect of that would be.

DR. CUMMINGS: You are probably referring to the use of anabolic steroids and the abuse of steroids in athletics. That's an interesting question because the pattern of abuse of steroids may in fact parallel the pattern of abuse that might be seen with the human growth hormone once that becomes commercially available. People might have that prescribed to increase their height to be a star athlete of one kind or another. When individuals who are already mature take anabolic steroids, it does change gene expression in genes that are related to some aspects of metabolism but none of those changes are inherited. And in the same way, insertion of growth hormone genes by somatic therapy would affect only the individual who was treated and not the offspring.

But if the individual were treated with growth hormone genes by germ cell therapy, they would pass that enhanced capacity on to their offspring. Experiments with transmitting growth hormone genes have already been done in animals. The first trials were done in mice and are now being used to try and raise superior strains of livestock. There are some experiments at the National Institutes of Health and the University of Pennsylvania on injecting or transferring human growth hormone genes into pig embryos to raise larger, leaner pigs. And in that case, the human gene put into a pig is transmitted from generation to generation.

BISHOP: First, I would like to make a commentary. If I am not mistaken, the Congregation for the Doctrine of the Faith says that it doesn't want to have a firm stand on the fact that from the beginning of the zygote there is a human person because it says that it is a philosophical concept and it doesn't want to make a stand from a philosophical concept. But it says that the zygote or the embryo should be considered as a person because it is human life and it has the dignity of a human life.

Secondly, I would like to ask a question. Some people who favor abortion say that the appearance of fetal brain tissue is very important because it is characteristic of being human. What would you say about this because these people affirm that until there is such tissue, it's not properly a human being so you can have abortions?

FATHER MORACZEWSKI: The Congregation of the Faith stated in the Declaration of Abortion (Footnote 19) that because there's disagreement among experts about the beginning of human life it is not possible to make a definitive assertion about the human zygote's personhood.

Whether there's agreement or disagreement, it is a philosophical question because it involves the presence of a nonmaterial principle which science by its current methods cannot directly study. While science avoids that particular issue, but there is no basic reason why we can't investigate it further.

I believe it is a question which biologists working with philosophers could recognize and jointly study. Personally, I'm convinced as a biologist and a philosopher that human life (i.e., human personhood) begins at the beginning as I described it in my talk. What the Congregation had said was just a cautionary note because when it was written in 1974, the evidence was less clear. Now, I admit there are other persons perhaps better versed in these matters than I who disagree with me but I'm stating my personal position and the supporting reasons.

With regard to the second part of your question, a number of persons would say that only when the primitive streak appears (about fourteen days) is that the beginning of what they believe to be true individuation. Continued development leads within a matter of days to the appearance of the beginning of the central nervous system. Other persons will say that only in the presence of encephalization or the beginning of the primitive brain, can one say you then have the beginning of a human person. But that, I think, is much too late because there is present an organism from the completion of fertilization onwards which is of human origin and which if allowed to live—apart from disease or disorder—will develop into an adult *human* organism, into an *adult* person.

Being a human organism does not require the actualization of the nervous system at that stage of development. Even Dr. Clifford Grobstein—who objects to human personhood from the beginning of individual life—states explicitly in his book that the human *zygote* is human to the core. It's already a human organism.

Dr. Cummings, is there any great danger that fertilized ovum would be used for research purposes? Is it going on now?

DR. CUMMINGS: Yes. That's already going on. There have been experiments done where the embryo is a small cluster of 6–8 cells. Researchers are experimenting on those embryos by removing one of the cells and using that cell to extract genetic material and using it to determine whether or not a defective gene is present. So in that sense that type of embryonic experimentation is going on. One of the embryomic cells is being destroyed. Basically, what you do is you go in with a micropipet and suck out a single cell and the rest remain.

If you watch that embryo develop *in vitro,* it will continue to develop. But, of course, it is kept under developmental conditions for only a few days so it's not clear whether the embryo has been fatally damaged or partially damaged or undamaged. But yes, that type of experimentation is going on.

FATHER MORACZEWSKI: The government Advisory Ethics Board some years ago (1979) recommended that this would be permissible as long as the embryo was not reimplanted, as long as the experiment was done before fourteen days and that the surviving embryo, in this case if one cell were removed, is not implanted into a woman to allow further development. Since this is done *in vitro,* an embryo that's been externalized dies not necessarily because one cell was removed, but because it was left in the environment where its development could not properly continue.

BISHOP: You were speaking about the fertilization being *in vitro,* also.

DR. CUMMINGS: Yes, that's right, These are fertilized *in vitro.*

BISHOP: How much of the identity of a person is affected when you take out one, two or three genes which are not functioning properly and you replace them with other genes from somebody else?

DR. CUMMINGS: I think that's part of the problem that needs to be resolved. I think when you transfer one gene and you're talking about a gene that's well characterized and you understand that it's a gene product that's necessary for normal functioning, I don't think many people will have problems with that.

The problems arise when you get into variations on the theme. Should we add or put in a few more genes? Or what happens when we find out that when you put the human gene in, it doesn't work very well and so you don't get a normal amount of gene product and you, therefore, cannot fully correct the defect? Those are the questions that I think need to be resolved especially if you get into situations where you consider germ cell therapy to change the heritability and the characteristics of future generations.

FATHER MORACZEWSKI: It would be somewhat analogous, I think, to planting a pig heart or a liver from another species into a human being. Only the scale is different but the idea is very similar as long as we're talking about *somatic* cell gene therapy and not reproductive cell therapy.

BISHOP: I'd like to have some comments on the case of a woman being a victim of incest going immediately to a doctor or to anyone and being cleaned out. Is she committing a sin? Is she committing an abortion?

FATHER MORACZEWSKI: Well, the assumption is, first of all, that if conception has already taken place and then one uses chemical or mechanical means to empty the uterus, a human being has been destroyed.

BISHOP: Why do you say that? Don't theologians disagree on the time of inception and the time line? Most people argue that way, I believe.

FATHER MORACZEWSKI: Well, while there may be disagreement on the exact time, nonetheless, the Church has certainly reiterated the fact that even though we may not be in full agreement as to exact moment of the inception of personhood, that human being once having started is to be treated as least as if it were a person because it is surely on its way unless its development has been impeded.

In practical order, my understanding is that human life which has begun should not be violated. And granted that the woman has been a victim of rape or incest, there's a third party involved and the Church's attitude, as I understand it, is that human life is precious and needs to be protected even though it was formed as a result of an unjust act done to the woman.

BISHOP: You're presuming that human life begins immediately with the intercourse?

FATHER MORACZEWSKI: Not quite. If one could prevent fertilization from taking place and we could know with moral certitude that fertilization has not in fact taken place, then one certainly could prevent the sperm from fertilizing the egg—if there were a possible and a practical way. That's one consideration. But if conception, that is to say if fertilization has already taken place such that a new human life is begun, then that human life is sacred and cannot be directly destroyed.

BISHOP: Could we have an explanation on this. From the moment fertilization how long?

FATHER MORACZEWSKI: The moment of fertilization? Well, as I was describing, it's the time when the new individual is formed and that's within a matter of less than twenty-four hours after the sperm has begun to penetrate the oocyte. It's a time we don't precisely know in any particular case. I mean, humanly speaking, that event cannot be timed that closely. That's why the caution has to be exercised if there is a reasonable likelihood that the woman has already conceived, that is to say, a new life already has begun. Because the fertilization process ordinarily begins in the fallopian tube and by the time the developing new life travels down to the uterus, three or four days have elapsed, at least according to the schemes that have been presented. Therefore, that new human life needs to be protected. Granted that there are many problems in terms of the practical way of how one deals compassionately with a woman who has been so violently attacked. Yet one cannot overlook that there's a third human individual involved.

BISHOP: Father Moraczewski, when we practically deal with directions to hospitals and some Catholic gynecologists that are asking this question, you seem to indicate that maybe we have as long as twenty-four hours. What is a morally safe outer limit in which we can give practical pastoral advice with regard to D&C and curettage or whatever is necessary?

FATHER MORACZEWSKI: Well, being an academic person and being asked practical questions doesn't always result in a good response. But I will attempt to address the issue. A woman comes into the emergency room and says she has been attacked and raped. All right, now what can we do? From what I have read, the medical evidence is that within five minutes after intercourse, sperm have already reached the fallopian tubes. Five minutes. That's rather fast. The sperm then swim up the fallopian tube and if the woman happens to be ovulating at that time the egg will soon begin descend that tube. Somewhere within that tube they meet and fertilization ordinarily takes place.

In the D&C procedure the lining of the uterus is scraped which makes it impossible for a fertilized egg to implant. But that's about 5 to 6 days later. So that if the woman comes in six hours after being raped and the uterus is scraped, which means that five days later the fertilized ovocyte arrives and finds that the uterus is inhospitable and that it cannot implant. In other words, it's an abortifacient procedure. So from these biological facts the best practical advice is a supportive talk with the woman trying to assure her that everything which can be done will be but that there is a human life at risk if she had ovulated in the past 24 hours or is apt to do so in the next 2 or 3 days.

I remember one woman who consulted me after a post rape and abortion. Reflecting back on that act, she said to me, well, I realize now that it was wrong. I thought then that I did the right thing. Because I now better appreciate what our Lord said: we have to love our enemies. Even if this new being were my enemy—which he is not—the very least act of love I could do is to allow him to live. That would be the advice I would give to women who have been raped: to do nothing that would destroy that new life.

BISHOP: On that last point, are you saying in effect, Father Albert, that there's nothing practically that you can say in those situations if you want to be on morally safe ground other than to counsel to see this life through to the end to birth?

FATHER MORACZEWSKI: Let me insert a condition. If it could be medically determined in the particular case that fertilization has yet not taken place (there are some situations where it can be determined, for example, in the case where the woman has already ovulated a couple of days before) and since we know that the egg doesn't last much more than twenty-four hours then any D&C would not have any abortifacient effect because she would not be ovulating again for some weeks. Also, if ovulation for the next few days could be prevented, that would be permissible.

BISHOP: You gave us an analogy, the pig heart or the pig liver and it seemed to me that that really isn't an apt analogy, if I understand the process correctly because that pig liver or pig heart wouldn't repeat itself, whereas, what you do genetically is going to repeat itself in future generations.

FATHER MORACZEWSKI: Dr. Cummings had made an important distinction between somatic and reproductive cell gene therapy. In *somatic* gene therapy we are talking about a developed human being. Here one looks at correcting the malfunction of a particular tissue, for example, the Islet cells of the pancreas which normally produce insulin. Then you're genetically altering only that one individual and that particular tissue.

As I said, it would be like transplanting a pig heart or a pig valve or whatever. Whereas, it's totally different if one involves the *reproductive* cell in gene therapy. Then you *are* influencing future generations, and that's an entirely different question.

DR. CUMMINGS: That's a distinction that has to be made: whether the genetic alteration will be in a somatic cell, that is, a cell of the body that will not be involved in transmitting genetic information to the next generation or whether this genetic alteration is taking place in a cell that gives rise to cells, say, sperm or egg or is an alteration in the sperm or egg itself.

It's the same thing as if someone gets cancer. They may have a genetic alteration in a liver cell that results in cancer. The outcome is terminal for them but that genetic defect is not passed on to their offspring if they should reproduce afterwards. That's an event that took place only in a liver cell and not in a sperm or egg. Somatic therapy, in effect, changes only cells in the body which are not transmitted or involved in the transmission of genetic information. So it would depend on which method was used to make this genetic alteration.

PARTICIPANT: We'd just like to add a little note on that whole question about the prevention of fertilization after rape. One aspect of the discussion is the possibility of a woman who will ovulate several days after the rape takes place and there would be some moral grounds for preventing that ovulation on that particular occasion. Certainly, I think that we would all agree that we have a moral obligation to try and prevent conception in cases of rape and incest. And there is, depending on the time frame, a window or a period where at least you can make certain actions that might do that. Sperm, although it reaches the fallopian tube within five minutes, could last for up to five days such that even if it's five days after rape, if an egg happens to appear in the fallopian tube at that time, you could also get fertilization then.

So one of the things you'd want to do is to postpone ovulation which is the process by which a woman produces an egg and discharges an egg into the fallopian tube. There are drugs you can use or, certainly, drugs which potentially can prevent ovulation or at least postpone ovulation.

There's not enough research that's been done on this because of the obvious alternative which is what is presently used and which is probably morally illicit which is the use of the day-after pill, DES. All those pills really do is prevent implantation so those pills are abortifacient. They do not postpone ovulation in the doses that they're given and the methods that they're given.

About three years ago there was a letter in the *New England Journal* about how a physician did a survey of Los Angeles hospitals, Catholic hospitals seeing how many would give this day-after pill and how many wouldn't and there was totally discrepancy: Four would and seven wouldn't and there's been some confusion about it. But the DES pill is definitely abortifacient. There are some other pills, DL nogestil (phonetics) which may in fact only act in postponing ovulation.

The other question is how long does fertilization take place. In vivo we don't know. In vitro, though, there are studies which say that between the time that a sperm enters the *Zona pellucida* and the joining of those two nuclei before you have a zygote takes about twelve hours at the very least.

So if there was a method (and curettage is not because all curettage will do is prevent later implantation) such as washing the fallopian tube to prevent that egg or that sperm-egg complex from going on to become a zygote that would be certainly a matter for a moral as well as medical investigation.

PART TWO

THE QUESTION OF EXCEPTIONLESS MORAL NORMS AND HUMAN DIGNITY

Chapter 8

ARE THERE EXCEPTIONLESS MORAL NORMS?

Germain Grisez, Ph.D.

I. A Look Back

All Catholic moralists agree on the exceptionlessness of some general norms (Love God and neighbor) and of norms which only exhort people to do what they know is right (Always be fair to others). But some today deny norms which received Catholic teaching proposes as exceptionless: One should never masturbate, fornicate, perform homosexual acts, engage in adultery, divorce and remarry, contracept, induce abortion, or otherwise directly kill innocent persons.[1] In what follows, I refer to these as "disputed norms." The question is: Considered *as exceptionless,* are the disputed norms true?[2]

During Vatican II, debate surfaced about contraception. There were initial attempts (including that of the majority of Paul VI's commission) to find some way to justify contraception without denying other disputed norms. But by some time in the 1970s, almost all Catholic thinkers who felt that contraception can be justified agreed that the way to justify it is to argue that none of the disputed norms is true.[3]

Today, theologians who deny the disputed norms claim to be the mainstream of Catholic moral theology.[4] In fact, in affluent countries they dominate most academic professional associations, scholarly publications, and institutions of higher education. Moreover, they enjoy considerable popularity, and some bishops agree with them. But John Paul II, many other bishops, many Catholic theologians and philosophers, and a substantial segment of other Catholics, even in affluent countries, still hold that the disputed norms are true.[5]

Some presentations in workshops of previous years sympathetically presented some arguments *against* the disputed norms.[6] My assignment is to provide an overview of arguments for the disputed norms' truth and a critique of the contrary arguments.[7]

II. Arguments That the Disputed Norms Are Not True

1) Most moral norms admit exceptions. For example, one should keep promises, but may break them for good reasons. Classical moral theology—the approved authors—developed the principle of double effect and even admitted exceptions to the norm against killing, when the killing is indirect or is done as capital punishment or in a just war. So, holding that all the disputed norms admit exceptions simply is a straightforward way of accomplishing what moral theology formerly accomplished deviously.[8]

2) Human nature and social conditions change. So, one cannot know that any norm is exceptionless. For example, the Church once condemned usury (meaning, the taking of interest), but today does not.[9]

3) The disputed norms point out acts which usually have bad consequences. But sometimes not choosing to do an act of these

sorts has worse consequences—a poor couple not using contraception has a baby they cannot care for. In such situations, one should choose the lesser evil. For to choose the greater evil is absurd.[10]

4) General principles can be clear and certain, but as one moves toward the concrete, circumstances complicate matters. So, St. Thomas teaches that prudent judgments can make exceptions to general norms.[11]

5) To suppose that the disputed norms are true is unreasonable. For it is to suppose that some choices would be wrong regardless of circumstances. This supposition leads to excluding some possibilities from deliberation before considering everything, which is unreasonable.[12]

6) The fundamental principle of morality is to love God and neighbor. But it does not seem that acts contrary to the disputed norms—for example, acts of masturbation—always are contrary to love of God or neighbor.[13]

7) The Holy Spirit is at work in the hearts of all Christians, and so their judgment on matters of faith and morals constitutes a *sensus fidelium.* But today many Catholics and other Christians deny the disputed norms. So, these norms cannot be essential to Christian morality.[14]

8) Not allowing exceptions to the disputed norms is rigid, not compassionate, and pastorally disastrous. Many people are leaving the Church over these peripheral issues.[15]

III. Faith Teaches that the Disputed Norms Are True

Vatican II provides ecclesiological premises for two arguments for the disputed norms' truth. The first of these is based on the infallibility of the People of God as a whole.

Scripture, tradition, and, until the present debate began, the whole magisterium agreed in teaching the disputed norms. Indeed, apart from the norm excluding remarriage after divorce, all Jews and Christians held and handed on the disputed norms until quite recently. Far from regarding them as peripheral, people of faith always believed that the disputed norms pertain to God's commandments, which they understood as stipulations of the covenant. So, to deny these norms is to say that the whole People of God held and handed on *as revealed* a set of norms which were actually false. Now, if that were so, the People of God as a whole erred in their faith. But that is impossible.[16] So, the disputed norms are true.

The second argument is that through many centuries popes and the bishops in communion with them taught the disputed norms as moral requirements reducible to the Ten Commandments, and so as pertaining to revelation, to be believed with divine and Catholic faith. That universal, constant, and most firm teaching meets the conditions which Vatican II articulated for the infallibility of the ordinary magisterium. So, although the disputed norms have not been solemnly defined, they have been infallibly taught.[17]

IV. An Explanation of the Truth of the Disputed Norms

The preceding argument only tries to show *that* the disputed norms are true. To understand *why* they are true, one must understand why any moral norms at all are true.

God made human persons to know him, love him, and serve him in this life, and to be happy with him forever in heaven. In heaven, faith and hope will pass away, but love will remain. Human free choices are self-determining and lasting, and so human persons in heaven (as in hell) will be shaped by the choices they made in this world. Indeed, as Vatican II teaches, all the good fruits of human nature and work will be found again, freed of evil and completed, when God refashions this universe into the new heavens and new earth.[18]

God initially creates people with unfulfilled potentialities so that they can help to create themselves, and in that way be more like him than if he created them from the start with greater perfection. Thus, in this world, God continues to create people through their own choices and acts. As Trent says, God's goodness is so great that he wants his gifts also to be our merits.[19] Therefore, everything we do in this world should be cooperation with God's creative work, directed by hope toward his kingdom.

To enable us to cooperate, God gives us freedom of choice, and also equips us with some natural knowledge of his plan. This human share in God's plan is "natural law." It is natural because it is based on our natural inclinations to goods which fulfill us. It is law because it consists of practical insights which direct our actions in regard to those basic goods. These insights direct us to choose to protect and promote these goods in ourselves and others, and never to choose to destroy, damage, or impede them.[20]

What are these goods which fulfill persons? Vatican II quotes the Preface of the Feast of Christ the King, which describes what God has in view as "a kingdom of truth and life, of holiness and grace, of justice, love and peace."[21]

One can explain and expand that list by looking at the various aspects of human nature, to whose capacities these goods correspond.[22]

As *animate,* we are organic substances. Life itself—its maintenance and its transmission—and health are one sort of basic good.

As *rational,* we can know reality and appreciate beauty. Knowledge of truth and esthetic experience are another sort of basic good.

As *simultaneously rational and animal,* we can transform the natural world by using things to express meanings and serve purposes. Excellence in work and play is another sort of basic good.

As *sexually differentiated and complementary persons,* we can unite into indissoluble couples from whom new persons emerge. Another sort of basic good is marriage including the children who spring from and fulfill marital communion.

As *agents through deliberation and choice,* we can strive to overcome personal and interpersonal conflict, or, to put the matter positively, we can try to foster various forms of harmony, and these also are sorts of basic good: friendship with God, justice and neighborliness with others, the harmony of one's feelings with reason, and the conformity of choice and action to conscience.

For two reasons, however, we need to know more of God's plan than natural law tells us.[23]

In the first place, natural law does not tell us the full significance of doing what is right in this world.[24] Only revelation makes it clear that our first responsibility is to love God perfectly and to love our neighbor, and that only such love will enable us to fulfill all the requirements of God's plan. Only revelation makes it clear that in making choices during this life, we have more at stake than earthly happiness, that we should seek the kingdom first of all and that other goods will be included in it, and that we must will only good in order to remain open to communion with God who is infinite good. Without revelation, we would not realize that just as God, although he sometimes permits evil, wills only good, so human persons, made in God's image, should never will anything bad, although they sometimes may accept something bad when it is inseparably connected with willing what is good.

In the second place, humankind is fallen and redeemed. So, the implications of natural law are different from what they would be in an unfallen world. Natural law remains the same: it still directs toward the goods which fulfill persons. But in the fallen world the possibility of realizing these goods is greatly reduced, and the need to struggle against the consequences of sin is greatly increased. Jesus' life, death, and resurrection show what this means, and his teaching explains it. To be truly good, fallen and redeemed human persons must conform to moral truths even when doing so sacrifices this-worldly fulfillment for the invisible, hoped-for kingdom, and so seems foolish.

Thus, specific norms of morality follow from our awareness of God's plan, an awareness which we have partly by spontaneous insight into the goods which fulfill us as human persons and partly by revelation, especially by Jesus' example and teaching.

Nevertheless, most of the moral norms which flow from natural law and the Gospel admit exceptions. All the specific, affirmative ones do. For they direct us to protect and promote the various goods which contribute to the full being of persons. But nobody can always and everywhere do at once everything suitable to serve these goods.

Many specific, negative norms also admit exceptions. For they forbid us to do what *ordinarily* violates love of others—for example, to appropriate their property for our own uses. However, since property does not directly fulfill persons, but is only a means to their fulfillment, sometimes the appropriation of others' property is compatible with love for them and required by love for ourselves or others in need.

However, some specific negative norms admit no exceptions. These are norms concerning kinds of actions which can never be chosen without a will at odds with one or more of the basic human goods. Since these goods are aspects of the full being of persons, a will at odds with them is contrary to love of God, of neighbor, or of one's self in communion with God and neighbor. Since God is absolutely good, one who loves him wills only good and never wills to destroy, damage, or impede any part of the being or full being of any person made in God's image.

For instance, denying one's faith and blasphemy are always wrong because they are contrary to love of God. Taking revenge—that is, harming others to get even—directly killing the innocent, and contraception are always wrong because they damage, destroy, or prevent the very being of another, and so are inconsistent with love of neighbor. Masturbation, fornication, and homosexual acts are always wrong because in them one treats one's own body, contrary to the truth of the matter, as if it were an instrument distinct from oneself to be used for gratifying experiences. Such treatment of one's body is inconsistent with love of self fulfilled in communion with God and neighbor. For those united in Christian marriage, adultery and divorce with remarriage are always wrong because they simultaneously violate the sacrament and marital fidelity.

These disputed norms play an important role in Christian life, for their very negations mark the boundaries of the field within which human persons can cooperate with God's creative work. For example, if married couples have no way of identifying marital love, they cannot pursue and foster it. But experience shows that attempts to define marital love positively regularly reduce it to certain skillful performances, psychological satisfactions, or social advantages. Even if couples manage to attain such goods, they only succeed in limited, joint projects, rather than share in the gift of the unique, unending communion which God wants to create with them and in them. So, God's plan defines marital love negatively, in terms of exclusive and permanent rights to marital communion.

Thus, the disputed norms excluding adultery and divorce with remarriage hold open the way for the constant growth and creative newness of marital love.[25]

V. Answers to Arguments Against the Disputed Norms

1) As has been explained, most moral norms do admit exceptions, but the disputed norms do not. To understand this more fully, one must notice that the disputed norms do not directly concern outward behavior, but rather concern willing at odds with goods which fulfill persons. The approved authors developed the principle of double effect precisely to identify acts in which one wills only good but incidentally brings about something bad.[26] So, in conceding that acts which indirectly bring about someone's death can be morally good, the approved authors did not admit an exception to the norm against killing the innocent. Capital punishment and the killing of combatants in a just war are not exceptions to the received norm, which concerns only innocent life. The tradition accepted the limitation of the inviolability of life to the lives of innocents because Scripture seems to say that God himself sets that limit.[27]

2) Nobody has shown that human nature has changed in any way that would falsify the disputed norms, nor has anybody even explained what such a change would be like. Social conditions do change, and such changes can affect the nature of human institutions such as money. So, interest-taking which would have been unjust in earlier times can be just today. In general, moral norms which concern human institutions can be falsified. However, the disputed norms concern, not human institutions, but divine ones: sex, marriage, and human life.[28]

3) It would be absurd to choose what one recognized as a greater evil. Indeed, if one finds something more good or less bad in every respect than something else one was considering, the latter loses its appeal, and one cannot choose it. But choices contrary to the disputed norms never are choices of something judged to be less bad in all respects than the consequences of following them.

Of course, sometimes those who follow a disputed norm accept bad consequences, such as suffering and death, in refusing to will something bad as a means of avoiding those bad consequences. Moreover, to avoid bad consequences, those who will only good sometimes must refrain from willing some good. For example, to avoid the bad consequences of having a baby, couples sometimes must abstain from marital intercourse. However, it is never clear that the bad consequences of conforming to a disputed norm will be greater than the bad consequences of violating it. For the consequences of human acts extend into the next world, and only God knows all of them. For example, those who try to justify contraception under certain circumstances compare possible futures with and without a possible baby. But they cannot foresee the possible futures of God's kingdom with and without that possible person. Thus, although those who will only good must take into account the good and bad consequences which they foresee, those who violate one of the disputed norms and will something bad cannot justify their choice on the grounds that the alternative is a greater evil.[29]

4) St. Thomas does teach that prudent judgments sometimes make exceptions to general norms. However, he also teaches the truth of the disputed norms. And the two are consistent, for, as has been explained, most moral norms admit exceptions, and prudent judgments make those exceptions when appropriate. But the prudent person has all the virtues, and so is not inclined to will anything bad. Thus, at the very beginning of any deliberation the prudent person excludes any possibility inconsistent with the disputed norms.[30]

5) Without considering everything, one would be unreasonable to exclude any possible act which one could choose while willing only good. However, one is reasonable in refusing even to consider actions excluded by the disputed norms. For, as has been explained, knowingly to choose such an action is to will something at odds with love of God, of neighbor, or of one's self in communion with God and neighbor. And, at the beginning of deliberation, the reasonable person rejects such possibilities as temptations. Nor do those who reject the disputed norms consider everything. They try to judge by what they foresee, but do not consider that they should cooperate with God's creative work according to his plan.

6) It is a mistake to regard isolated outward performances as if they were complete moral acts. Morality chiefly is in the heart—that is, in deliberate willing. Sometimes an act contrary to one of the disputed norms—for example, an act of masturbation—is not contrary to love of God or neighbor because the agent lacks sufficient reflection or full consent or both. It does not follow that such an act is morally good, but rather that it falls short of being a morally significant act. But if one deliberately masturbates, one fantasizes and wills others to be sex objects. And, in general, one who deliberately wills something bad contrary to one of the disputed norms implicitly wills a whole set of unrecognized implications. For instance, in willing to treat one's own body as a subpersonal thing, one implicitly wills that others' bodies have that status. But for the human body to have that status is inconsistent with its having the status implied for it by central truths of Christian faith: the Word becoming flesh, his bodily presence in the Eucharist and our need to receive it, his bodily resurrection and our hoped for share in it, and so on.[31]

7) Although some Catholics reject the disputed norms, many still hold that trying to live by them is essential.[32] Now, if the Holy Spirit works in all the faithful, still he does not contradict himself. So, one must discern which group's judgment manifests the Spirit's action.[33] Those who accept the disputed norms agree with their ancestors in faith, who handed these norms on; those who reject them agree with people who gradually abandoned the tradition and who today make up the nonbelieving world. Insofar as the tradition of faith and the contemporary nonbelieving world contradict one another, it is reasonable to judge that the former rather than the latter manifests the Spirit's working. So, it is reasonable to discern the *sensus fidei* in believers who accept the disputed norms, rather than to regard as *sensus fidelium* the opinion of those who reject them.

8) Those who argue that not allowing exceptions to the disputed norms is too rigid, not compassionate, and pastorally disastrous assume that these norms are like positive laws, which the Church can either enforce, mitigate, or repeal. But since the disputed norms are truths pertaining to God's plan, not laws, continuing to teach them is helpful, not rigid. Teaching them also is compassionate, because it opposes great human evils such as mean-

ingless sex, killing the unborn, and destruction of families. Moreover, teaching the disputed norms is pastorally necessary because God has written them on people's hearts, and so failing to teach them does not repeal them, but only makes it harder for people to resist temptations and easier for them to rationalize conformity to the world, which they nevertheless half realize is divergence from the mind of Christ.[34] Besides, every Christian can live up to the disputed norms if he or she really wants to do so, because God provides sufficient grace.[35] Finally, some Catholics are leaving the Church, but the explanation is the general process of secularization, which is affecting most mainline churches in affluent societies.[36]

VI. A Look Ahead

The preceding overview of arguments for the disputed norms' truth and critique of arguments against them hardly exhausts the subject. However, this sketch should clarify several points.

First, the issue is more complex than one might think. Second, the Church is divided on the issue. Third, this division is bad. It impedes evangelization and catechesis, anguishes many pastors, and confuses the faithful. Fourth, the issue does not concern something peripheral on which the Church can simply agree to disagree.

I began by looking back to the origin of this issue around the time of Vatican II. Looking ahead, I think the resolution must come by a collegial effort of the pope and bishops, either in Vatican III or by some other form of collegial effort. That effort will need the help of teams of theologians who hold the opposing views. Those on each team should be asked to articulate their views fully and to criticize the arguments and counterarguments of their opponents.[37] Only with the help of such full theological debate will the pope and bishops completely understand the opposing positions and how each is related to the central truth and reality of Catholic faith—Jesus and his kingdom.

Until now, it seems to me, the situation has not been squarely faced. There seems to be a widespread fear of facing it.[38] However, if all the bishops set to work in union with the pope, one can be sure that the collegial effort will succeed.[39] For Jesus, who is faithful, promised to stay with his Church. At the beginning, he sent the Holy Spirit with the sure gift of truth. He will not fail to provide this gift today.

Notes

1. The best single brief presentation of the whole argument against such exceptionless moral norms is given by Fuchs (1971), which is criticized specifically and in detail by Grisez (1985b).

2. Those who deny the disputed norms do not necessarily wish to assert that the acts which those norms exclude are generally good or permissible: see Curran (1986) 255–58 for a summary of his own views (with references to his prior works) emphasizing the modesty of his dissent.

3. The faithful at large appear to have followed. A 1987 Gallup poll (*National Catholic Reporter,* 11 September 1987, 8) reports not only that 66% of Catholics in the United States believe one can be a good Catholic without obeying the Church's teaching on contraception but also that 57% answer similarly with respect to remarriage after divorce and 39% with respect to abortion. Other polls (see Gallup and Castelli [1987] 51 and 182) indicated that by 1985 66% of Catholics in the United States wanted the Church to allow divorced Catholics to remarry and 58% approved of premarital intercourse.

4. See Sullivan (1983) 152 and 227–28 (n. 46). Curran (1986) convincingly argues that his views are very widely shared; moreover, a statement supporting him which he reprints (282–84), signed by some past presidents of the Catholic Theological Society of America and of the College Theology Society and by over 750 other theologians, makes the point (283) that "there are very many Catholic theologians who do dissent from noninfallible teachings."

5. The recent magisterium has affirmed the general proposition that there are exceptionless specific moral norms: Congregation for the Clergy, *Directorium catechisticum generale* (11 April 1971), n. 63 (*AAS* 64 [1972] 136): "Edoceri insuper debeat ipsa christianorum conscientia normas etiam adesse absolutas, seu in omni casu et pro omnibus obligantes"; John Paul II, *Reconciliatio et paenitentia,* 17 (*AAS* 77 [1985] 221–22): "Sunt enim actus, qui per se ipsos et in se ipsis, extra adiuncta, propter objectum suum semper sunt graviter illiciti. Hi actus, si sufficienti cum conscientia ac libertate ponuntur, semper gravem inferunt culpam." And the Pope cites the Council of Trent (DS 1544), which in rejecting the view that grace is lost only by unbelief, cites 1 Cor 6:9 for the proposition that also excluded from the kingdom are "those with faith who are fornicators, adulterers, effeminate, sodomites, thieves, covetous, drunkards, evil-tongued, greedy."

6. See McKeever (1981) 211–22; Cahill (1984) 121–35.

7. Three books undertaking the same task as this brief paper: Pinckaers (1986), May (1989), and Finnis (1990).

8. See Curran (1975) 173–209; Schüller (1978); McCormick (1981) 453, 506, 542, 711–13; Scholz (1984).

9. See Rahner (1976) 14–15; Sullivan (1983) 152; Noonan (1966). The argument often involves a schema according to which a shift in consciousness has been (must be?) made from a "classicist" world view to "historical consciousness"; see Lonergan (1967); Curran (1970) 116–36.

10. This argument expresses the theory of "consequentialism" or "proportionalism." For a very sympathetic account of it with many references to its chief proponents: Hoose

(1987). The development of the theory's leading American proponent can be followed in McCormick (1981) 349–67; 529–44; 709–11; and McCormick (1978) 35–50 and 193–267. For a very easily understandable statement of the theory, see the work (introduced by Curran) of O'Connell (1978) 144–73.

11. For this and related arguments against exceptionless norms using the authority of St. Thomas, see Janssens (1972) 125–26, 133, 139–41; (1977) 232; (1982) 38–40; (1988) 355–56; Häring (1978) 363; McCormick (1984) 115, 169; Scholz (1979) 166–69, 173, 178; Fuchs (1983) 192–94; Mahoney (1987) 241; Milhaven (1970) 141–72; Dedek (1979) 408–9.

12. Janssens (1972) 144; Janssens (1977) 231; Vacek (1985) 313; Mahoney (1987) 309–321; McCormick (1981) 700–701.

13. See Curran (1970) 7–26, 167–80; Häring (1978) 392–410.

14. The 30 July 1968 statement by certain Catholic theologians of dissent form *Humanae vitae*—see Curran et al. (1969) 25—includes the *sensus fidelium* argument without using the phrase: "No real importance is afforded the witness of the life of the Church in its totality; the special witness of many Catholic couples is neglected; it fails to acknowledge the witness of the separated Christian churches and ecclesial communities; it is insensitive to the witness of many men of good will; it pays insufficient attention to the ethical import of modern science." The *sensus fidelium* argument is protean; dissenting theology and its journalistic popularizers rely heavily on it and articulate it in various forms: "Moral norms must be drawn from *experience*"; "Moral teachings require *reception* on the part of the faithful to be obligatory"; "Cardinal Newman endorsed dissent when he spoke of '*consulting the faithful* in matters of doctrine' "; and so forth.

15. Many make this argument, but no one more passionately and repeatedly since the contraception controversy began than Bernard Häring, C.Ss.R. See, e.g., Häring (1989). Andrew Greeley et al. (1976) 313–27 argues *post hoc ergo propter hoc* that *Humanae vitae* caused the "declining Church"; they fail to consider the possibility that dissent contributed to the decline.

16. *Lumen gentium,* 12: "The body of the faithful as a whole, anointed as they are by the Holy One (cf. Jn 2:20, 27), cannot err in matters of belief. Thanks to a supernatural sense of the faith which characterizes the People as a whole, it manifests this unerring quality when, 'from the bishops down to the last member of the laity,' [note omitted] it shows universal agreement in matters of faith and morals." If the whole body of truth concerning faith and morals on which the Church at any time universally agrees were not infallibly held and handed on, the Church's pastors would not have been able to settle disputes when they arose by making solemn definitions based on what the whole Church believed in previous times.

17. *Lumen gentium,* 25. See Ford and Grisez (1978) for the full development of this line of argument, Sullivan (1983) 119–52 for a critique of the Ford-Grisez argument, and Grisez (1985a) for the response to Sullivan's critique; for a summary of other theological debate, see Grisez (1988) 12–16. Most dissenting theologians virtually ignored the Ford-Grisez argument. McCormick commented—(1981) 777—on it and on Joseph Komonchak's article which appeared in the same issue of *Theological Studies:* "It is noteworthy that these two studies are basically essays in ecclesiology. [Note omitted.] It would be immodest for a moral theologian to attempt to referee such a dispute, though it is clear that many theologians (what Komonchak calls 'something like a *consensus theologorum*') would favor the Komonchak thesis." Since the two articles appeared at the same time and since McCormick was commenting on both, neither he nor Komonchak was referring to a consensus of opinion about the Ford-Grisez argument among those who had *studied* it. Rather, Komonchak's invocation of an opposing consensus and McCormick's confident prediction that theologians

129

would favor Komonchak's thesis meant that they were sure that the Ford-Grisez argument would be rejected by theologians without studying it, and they apparently were right. Even Charles Curran, who on other occasions shared in fair debate, ignored the Ford-Grisez argument, for in a subsequent book—Curran (1982) 5—concerning the relationship between the magisterium and theology, in delimiting the subject to be treated, Curran blandly claimed that "all admit that the investigations of theologians have not involved the infallible teaching office of the Church"—precisely what Ford and I deny.

18. See *Gaudium et spes,* 38–39; see Grisez (1983) 459–71 and 807–30.

19. DS 1548/810.

20. See Grisez (1983) 41–72 and 173–228. A simple, strictly philosophical presentation of Grisez's ethical theory: Grisez and Shaw (1988).

21. *Gaudium et spes,* 39.

22. See Grisez (1983) 115–40. For an important clarification of the basic goods, see Grisez, Boyle, and Finnis (1987) 106–17 and 131–41.

23. See Grisez (1983) 599–682; Grisez (1984a).

24. See Grisez (1966).

25. See Grisez (1985b) 175–77, 191–93.

26. On this, see Boyle (1984).

27. Beginning with: "Whoever sheds the blood of man, by man shall his blood be shed; for God made man in his own image" Gn 9:6. For a compact summary of the tradition on the intentional killing of the innocent, see Grisez (1987) 292–99. For the argument that, despite apparent tradition, *all* intentional killing, even as capital punishment or in warfare, is wrong: Grisez (1970); Grisez and Boyle (1979) 336–441; Finnis, Boyle, and Grisez (1987) 297–319.

28. See Grisez (1983) 182–83, 859, 869 (n. 62) and 891–94 including relevant notes; Grisez (1985b) 169–77; Finnis (1980) 139–42.

29. For a very helpful summary of the various arguments against proportionalism: Kiely (1985). For fuller critiques of consequentialism or proportionalism: Grisez (1978); Grisez (1980); Grisez (1983) 141–71, including a critique (161–64) of McCormick's most cautious statement of his view (in McCormick [1978] 193–267); Finnis (1983) 80–120, including (99–104) a critique of McCormick (1978); Finnis, Boyle, and Grisez (1987) 238–72. For an explanation of the moral difference between contraception and natural family planning: Grisez, Boyle, Finnis, and May (1988). For a critique of proportionalism from a more strictly Thomistic viewpoint, see Pinckaers (1982); in the course of this article, Pinckaers makes clear how far St. Thomas is from the entire outlook of the proportionalists. Some other theological critiques of proportionalism: Connery (1973) and (1981); Citterio (1982); Composta (1981); Zalba (1982); Ermecke (1973).

30. For replies to the arguments which invoke the authority of St. Thomas, see the massive work of Belmans (1980); also see Lee (1981); May (1984); Grisez (1983) 148–49, 268–69.

31. See Grisez (1977); Grisez (1984b).

32. A poll of Catholics in the United States, taken shortly after the publication of *Humanae vitae* in 1968 (*National Catholic Reporter,* 11 September 1968, 9), found 25% answering "No" to the question: "Do you think it is possible to practice artificial methods of birth control and still be a good Catholic?" A similar 1987 poll, published exactly nineteen years later (*National Catholic Reporter,* 11 September 1987, 8), found 27% answering "No" to an almost identical question. The difference of two percentage points is hardly significant, but the constancy of this substantial minority's sense of faith is quite significant. Moreover, it is more impressive when one takes into account the fact that many of the more mature

members of the population polled in 1968 had died by 1987 and their places were taken by people too young in 1968 to be represented in a poll.

33. The supernatural sense of faith (cf. *Lumen gentium,* 12) is not to be confused with the consensus even of a majority of the faithful in affluent countries at the present time: see John Paul II, *Familiaris consortio,* 5, *AAS* 74 (1982) 85–86.

34. Paul VI and John Paul II teach (*Humanae vitae,* 29, *AAS* 60 [1968] 501; *Familiaris consortio,* 33, *AAS* 74 [1982] 121): "To diminish in no way the saving teaching of Christ constitutes an eminent form of charity for souls."

35. To deny this, as many seem to do today, is heresy (see DS 1536–39/804, 1568/828). John Paul II, "Address to participants in a seminar on 'Responsible Parenthood'" (17 September 1983), *Insegnamenti di Giovanni Paolo II,* vol. 6, part 2, 564; *L'Osservatore Romano,* Eng. ed., 10 October 1983, 7, forcefully recalls Catholic teaching concerning grace: "To maintain that situations exist in which it is not, *de facto,* possible for the spouses to be faithful to *all* the requirements of the truth of conjugal love is equivalent to forgetting this event of grace which characterizes the New Covenant: the grace of the Holy Spirit makes possible that which is not possible to man, left solely to his own powers. It is therefore necessary to support the spouses in their spiritual lives, to invite them to resort frequently to the Sacraments of Confession and the Eucharist for a continual return, a permanent conversion to the truth of conjugal love."

36. Roof and McKinney (1987) 170: "The big 'winner' in the switching game is the growing secular constituency.... The liberal religious traditions especially have a serious institutional problem of holding their own.... Liberal Protestantism's greatest losses come from those dropping out of religion altogether. But Catholics and Jews, and to a lesser extent some conservative Protestants, also lose considerable numbers to the nonaffiliate ranks. What was once a liberal Protestant 'problem' is now more generally one for the mainline faiths."

37. Unless the magisterium takes the initiative to organize theological debate on the issues which divide the two camps, it will not occur, not because of the human failings of either group of theologians, but because both camps realize that the theological argument has gone as far as it can go, because the issues now go to first principles: what faith is and how it is handed on.

38. The Holy See seems to be following a strategy of trying to appoint "better bishops." If so, that strategy will not solve the problem. For, first, even if all bishops eventually agree with John Paul II on matters disputed among theologians, the problems which have been raised will not have been resolved. And, second, since a bishop who begins by agreeing with the Pope usually cannot eliminate from his diocese all dissenting theologians (and all the priests and teachers who follow them), he can hardly avoid cooperating with them, and in doing so undercutting his own teaching efforts. Such a pastor is hardly acting consistently. Hence, he himself is likely to experience strong tendencies to consider dissenting opinions somehow acceptable and gradually to yield to them, with the bad result that there is a constant drift of bishops toward dissenting opinions.

39. For a much fuller description of the problem and the possible way to solve it: Grisez (1986). It is important to note that John Paul II has made it clear that he *believes* the teaching on contraception—that is, accepts it as part of the Catholic faith. In *Familiaris consortio,* 29, *AAS* 74 (1982) 115, he reaffirms "in continuity with the living tradition of the ecclesial community throughout history... the Church's teaching and norm, always old yet always new, regarding marriage and regarding the transmission of human life." He cites proposition 22 of the 1980 Synod of Bishops: "this Sacred Synod, gathered together with the Successor of Peter in the unity of faith, firmly holds what has been set forth in the Second

Vatican Council (cf. *Gaudium et spes,* 50) and afterwards in the Encyclical *Humanae Vitae,* particularly that love between husband and wife must be fully human, exclusive and open to new life (*Humanae Vitae,* 11; cf. 9, 12)." The phrase, "in continuity with the living tradition of the ecclesial community throughout history," suggests John Paul II's position on the status of the Catholic teaching concerning contraception. Elsewhere, he makes his position fully explicit. Nearing the end of his four-year long catechesis on the redemption of the body and on marriage—John Paul II, General Audience (18 July 1984), *Insegnamenti di Giovanni Paolo II,* vol. 7, part 2, 102; *L'Osservatore Romano,* Eng. ed., 23 July 1984, 1—he comments on *Humanae vitae,* noting that Paul VI stressed that the norm concerning contraception pertains to natural law, whose interpretation is within the magisterium's competence. Pope John Paul then adds: "However, we can say more. Even if the moral law, formulated in this way in the Encyclical *Humanae Vitae,* is not found literally in Sacred Scripture, nonetheless, from the fact that it is contained in Tradition and—as Pope Paul VI writes—has been 'very often expounded by the Magisterium' (*HV,* n. 12) to the faithful, it follows that this norm *is in accordance with the sum total of revealed doctrine contained in biblical sources* (cf. *HV,* n. 4). It is a question here not only of the sum total of the moral doctrine contained in Sacred Scripture, of its essential premises and general character of its content, but of that fuller context to which we have previously dedicated numerous analyses when speaking about the 'theology of the body.' Precisely against the background of this full context it becomes evident that the above-mentioned moral norm belongs not only to the natural moral law, but also to the *moral order revealed by God:* also from this point of view, it could not be different, but solely what is handed down by Tradition and the Mag.sterium and, in our days, the Encyclical *Humanae vitae* as a modern document of this Magisterium. [Emphasis his.]" Here John Paul II reasons from the manner in which the Church has taught concerning contraception to that teaching's being consonant with the whole of revealed doctrine, and then from relevant contents of Scripture, which he had expounded in detail, to the norm's belonging to the "moral order revealed by God." This papal belief powerfully confirms the thesis of Ford and Grisez (1978).

Bibliography

Belmans, Theo G., O. Praem., *Le Sens Objectif de l'Agir Humain: Pour Relire la Morale Conjugale de Saint Thomas,* Studi Tomistici, 8 (Vatican City: Libreria Editrice Vaticana, 1980).

Boyle, Joseph, "The Principle of Double Effect: Good Actions Entangled in Evil," in *Moral Theology Today: Certitudes and Doubts* (St. Louis, Missouri: Pope John Center, 1984), 243–60.

Cahill, Lisa Sowle, "Contemporary Challenges to Exceptionless Moral Norms," in *Moral Theology Today: Certitudes and Doubts* (St. Louis, Missouri: Pope John Center, 1984), 121–35.

Citterio, Ferdinando, "La revisione critica dei tradizionali principi morali alle luce della teoria del 'compromesso etico,'" *Scuola cattolica,* 110 (1982), 29–64.

Composta, Dario, "Il consequenzialismo: Una nuova corrente della 'Nuova Morale,'" *Divinitas,* 25 (1981), 127–56.

Connery, John R., S.J., "Morality of Consequences: A Critical Appraisal," *Theological Studies,* 34 (1973), 396–414.

———, "Catholic Ethics: Has the Norm for Rule-Making Changed?" *Theological Studies,* 42 (1981), 232–50.

Curran, Charles E., *Contemporary Problems in Moral Theology* (Notre Dame, Indiana: Fides, 1970).

————, *Ongoing Revision in Moral Theology* (Notre Dame, Indiana: Fides/Claretian, 1975).

————, *Moral Theology: A Continuing Journey* (Notre Dame, Indiana: University of Notre Dame, 1982).

————, *Faithful Dissent* (Kansas City, Missouri: Sheed and Ward, 1986).

Dedek, John F., "Intrinsically Evil Acts: An Historical Study of the Mind of St. Thomas," *Thomist,* 43 (1979), 385–413.

Ermecke, Gustav, "Das Problem der Universalität oder Allgemeingültigkeit sittlicher Normen innerweltlicher Lebensgestaltung," *Münchener theologische Zeitschrift,* 24 (1973), 1–24.

Finnis, John, "Natural Law, Objective Morality, and Vatican II," in May (1980) 113–49.

————, *Fundamentals of Ethics* (Washington, D.C.: Georgetown University Press, 1983).

————, *Moral Absolutes: Tradition, Revision and Truth,* forthcoming (1990).

Finnis, John, Joseph Boyle, and Germain Grisez, *Nuclear Deterrence, Morality and Realism* (Oxford and New York: Oxford University Press, 1987).

Ford, John C., S.J., and Germain Grisez, "Contraception and the Infallibility of the Ordinary Magisterium," *Theological Studies,* 39 (1978), 258–312.

Fuchs, Josef, S.J., "The Absoluteness of Moral Terms," *Gregorianum,* 52 (1971), 415–57; reprinted under the title "The Absoluteness of Behavioral Moral Norms," in Fuchs (1983) 115–52.

————, *Personal Responsibility and Christian Morality* (Washington, D.C.: Georgetown University Press, 1983).

Gallup, George, Jr., and Jim Castelli, *The American Catholic People: Their Beliefs, Practices, and Values* (Garden City, N.Y.: Doubleday, 1987).

Greeley, Andrew, et al., *Catholic Schools in a Declining Church* (Kansas City, Missouri: Sheed and Ward, 1976).

Grisez, Germain, "Man, Natural End of," *New Catholic Encyclopedia* (1966) 9:132–38.

————, "Toward a Consistent Natural-Law Ethics of Killing," *American Journal of Jurisprudence,* 15 (1970), 64–96.

————, "Dualism and the New Morality," *Atti del Congresso Internazionale Tommaso d'Aquino nel suo Settimo Centenario,* vol. 5, *L'Agire Morale* (Naples: Edizioni Domenicane Italiane, 1977), 323–30.

————, "Against Consequentialism," *American Journal of Jurisprudence,* 23 (1978), 21–72.

————, "Christian Moral Theology and Consequentialism," in May (1980) 293–327.

————, *Way of the Lord Jesus,* vol. 1, *Christian Moral Principles* (Chicago: Franciscan Herald Press, 1983).

————, "Presidential Address: Practical Reason and Faith," *Proceedings of the American Catholic Philosophical Association,* 58 (1984a), 2–14.

————, "Turmoil in the Church," *Homiletic and Pastoral Review,* 85 (November 1984b), 12–22.

————, "Infallibility and Specific Moral Norms: A Review Discussion," *Thomist,* 49 (1985a), 248–87.

————, "Moral Absolutes: A Critique of the View of Josef Fuchs, S.J.," *Rivista di Studi sulla Persona e la Famiglia: Anthropos* (now *Anthropotes*), 1 (1985b), 155–201.

————, "How to Deal with Theological Dissent," *Homiletic and Pastoral Review,* part 1, 87 (November 1986), 19–29; part 2, 87 (December 1986), 49–61.

————, "The Definability of the Proposition: The Intentional Killing of an Innocent Human Being Is Always Grave Matter," in *Atti del Congresso Internazionale di Teologia Morale: Persona, Verità e Morale* (Rome: Città Nuova Editrice, 1987), 291–313.

133

————, "General Introduction," in John C. Ford, S.J., Germain Grisez, Joseph Boyle, John Finnis, and William E. May, *The Teaching of "Humanae vitae": A Defense* (San Francisco: Ignatius Press, 1988), 7–32.

Grisez, Germain, and Joseph M. Boyle, Jr., *Life and Death with Liberty and Justice: A Contribution to the Euthanasia Debate* (Notre Dame, Indiana: University of Notre Dame Press, 1979).

Grisez, Germain, Joseph Boyle, and John Finnis, "Practical Principles, Moral Truth, and Ultimate Ends," *American Journal of Jurisprudence,* 32 (1987), 99–151.

Grisez, Germain, Joseph Boyle, John Finnis, and William E. May, " 'Every Marital Act Ought to Be Open to New Life': Toward a Clearer Understanding," *Thomist,* 52 (1988), 365–426.

Grisez, Germain, and Russell Shaw, *Beyond the New Morality: The Responsibilities of Freedom* (Notre Dame, Indiana: University of Notre Dame Press, 3rd ed., 1988).

Häring, Bernard, C.Ss.R., *Free and Faithful in Christ: Moral Theology for Clergy and Laity,* vol. 1, *General Moral Theology* (New York: Seabury Press, 1978).

————, "Does God Condemn Contraception? A Message for the Whole Church," *Commonweal,* 116 (15 February 1989), 69–71.

Hoose, Bernard, *Proportionalism: The American Debate and Its European Roots* (Washington, D.C.: Georgetown University Press, 1987).

Janssens, Louis, "Ontic Evil and Moral Evil," *Louvain Studies,* 4 (1972), 115–56.

————, "Norms and Priorities in a Love Ethic," *Louvain Studies,* 6 (1977), 207–38.

————, "Saint Thomas Aquinas and the Question of Proportionality," *Louvain Studies,* 9 (1982), 26–46.

————, "A Moral Understanding of Some Arguments of St. Thomas," *Ephemerides Theologicae Lovaniensis,* 64 (1988), 354–60.

Kiely, Bartholomew M., S.J., "The Impracticability of Consequentialism," *Gregorianum,* 66 (1985), 655–86.

Lee, Patrick, "Permanence of the Ten Commandments: St. Thomas and His Modern Commentators," *Theological Studies,* 42 (1981), 422–43.

Lonergan, Bernard, S.J., "The Transition from a Classicist World-View to Historical Mindedness," in *Law for Liberty,* ed. James E. Biechler (Baltimore, Md.: Helicon, 1967), 126–33.

McCormick, Richard A., S.J., "Ambiguity in Moral Choice" and "A Commentary on the Commentaries," in McCormick and Ramsey (1978).

————, *Notes on Moral Theology: 1965–80* (Washington, D.C.: University Press of America, 1981).

————, *Notes on Moral Theology: 1981–84* (Washington, D.C.: University Press of America, 1984).

McCormick, Richard A., S.J., and Paul Ramsey, eds., *Doing Evil to Achieve Good: Moral Choice in Conflict Situations* (Chicago: Loyola University Press, 1978).

McKeever, Paul E., "Proportionalism As a Methodology in Catholic Moral Theology," in *Human Sexuality and Personhood* (St. Louis, Missouri: Pope John Center, 1981).

Mahoney, John, S.J., *The Making of Moral Theology* (Oxford: Oxford University Press, 1987).

May, William E., ed., *Principles of Catholic Moral Life* (Chicago: Franciscan Herald Press, 1980).

————, "Aquinas and Janssens on the Moral Meaning of Human Acts," *Thomist,* 48 (1984), 566–606.

————, *Moral Absolutes: Catholic Tradition, Current Trends, and the Truth,* The Père Marquette Lecture in Theology, 1989 (Milwaukee, Wis.: Marquette University Press, 1989).

Milhaven, John Giles, *Toward a New Catholic Morality* (Garden City, N.Y.: Doubleday, 1970).

Noonan, John T., Jr., "Authority, Usury, and Contraception," *Cross Currents,* 16 (1966), 55–79.

O'Connell, Timothy E., *Principles for a Catholic Morality* (New York, N.Y.: Seabury Press, 1978).

Pinckaers, Servais, O.P., "La question des actes intrinsèquement mauvais et le 'proportionnalisme,'" *Revue Thomiste,* 82 (1982), 181–212.

——, *Ce qu'on ne peut jamais faire: La question des actes intrinsèquement mauvais: Histoire et discussion* (Fribourg, Switzerland: Éditions Universitaires, 1986).

Rahner, Karl, S.J., "Basic Observations on the Subject of the Changeable and Unchangeable Factors in the Church," in *Theological Investigations,* vol. 14, *Ecclesiology, Questions in the Church, The Church in the World,* trans. David Bourke (New York: Seabury Press, 1976), ch. 1.

Roof, Wade Clark, and William McKinney, *American Mainline Religion: Its Changing Shape and Future* (New Brunswick, N.J.: Rutgers University Press, 1987).

Scholz, Franz, "Problems on Norms Raised by Ethical Borderline Situations: Beginnings of a Solution in Thomas Aquinas and Bonaventure," in Charles Curran and Richard A. McCormick, S.J., eds., *Readings in Moral Theology No. 1: Moral Norms and Catholic Tradition* (New York: Paulist Press, 1979), 158–183.

——, "Gemeinsames, Trennendes, Missverstandenes," *Theologie der Gegenwart,* 27 (1984), 209–20.

Schüller, Bruno, S.J., "The Double Effect in Catholic Thought: a Reevaluation," in McCormick and Ramsey (1978) 165–92.

Sullivan, Francis A., S.J., *Magisterium: Teaching Authority in the Church* (New York: Paulist Press, 1983).

Vacek, Edward, S.J., "Proportionalism: One View of the Debate," *Theological Studies,* 46 (1985), 287–314.

Zalba, Marcelino, S.J., "Principia ethica in crisim vocata intra (propter?) crisim morum," *Periodica de Re Morali, Canonica, Liturgica,* 71 (1982), 25–63 and 319–57.

Chapter 9

CONSISTENT ETHICS OF LIFE IN HEALTH CARE

John Haas, Ph.D.

One of the most intractable, complex and seemingly insoluble problems facing the United States today is the problem of homelessness. It is a national scandal and an embarrassment to the United States throughout the world. Cardinal Joseph Bernardin has regularly and forcefully maintained that a consistent ethic of life must be seen not only in the narrow field of medical ethics but also in the broader domain of social justice.[1] We cannot be for prenatal life without being just as fiercely committed to postnatal life. The Catholic Church cannot insist that it would be immoral to contracept or abort children without also insisting that we as a society must see that these children are also clothed, fed and housed. The case for a linkage between the various life issues advanced so insistently by Cardinal Bernardin has been one of the most significant developments in the moral posture of the Church in this country following the Council. In this regard, one of the most dismaying aspects of homelessness in America today are the numbers of women and their children who are joining their ranks. Some estimate that women with children now constitute 25% of the homeless in the United States.

Such social problems as homelessness prove to be so intractable because of the complexity of social life and the almost countless variables which enter into social situations. The injunction to care for the homeless allows a bewildering array of possible solutions. Some, however, have had adverse effects on other social groups. There have been attempted solutions which have led to the destablization of residential communities. The McKinney Act mandated the federal government to turn over thousands of empty, government-owned buildings to homeless advocates to be used as kitchens, health clinics and transitional clinics. However, bureaucratic inefficiencies at the Department of Housing and Urban Development, lack of coordination among various government agencies and lack of clarity in the law itself as to who qualifies as a homeless provider group have all conspired to prevent the achieving of the goals which the law had sought.

As people of good-will struggle to find solutions to housing and medical care for the homeless, they all agree on certain fundamental guiding principles. Whatever course of action the homeless advocates or government agencies or city planners or land developers may debate, whatever particular policies they may decide to cooperate on or disagree over, there is, however, one, absolute principle upon which they are so fundamentally agreed that it is never even discussed. All are of one mind that the solution to the problem of homelessness does not lie in killing the homeless. The statement just made may well be judged to be absurd. After all, it will be insisted, who would ever advocate such a solution to a terrible social problem? Yet it must surely be agreed that before any solution could possibly be proposed or attempted, there must be this absolute, minimal commitment on the part of all concerned with the problems of the homeless. Whatever the disagreements over the bewildering array of possible solutions to the problems of the homeless and no matter how long it may take to solve the problem and no matter what the social costs might be, there must be agreement on one thing—the innocent cannot be killed as a means to solving this problem. Is this too much to ask?

Remarkably, in today's society, it seems to be! The Catholic Church says, "Yes, we are faced with a bewildering array of problems in health care. There are grave problems associated with unwanted pregnancies, genetic defects, the prolongation of life, artificial hydration and nutrition for the irreversibly comatose. We want to work with the rest of society toward a solution to these problems. However, there is just one condition for our cooperation. There is one principle we will not violate. As we seek common solutions to these problems let us agree that we will never directly kill the innocent."

Here can be seen the root and core of a consistent ethic of life in Catholic health care. The prohibition against the direct taking of innocent human life does not answer all the problems surrounding the life issues in health care by any means. It is indeed the absolute minimum that we can ask for. As Cardinal Bernardin has so insistently argued, we must go beyond it. But for the love of God, by all that is good and decent and holy, it is the absolute, barest minimum upon which the Church must insist in facing the complex questions of health care—Do not kill the innocent!

Here one can see a difference between positive precepts admitting of exceptions and certain negative precepts admitting of no exceptions.[2] Some proposed actions can so violate fundamental human goods that they render virtually meaningless any other proposals which may be addressed to the alleviation of social problems. Such proposed actions must be absolutely and at all times prohibited.

The consistent life ethic of the Catholic Church *may* appear inconsistent to many in contemporary society because they do not share this fundamental commitment to the value of human life. The Church insists that innocent human life is inviolable and may never be directly destroyed. What may look like a lack of compassion in refusing to abort a defective fetus or in refusing to provide a lethal dose of morphine to one suffering from terminal cancer is actually a commitment to the basic, fundamental good of human life in its entirety, physical, emotional, spiritual. The Church insists on the inviolability of this good because of its inherent value and because it sees that the advocacy of specific policies or social programs are simply meaningless without it—as meaningless as proposals to alleviate the problem of homelessness by killing off some of the homeless. The recognition of the inviolability of innocent life is at the very heart of the Church's consistent ethic of life.

The Church is, of course, perfectly capable of developing solidly rational arguments to defend its position. Without making any reference to God or revelation it can insist with Immanuel Kant that unless every person is treated as an end in him or herself and never used as a means toward an end, civilized social life is impossible.[3] There is no other institution in the modern world which is so consistently and comprehensively rational in its approach to moral problems generally and medical ethics problems in particular. Indeed, it was this dispassionate, rational reflection inherent within our Catholic tradition which led certain Evangelical leaders to complain during the Pope's pastoral visit in 1987 that he sounded no different than a secular humanist.

Yet we all know the reaction of the secular humanist to the consistent life ethic of the Catholic Church. It is too imbued with religious belief ever to be applicable in a pluralist society. The secularist complains that the Catholic life ethic is predicated on unverifiable religious beliefs such as the immortal soul which supposedly imparts transcendent value to the human person. The Church is accused of treating something which is no more than vegetative life, an irreversibly comatose individual, as some kind of sacred reality which ought not to be violated.

Of course, both the Evangelical leader and the secular humanist are correct in their assessment of the consistent life ethic of the Catholic. The Church surpasses any other contemporary institution not only in its rational, consistent and comprehensive approach to medical-moral and social questions, it also displays the most intense awareness of the sacred in our midst.

When the Catholic Church insists that innocent human life is sacred, it is not simply mouthing a common platitude but is making a profession of faith, it is expressing a religious awe which partakes of that very awe which is manifested in the face of Divinity itself. The sacral quality of innocent human life is so intense that the Church safeguards it with all the prohibitions which one might expect from the tabus of a primitive religion.[4] But the application of an almost rarefied rationality as well as a sublime religious veneration to the human subject/object of moral choices in health care is no sign of inconsistency in the Catholic tradition, but rather an expression of what the human person is in his fullness as "homo intelligens et religiosus." In the presence of human life, the Catholic stands in religious awe as before God, for the Catholic realizes that one stands in the true presence of the "imago Dei", the very image of God on earth.[5] Human life is sacred because it has truly come from the hand of God and mirrors His own perfections.

In our technological society, human life, long stripped of its sacral significance by the reigning speculations of the likes of Darwin and Freud and Feuerbach, has come to be seen as just another product usually still reproduced in the primitive way, but now susceptible to the wonderful production techniques of the "homo technicus." Measurable, quantifiable, manipulative techniques of fertility drugs, ova aspiration, sperm collection, nutrient serums in petri dishes have replaced the religious awe of the Psalmist:

> Truly you have formed my inmost being;
>   you knit me in my mother's womb.
> I give you thanks that I am fearfully,
>   wonderfully made;
>   wonderful are your works.
> My soul also you knew full well;
>   nor was my frame unknown to you
> When I was made in secret,
>   when I was fashioned in the depths of the earth.[6]

Even those still using the "primitive" method of reproduction and not availing themselves of new technologies have unfortunately developed the deadly attitude that *they* are the creators of that which has arisen from their carnal activities and that they are entitled to nurture it—or destroy it—according to their own designs.

They are, of course, mistaken. All human life is sacred and has come from the hand of God, whether conceived within the body of an abortion rights activist attorney, in a petri dish or in the fallopian tube of a high school senior after the Homecoming Dance.

Even the prearranged and intentional activity of a married couple seeking children does not create human life. The married couple give themselves to one another, while God, and He alone, gifts them with new life.

It seems the Catholic Church was almost prophetically aware of the day when technology would develop to such a point that human pride would surrender to the unspeakable folly of thinking that the human person had become the creator. The Church has consistently rejected the doctrine of traducianism, which holds that a child receives all of life, body and soul, from its parents. The rejection of traducianism insists on the direct act of God in the creation of each individual soul, in that which truly constitutes each individual a human being, an "imago Dei", a rational, willing, loving creature of inestimable value and an eternal destiny.[7] God has loved each single one of us into existence.

The received, magisterial doctrine of creationism maintains that no one is a mistake, a fluke, a mere accident in a cosmic swirl of gas and dust and fire, but a "creatura Dei". The doctrine of the incarnation carries us even further. In a way surpassing all understanding God has loved us to the point of a total outpouring, a "kenosis", of Himself. Human life is of such incomparable value that God lavished not only an entire universe on us, but His very Self. "Fear not, for I have redeemed you; I have called you by name: you are mine... [b]ecause you are precious in my eyes and glorious, and because I love you."[8]

Anyone, not only the religious person, should be able to recognize and acknowledge the incomparable value of each, individual human life. Anyone should be able to understand that it is incommensurable with any other value. It cannot be placed in the scales and found wanting. It cannot be measured against any assemblage of other goods, no matter how impressive or appealing, and found to be liable to direct violation. As said previously, if innocent human life can be subjected to assault and destruction, then no other proposal for moral action makes any sense, no other proposal for moral action can be compelling, for it too could be overturned by another arbitrary assemblage of goods.

Yet not everyone does see and appreciate the absolute inviolability of each innocent human life. We as Catholics are blessed with the gift of revelation showing us the value of each life in the sight of God. What reason shows us should be inviolable for its own sake and the sake of all other human goods—individual and social—revelation shows us to be of truly inestimable worth. What reason shows us to be true with its dispassionate objectivity, God reveals in searing light, a truth white-hot in its intensity admitting of no exception, no compromise. "Thou shalt not murder."

From this indisputable truth known through reason and confirmed through revelation so as not to leave the slightest possibility of doubt the Catholic Church has derived its consistent life ethic in health care. The fabled and noble pagan Hippocrates knew the same from reason and religious sensibility. In his oath for physicians he formulates a basic principle for the practice of the medical art which is grounded in morality. "Primum non nocere."[9] "First, do no harm." The Mosaic Code is stark in its simplicity as well, as it articulates a clear moral prohibition. "Non occides."[10] "Thou shalt not kill."

From these natural and supernatural insights the Catholic Church has formulated its consistent life ethic in health care. "One may never directly take an innocent human life."

This uncompromising and uncompromised principle has helped give rise to much of the entire, impressive structure of carefully developed and refined speculation in the area of health care ethics. It is because the Catholic is totally averse to violating in any direct way the fundamental good of human life while still having to live in an imperfect world that he has developed and refined such distinctions as those between remote or proximate, material or formal cooperation in evil. It is largely because the Catholic shrinks from the very thought of violating the basic, fundamental good of life that he has developed the doctrine of totality, the indirect voluntary, the distinctions between ordinary and extraordinary means of prolonging life, the principle of double effect.

Non-Catholics will often dismiss all these distinctions as nothing but semantics, crass, even cynical, rationalizations to allow the Catholic to do something which the Church actually considers to be a sin. "At least we are more honest," the classical Protestant will declare. "We cannot escape sin. Luther and Calvin taught us that the human person is totally depraved. We need not spin out such torturous devices as the principle of double effect to help us avoid sin. We can't avoid sin. Hence, we do the best we can, realizing that it involves sin, and we throw ourselves on God's mercy." As Luther said, "*Pecca fortiter*! Sin for all you are worth. God can forgive only a lusty sinner."[11]

The Catholic response is that we can, with God's grace, avoid sin. There is no necessity to sinning. What appear to be intractible situations in which sin cannot be avoided only appear to be such. The principle of double effect, for example, was developed to help the Catholic know when a person might posit an act when it is foreseen that evil will be one of the consequences of the act. The presupposition of the principle is that sin *can* be avoided. And despite the fact that it is foreseen that an evil can result from the posited act, the first condition of the principle is that the intended and executed act itself must be good, or at least not evil. Consequently, another presupposition of this principle is that there are some human acts which are intrinsically evil and which cannot be chosen because in and of themselves they impede in some way the realization of goods necessary for the actualization of a person's potential for fulfillment.

Another condition of the principle of double effect, of course, insists upon the rectitude of the intention of the actor, i.e., he or she only intends the good effect which is proposed and merely permits the unintended, but foreseen, evil consequence, as Jesus did when He went up to Jerusalem before His passion, freely accepting, but not intending His own death.

Another of the four conditions which must be fulfilled, still insisting that evil may never be done that good may come of it, tells one that the evil resulting from the action cannot be the means to the good. This is usually expressed by saying that the good must be realized prior to, or at least simultaneously with, the unintended evil.

Finally, even though all these conditions have been met, the proposed good act still may not be posited in light of the unintended evil side effect *unless* there is a proportionately grave reason for so acting.

The consequentialists, of course, collapse the entire principle of double effect into this final condition. They argue that there are premoral or ontic evils which one may choose as instrumental means to realize a proportionately greater good. However, as the moral agent chooses a premoral evil the act takes on moral significance. If one chose what the consequentialists call an ontic evil, even as an instrumental good, the act would be immoral regardless of the consequences. An "actus humanus" as distinct from an "actus hominis" has moral significance by virtue of the choice of the moral object which is either a true good or a wrongly perceived good the choosing of which has its own moral significance, not merely that moral significance which might be derived from a more distant end.

Secondly, some consequentialist theologians, such as Bruno Schueller, conceive the principle of double effect as the attempt to combine two disparate moral methodologies, the deontological and the consequentialist. Schueller argues that the first condition of the principle, i.e., that the proposed act itself must be good, is expressive of the deontological or legalistic approach to ethics and the final condition, i.e., there must be a proportionately grave reason for positing a good act when an evil consequence is foreseen, that of the consequentialist. He inaccurately argues that the posited act causes in the same way both the good and evil effect denying any moral significance to the notion of simply permitting evil as an unintended side effect of the posited act. As Schueller writes, "I am strongly inclined to believe that in point of fact *'intend as a means' and 'permit,' when referring to a nonmoral evil, denote exactly the same mental attitude."*[12] Of course, what is being permitted according to the classical teaching of the principle of double effect is not simply a nonmoral evil. What is permitted *would be a moral evil* were it chosen. The unintended death of an infant resulting from a hysterectomy necessary to save the life of the mother is an evil only in an analogous sense. It is not a moral evil at all. It may be viewed as unfortunate, indeed even as tragic by the parents and physician, but it is not an evil in the moral sense. However, it would be a moral evil if it were chosen end or as a means to any other end. The use of the term premoral or ontic evil to refer to the means chosen to attain what the consequentialists call a proportionately greater good only clouds the decision-making process and denies the morally relevant distinction between intending and permitting.

One of the fundamental manifestations of true evil consists in freely choosing to act in such a way as to assault or impede a fundamental good which serves as the basis for meaningful human actions and fulfillment and which itself shares derivatively in the goodness of the Creator Himself. This is what the person who wants to be moral must avoid at all costs. This is what receives the dreaded appellation of sin. And the person who desires to be moral is willing to endure anything rather than commit sin.

The Catholic Church has developed such a consistent ethic of life because it knows that if certain acts are freely chosen and perpetrated, acts known as mortal sins, then all other good acts are rendered morally meaningless. To return to our earlier example, "Yes, let us by all means help the homeless. But as we undertake the difficult task of finding solutions, please let us agree on one thing. We will not attempt to alleviate the problem of homelessness by killing off some of the homeless." As outrageous as it sounds, it is to such absurd levels that we have been reduced in current moral debate in the public arena—and sometimes even within the Church.

I was once on a radio series dealing with ethical and public policy questions sponsored by a large Eastern university. This particular program dealt with the treatment of handicapped newborns. After the opening discussion, a student posed the following question: "Since an ounce of prevention is worth a pound of cure, why not allow abortions to eliminate birth defects?" Of course I pointed out that abortion does not eliminate birth defects, but rather the persons suffering from the defect. I wanted to say, "Yes, let us by all means strive to overcome birth defects and the problems associated with them, but as we struggle to find solutions, let us agree on just one thing. Please, let us not kill the ones we claim we want to help!"

At the beginning of the radio program the moderator presented my opponent and me with an actual moral dilemma of which she had been aware. Twins were born joined at the chest. We were asked what we would do. My opposite, an attorney, said she would allow the newborns to die. I responded that the newborns would have to be cared for as any other children, hoping that one day they could be separated. After the program I asked the moderator, a professor of political science and public policy, what had been the outcome of the dilemma she had presented to us. She said that the children had indeed been cared for and that after a couple of years the doctors surgically separated the twins, although one of them died from the procedure. "Oh," I said. "Then in light of the outcome you would have agreed with my response." "Oh no," she said. "Even knowing the results I would have let them die."

In the face of such attitudes where do we find common ground with others in our society for developing a consistent life ethic in health care? Because of the gift of revelation and the magisterium, the Catholic Church has a clarity of vision in such matters which no other institution can parallel. The non-believers around us suppose themselves to be choosing rightly in the pursuit of moral health care. They see themselves as choosing goods, such as saving the parents of Siamese twins the expense and emotional distress of caring for them or as putting a suffering, terminally ill cancer patient out of his misery through an act of euthanasia. Pain and suffering and confusion can cloud the insights of people wanting to pursue the good. The Catholic Church, however, bears witness to the fact that it is meaningless to choose any specific goods if it means an assault upon other basic, fundamental goods essential to human flourishing.[13]

This witness is not always easily intelligible to the secular world. A university professor one time asked me in all seriousness: "Why does the Catholic Church teach that the life of the unborn child is to be preferred to the life of the mother?" The answer required an explanation that the Catholic Church holds no such position. Neither life can be preferred over the other. There are simply no factors which can render one life more valuable than another so that the one could be destroyed for the sake of the other. Everything must be done to preserve the life of both. Sometimes procedures are allowed under the principle of double effect which would carry possible, unintended adverse side effects, but no innocent human life can be taken for the sake of another. As illustrative of this point, the "Ethical and Religious Directives for Catholic Health Facilities" states:

> Cesarean section for the removal of a viable fetus is permitted, even with risk to the life of the mother, when necessary for successful delivery. It is likewise permitted, even with risk for the child, when necessary for the safety of the mother.[14]

This uncompromising and uncompromised commitment to life is seen throughout the development of modern refinements in the ethics of health care. The limited scope of these remarks permit reference to only a few. It was to avoid any possibility of directly taking an innocent life that Pius XII in 1957 formulated the distinction between ordinary and extraordinary means of prolonging life.[15] Respect for the value of human life led the Second Vatican Council to condemn unequivocally "all offenses against life itself, such as murder, genocide, abortion, euthanasia, and wilful suicide."[16] The inviolability of innocent life provides the foundation for the "Declaration on Procured Abortion" in 1974[17] and the "Declaration on Euthanasia" in 1980.[18] The commitment to life received unprecedented refinement in 1987 in "Donum Vitae" which provides a moral analysis of various technologies of reproduction.[19] Not only did that document understandably reject the direct assaults on nascent life often involved in procedures attempting to overcome infertility such as "in vitro" fertilization, it also cautioned against any approach which would reduce human reproduction to a technological procedure which would render human life a product of human manipulation. Human life is too precious and too lofty ever to be something "made."[20] It is in the strictest sense a divine gift arising from—not produced by—the act in which a husband and a wife make a gift of themselves to one another.

It was reverence of human life which led the bishops of the United States at their most recent national convention to craft a particularly strong document in defense of the unborn against the assault of abortion.[21]

Even now, the ponderous reflection of Catholic teachers and moralists and pastors on the question when the provision of artificial hydration and nutrition is no longer morally obligatory is guided by the absolute aversion to killing an innocent human life. The current study manifests intense rationality mingled with religious awe. Can artificial hydration and nutrition be viewed as treatment in one circumstance and care in another? Is the distinction between treatment and care possible or, if possible, relevant in settling this question? To what extent is the distinction between ordinary and extraordinary means applicable? How certain must the physician be that the patient will die of his underlying pathological condition rather than dying of starvation or dehydration before terminating artificial hydration and nutrition? The questions continue to multiply.

The Catholic Church commits tremendous resources in terms of personnel, money, institutions and time struggling with these questions because it shudders at the thought of ever advocating the direct, intentional destruction of even one innocent human life. The world cannot understand this. It accuses the Church of rigidity on one hand or, on the other, of inconsistency arising from a convoluted casuistry allowing all kinds of exceptions to what are supposed to be exceptionless norms. The world claims the Church is too motivated by abstract religious sentiment or that it has fallen prey to crass vitalism, physicalism or biologism by insisting that life at *all* stages of its development and dying processes must be equally respected.

Neither of these accusations is correct, of course. There are glints of the truth in both, however. There is no denying the reverence of the Church before the transcendent value of an immortal soul. But the soul is no abstract construct of religious sentiment. It is a constitutive, inseparable element with the body comprising a human being. It is, as St. Thomas tells us, the form of the body; it is created by God and is that which determines a human being a human being.[22] If a person is alive then, regardless of his condition, he is entitled to the reverence due to the "imago Dei." Nothing extraordinary need be done to prolong the life of a dying person, but nothing may be done which will directly and intentionally terminate his or her life either. All the palliative measures available are appropriate, but never may a creature dare to snuff out the image of the Creator.

Having formulated the principle that one may never directly take an innocent human life, and having developed norms to guide the application of that principle in a fallen and disordered world, the Church is absolutely consistent in its application, although not always without anguish over the circumstances in which it must be applied.

The principle is applied by the Church consistently at the beginnings of life. Contraception is immoral because it always involves the positing of an act other than the freely chosen marital

148

act, which act is directed against the realization of the good of human life which otherwise might result from such an act.[23] Abortion is a senseless deed in that it constitutes a direct assault upon a fundamental human good, the cherishing and nurturing of which leads to our own fulfillment as well as that of the nascent life. "In vitro" fertilization almost always involves the intentional discarding of any embryos which are abnormal or unlikely to survive. "In vitro" fertilization always manifests a lack of respect due the dignity of life by reducing it to being a mere product of technology. Surrogate mothering reduces a child to mere chattel as its mother surrenders it for a fee. The withholding of standard care for disabled new-borns is to treat them as less than human.

The norm against the direct taking of an innocent human life has been applied just as vigorously and consistently at the end of life's spectrum. Death and dying issues can be particularly complex, but the Church has struggled to apply its life ethic as consistently as possible. For example, the dying process of an individual cannot be hastened in order to obtain his or her organs for transplant. Many safeguards have been developed to assure everyone that a potential donor is truly dead before his organs are removed. A physician on a transplant team cannot be the one to declare a potential donor to be dead. Since he would have such a vested interest in the availability of the organs, his sound judgment and sense of fairness might be adversely affected.

Because of the sophistication of new medical technologies, new criteria for determining death have had to be developed. The criterion of brain death has been almost universally accepted and even it has a number of safeguards associated with it.

All these positions, and many more, have been formulated out of a respect for innocent human life and an aversion ever to take it unjustifiably.

The consistent life ethic has also been applied more vigorously in the area of social justice due in large part to the call and witness of Cardinal Bernardin. The Catholic Health Association has recently developed a Social Accountability Budgeting Process so that Catholic hospitals may more adequately monitor the extent to which they do indeed apply and consistent ethic of life to all aspects of health care including providing medical services to the indigent and "underserviced."

149

Of course, many Catholic health facilities have long had an exemplary record of witnessing to a consistent ethic of life. The Daughters of Charity National Health System, the largest nonprofit health delivery system in the country, in 1988 provided $79.1 million worth of charity care.

There is no institution in the United States other than the Catholic Church which has a more consistent life ethic in health care in the narrow domain of medical ethics or the broader one of social justice. The health facilities and agencies of the Archdiocese of New York, for example, do not make contraception or abortion available to their clientele. The Archdiocese provides a beautiful witness to a consistent ethic of life. However, it did not stop simply at the prohibition of contraception and abortion as a way of affirming life. In October 1984, Cardinal John O'Connor of New York committed his archdiocese to providing "free confidential help of highest quality" to any single or married woman facing an unplanned pregnancy. The Cardinal addressed any woman with a difficult pregnancy, "The Archdiocese of New York is prepared to do everything in its power to help you and your unborn baby, to make absolutely certain that you need never feel that you must have an abortion."[24]

There are few things as compelling as consistency in word and deed. It bespeaks an integrity which has irresistible moral appeal. Rational argument will never win over to a consistent ethic of life a society as jaded, hedonistic and self-serving as our own. What is needed today is conversion. Rational argument will not win over our society, but the power of the Lord of life will, manifested in an institution which lives with consistency and integrity the sacrificial life of Christ Himself. There are countless ways in which the Church does indeed manifest its commitment to life and consistently applies that commitment. But today, before any initiatives on behalf of the needy can be realized, before there can be a consistent ethic of life in health care in the realm of medical ethics and social justice, before any of this, there must be life. It would provide an astounding example to the world and stop the mouths of many critics if every diocese in the Church in this country were able to make the same offer of care for women contemplating abortion that New York has done, perhaps with the wealthier dioceses helping the poorer. I have no idea if such a thing would be possible or what the mechanism would be, but it would constitute a staggering witness to life if the entire National Conference of Catholic Bishops could pledge itself to providing whatever resources would be necessary to help a woman opt for life rather than abortion.

The Church confounds the world because she loves life unreservedly, with a fervor and an intensity which simply has no equal in our secular society. The Church baffles the world because she has such an abhorrence of sin that she will counsel anything before she will counsel sin. Theologies of compromise with evil cannot comprehend the unbridgeable abyss which exists between choosing moral evil and suffering any kind of affliction, natural or personal. Jesus taught it, however. "If your right eye causes you to sin, tear it out and throw it away. It is better for you to lose one of your members than to have your whole body thrown into Gehenna."[25] The seven martyred brothers recorded in Maccabees knew it. Each accepted the ripping out of his tongue, the severing of his hands and a torturous death rather than violate the faith of their forefathers. "(The young man) put out his tongue at once when told to do so, and bravely held out his hands, as he spoke these noble words: 'It was from Heaven that I received these; for the sake of His laws I disdain them; from Him I hope to receive them again.' "[26] John Cardinal Newman taught the same. "The Catholic Church holds it better for the sun and moon to drop from heaven, for the earth to fail, and for all the many millions on it to die of starvation in extremist agony, as far as temporal affliction goes, than that one soul, I will not say, should be lost, but should commit one single venial sin, should tell one wilful untruth, or should steal one poor farthing without excuse."[27]

Those are hard words, but they teach that there is simply no commensurability between natural evil and moral evil. The Christian should be willing to suffer any natural disaster or injustice rather than commit one sin. It is this uncompromising commitment to what is good and the steadfast unwillingness to hurt or damage or destroy fundamental human goods even to gain the world itself that will win the world back to sanity. It is such commitment to the moral good which has enabled the crafting of a consistent ethic of life in health care and the ongoing refinement and development of it. Catholics may boast a consistent ethic of life, for they know that it profits nothing to gain the whole world, even in terms of the most efficient social utopia imaginable, if in the process they have lost their soul.

Notes

1. Cf. the Gannon Lecture given at Fordham University by Cardinal Joseph Bernardin, December 6, 1983, printed in *Origins*, December 29, 1983, pp. 491–494. Cf. also "Health Care and the Consistent Ethic of Life" by Cardinal Bernardin in *Origins*, June 6, 1985.

2. Cf. John Finnis, "The Consistent Ethic: A Philosophical Critique" in Joseph Cardinal Bernardin, et al. *Consistent Ethic of Life* (Kansas City, Mo.: Sheed & Ward, 1988).

3. "So act as to treat humanity, both in your own person and in that of any other person, always as an end also, never as a means only." Walter Kaufmann, ed., *Philosophical Classics: Bacon to Kant* (Englewood Cliffs, N.J.: Prentice-Hall, Inc., 1965), p. 584. Cf. Kant's *Saemmtliche Werke*, ed. Karl Rosenkranz and F. W. Schubert, Vol. III (1838), p. 57.

4. "Tabu" means literally "marked off" from the Polynesian "ta" or mark and "pu" or exceedingly. If a person, place or thing is tabu it means it is marked off from the realm of the ordinary and must be approached with exceeding caution. The mere touching of an object which is tabu can be quite dangerous, leading even to death. However, this expresses only the negative aspect of tabu. An object is under a tabu because of the positive aspect of "mana" or the sublime, wonder-working aspect of the supernatural. "Negatively, the supernatural is 'tabu', bot to be lightly approached because (positively) it is 'mana'—instinct with a power above the ordinary." R. H. Codrington, *The Melanesians* (Oxford: Clarendon Press, 1969), p. 188. Cf. also J. G. Frazer, *The Golden Bough* (12 volumes, 1911–15), especially volume 3, *Taboo and the Perils of the Soul.*

5. Cf. Genesis 1:26ff and *Gaudium et spes*, #12.

6. Psalm 139:13–15.

7. The question of the creation of the soul is a complex and difficult one with a number of the Fathers of the Church actually holding erroneous positions. Tertullian taught materialistic traducianism (*De anima* 9–41) and Gregory of Nyssa seems to favor it (*De hom. opif.* 29). Augustine rejected the materialistic traducianism of Tertullian, but suggested a spiritual generationism (*Epist.* 190.4.15) which held that the soul originates from the substance of the soul of the parents. Augustine held this view because of his doctrine of original sin. He thought the doctrine of the immediate creation of the soul by God would mean the participation by God in the creation of evil. Traducianism (and the closely allied generationism) has been condemned by the ordinary magisterium of the Church which teaches creationism. Cf. the condemnation of traducianism in Denz. 360–361 (Anastasius II, Ep. "Bonum atque iucundum" to the Bishop Galliae, 23 August 498), Denz. 1007 (Benedict XII, "Libellus 'Cum dudum'" to Armenios, August 1341), Denz. 3220–24 (Leo XIII, Decree of the Holy Office "Post obitum", 14 December 1887, against the errors of Antonio Rosmini). The doctrine taught authoritatively by the ordinary magisterium is that of creationism.

8. Isaiah 43:4.

9. *Hippocratic Oath.*

10. Exodus 20:13.

11. Roland H. Bainton, *Here I Stand. A Life of Martin Luther* (New York: Mentor Books, 1959), p. 175.

12. Bruno Schueller, "The Double Effect in Catholic Thought: A Reevaluation" in *Doing Evil to Achieve Good*, ed. Richard McCormick (Chicago: Loyola University Press, 1978), p. 191.

13. Cf. Germain Grisez, *The Way of the Lord Jesus* (Chicago: Franciscan Herald Press, 1983), especially his discussion of the "eighth mode of responsibility", pp. 216ff.

14. "Ethical and Religious Directives for Catholic Health Facilities," United States Catholic Conference, Washington, D.C., 1971, #15.

15. Pius XII, November 24, 1975. "Prolongation of Life: Allocution to an International Congress of Anesthesiologists," *The Pope Speaks* 4:393–398.

16. *Gaudium et spes*, #27.

17. Congregation for the Doctrine of the Faith, May 1974. Translated into English in *Osservatore Romano*, December 5, 1974.

18. Congregation for the Doctrine of the Faith.

19. Congregation for the Doctrine of the Faith, February 22, 1987. Translated into English in *Origins* Vol. 16: No. 40, March 19, 1987.

20. Cf. William E. May, "Catholic Moral Teaching on *In Vitro* Fertilization" in *Reproductive Technologies, Marriage and the Church* (Braintree, Mass.: The Pope John Center, 1988).

21. National Conference of Catholic Bishops, November 1989, Baltimore, Maryland.

22. "... anima forma corporis", S.T. Ia, 76, 1. Cf. also *Gaudium et spes*, #14.

23. Cf. Germain Grisez, et al., " 'Every Marital Act Ought to be Open to New Life': Toward a Clearer Understanding", in *The Teaching of Humanae Vitae: A Defense* by John C. Ford, et al. (San Francisco: Ignatius Press, 1988).

24. Cf. *Origins*, Vol. 14: No. 19, October 25, 1984, pp. 291ff.

25. Matthew 5:29.

26. II Maccabees 9:11.

27. John Henry Newman, *Apologia Pro Vita Sua* (London: Longmans, Green, and Co., 1904), p. 153.

Chapter 10

PASTORAL CONCERNS
MORAL NORMS: EXCEPTIONLESS AND
CONSISTENTLY PRO-LIFE

BISHOP: I'd like to address a question to each of the speakers, if I may. First of all, Dr. Haas, before I even ask the question, I want to say how pleased I was in hearing you emphasize the direct intervention of God in the creation of each human being and in the creation of the soul. With regard to your emphasis on the inviolability of innocent human life, the absolute sacredness of it: I'm still not sure how I would answer the problem of an insane aggressor, who is an adult, large, violent, who is threatening me or an innocent person with a meat axe or a gun or a grenade. According to definition, he would be innocent. I'm speaking about protecting ourselves and the right we have to defend ourselves even, if necessary, to the extent of taking his life.

DR. HAAS: The principle we have articulated is that one may never directly take the life of an innocent human being. One of the qualifiers in that principle is "innocent," but another qualifier is

154

"direct" so that, for example, you would try to protect yourself, it's an act of self-defense. You're trying to stop this assailant from harming you. And if in the process of stopping him from harming you, the unintended side effect might be his death, that would be something that you might be willing to accept.

BISHOP: No. I mean he's coming for me and he's five feet away and I'm going to shoot him.

DR. HAAS: The question is whether you're intending to kill him. I would think that what you really want to do is stop him not to kill him. In other words, the act that you're formulating is to *stop* this aggressor not to *kill* the aggressor. When St. Thomas writes about the right to self defense in the *Summa*, he talks about our not using any more violence than is necessary to prevent the assault. Our moral act is formulated interiorly in terms of the object, that is, what it is we want to accomplish. I would say here that what you want to accomplish is to stop this assailant not to kill him.

BISHOP: What about the child in the womb who is directly threatening the life of the woman. And could you say that same thing, that I'm not really intending to kill the child? I'm only intending the good effect? I don't think so. I mean that would seem to me to be direct.

DR. HAAS: Of course, it depends on the procedure we're talking about. The Church has never allowed the direct taking of a child even when it's threatening the life of the mother.

BISHOP: I know that.

DR. HAAS: It has never permitted that. But depending on the circumstances, it allows a whole number of procedures which could be determined by the practitioners of medicine to be the most effective way to try to save the woman's life and not kill the child while the probable unintended effect of that act would also be the death of the child.

BISHOP: But it would seem to me to be direct. I can't see it as an involuntary act on my part.

DR. HAAS: Well, would you be intending to kill the person? Would that be your intent or merely to stop him?

BISHOP: Stop, of course.

But know that I'm stopping him by killing him. I can't be very careful. I'm not a good shot.

DR. HAAS: You'll probably miss him then. You know, St. Peter wasn't a very good swordsman either. He only got the ear instead of the head. In a crisis situation, you don't have to put yourself at risk by taking more time to see that you're only going to harm him or slow him down rather than actually kill him. You just have to stop him, and it seems to me that is what your intent has to be.

BISHOP: Dr. Grisez, if I may ask you, in your call for or a serious suggestion as to some kind of a convocation, whether it's the Third Vatican Council or the gathering of theologians, how would you advertise that? What would you say? What are your expectations in calling such? Would this be a true dialogue? A true searching for the truth or what would be the nature of this convocation?

DR. GRISEZ: The presupposition of my proposal is that there is a real division over disputed questions, such as whether it's ever permissible to choose to kill the unborn, whether it's ever permissible to divorce and remarry, whether it's ever permissible to engage in homosexual acts. The pope and the bishops who agree with him on these matters are really divided from a fairly substantial number of bishops, not just one or two in the whole world, who disagree with him on these issues. Also, I think there's a fair number of bishops who are confused and would say: I don't want to disagree with the Pope, but I'm not sure all these received teachings are right, either.

BISHOP: Would this not be somewhat counterproductive, therefore?

DR. GRISEZ: If there really is a division, it seems to me absolutely essential that the Pope and all the bishops get back together once more. That doesn't mean they have to be personally present at the same meeting—a Vatican Council III. It may be done another way. But somehow they have to come to agreement. And the first thing they have to do is to admit to themselves and to one another: We're divided about important matters. As long as they don't admit this, they're rather like a family in which the husband and father has been drinking too much and really is an alcoholic but pretends he isn't. The wife knows they've got real trouble but she continues to pretend everything is all right. The children are more and more upset; they know something is wrong with Dad. But nobody wants to say: Dad's an alcoholic. The Church is like that today. There's a real division but no one wants to say: We're really divided. That's bad, and we have to face up to it and do something about it.

BISHOP: To do what about it?

DR. GRISEZ: What I propose is not a one-sided approach, because there really are serious problems in moral theology itself. Charlie Curran didn't start saying different things than I say because he is stupid or because he's a bad person. Charlie Curran started saying different things than I say because he's looking at the same problems I'm looking at, doing his best to answer them, and coming up with different answers. He's trying to do his job. I'm trying to do my job. We disagree.

No matter what eventually you and the Holy Father and every other bishop in the world agree to, provided you all agree, I'm willing to say: That's my faith too, and I'll die for it. And I'm pretty sure Charlie Curran would say: That's my faith too, and I'll die for it.

First you must face up to the disagreement. Then, give me and those who disagree a chance to come before you and the Holy Father—a representative body of bishops, not all of them—and present our views and argue with each other. Sit still and listen until you learn what the issues are, and what we think about them. Ask us questions, and make us answer until you've heard all you want to hear. When that's done, both sides will have had a very fair opportunity to tell you what they're thinking. Then, throw us out. Send us home.

Then, sit down with the Holy Father. And ask yourself this very important question: What is the Catholic faith here? What is it that we believe? What is it that the Lord teaches is our way of life? How does what these theologians are saying relate to that? What must we tell Christian people they need to do to be saved? We don't want to tell them anything more than that, but we don't dare tell them anything less.

You'll be able to walk out of there and with full confidence and real sincerity say: We believe and the Holy Spirit teaches. And then there won't be any question about what we can do and what we can't do.

BISHOP: Dr. Grisez, I think that little footnote 38 you gave in your text is probably more pregnant than perhaps the size of it would suggest, because it's out of that kind of a context that you're doing theology, at least in part. There is a definite sense of frustration that persons such as yourself feel with this particular group of people—

Somehow or other the course of events is such that Bishops can get swept along. You are no longer that prophetic person or that teaching person in the diocese you should be. I'd like you to comment on what I'm saying.

DR. GRISEZ: If I were a bishop today, I think I'd probably not do any better than most of you do. I think it's a very difficult situation. I would look around the diocese and see that there are some theologians who agree with the Pope and are very energetic in defending him and there are some who disagree with him and teach accordingly. I'd see that I've got quite a few priests who agree with dissenting theologians. They may not be loudmouths but they do agree with dissenting theologians and put their views into pastoral practice. And I've got some that support the Pope. I'd see that I've got teachers in the schools who are teaching the kids, even kids eight and ten years old, dissenting theology and I've got teachers who are teaching the Baltimore Catechism.

For God's sake, what a mess I've got here! That's the first thing.

You've got these people from *The Wanderer* on your back and they're saying you've got to fire all these dissenters and you can't possibly do that. It's insane. Discipline can't straighten out this kind of problem. Frankly, I don't know what I would do. I wouldn't try to fire all these people. Cardinal O'Boyle tried to discipline a few people and look what happened to him. (I was working for him that year and saw the whole thing close up.) I wouldn't want to go through that. I wouldn't want anybody in this room to go through that. And it didn't help much, I'm sorry to say. So, I've become convinced that that's not the way to go.

I'm not frustrated with bishops. I'm not angry at anybody. And I'm not criticizing our Holy Father. I think he's done the very best he can. But I do think that we've got a problem and the problem is that there's division in the magisterium and only the Pope and bishops can overcome that division. What I'm saying is: Face up to the problem. Recognize that you and the Pope and other bishops in the world are going to have to get together, face the problem, and overcome the division.

I have heard the line, "The Holy See seems to be following a policy of trying to appoint 'better bishops.'" That strategy isn't going to work and it's not going to work for two reasons:

First, bishop appointments don't answer Charlie Curran's questions. They don't answer my arguments. They don't answer anything. And the questions have to be answered. The modernist controversy should have taught the Church one thing: Questions must be faced up to and answered. They won't go away.

Second, if I were a bishop today, I would begin to feel after a while that dissenting opinions can't be all that bad. We've got to live with them. And pretty soon these *Wanderer* people would get on my back and I'd say: They're worse than the dissenters. And in some ways they are. They've even condemned me. Can you believe that?

(Laughter.)

BISHOP: I thought when you were describing the kind of forum that could address this situation, if we assess it accurately, would be a general council and that's all. What other way could you see doing that? Because it is something that probably is affecting the entire church in varying degrees. These issues that we were talking about here were quite deliberately set aside in the last general council for the most part, not entirely, but for the most part.

I would appreciate your reaction to the implicit questions that are in these remarks.

DR. GRISEZ: I don't mean to say that the only thing to do is to summon Vatican III. That might not be a good thing to do. There might be very good reasons not to take that route. I have suggested elsewhere that a new use of the Synod of Bishops could be made.

I think it would be a very desirable thing if the members of the Synod were elected in a different way than they have been. I think it would be good if the bishops of the world were divided by chance into groups of ten or so. Those groups would meet to discuss the problem that was going to be treated, and each group would elect one of its own members to be in the Synod. The Holy Father could also have some people that he wants, but essentially, it would be a representative body made up of bishops that were chosen by small groups of bishops who had thought about the topic of the Synod session and prayed about it.

The session could take up one question—for example, the question of the definability of the proposition that it's always wrong intentionally to kill the innocent. I think that proposition is terribly important and that it could be solemnly defined. If there were a representative body of bishops meeting in a Synod, they could hold a good debate by theologians, a really fair debate. Then they could come to a firm conclusion on that issue and recommend to the Holy Father what to do. He could prepare a document and circulate it to all the bishops for comments. And I think he could then issue a solemn definition which every bishop in the world would support. Now if that happened, I think it would totally change the present theological situation, and many other matters that are in debate would begin to be discussed in a different way.

A few years later, another session of the Synod might take up some other debated proposition. I think if you defined just two or three propositions that are particularly important, that would have the effect of clearing the confusion out of the whole area.

Now, a further point. This doesn't necessarily require a solemn definition and you could start doing something useful even without having the Pope involved. The National Conference of Catholic Bishops has never had a debate between theologians representing the two sides. You go to Collegeville now and then. You could spend a day, giving Charlie Curran and me two hours apiece to present our positions, and then thinking about it and talking about it. And you could spend another day asking us questions until you're tired of hearing us, and then talking about it and thinking about it.

I think that would be an instructive exercise and that Charlie and I would be happy to cooperate in doing it. We actually respect each other, and he takes the same attitude toward me that I do toward him. We disagree because theology cannot settle these issues. We theologians can only do our best. Only the Pope and you bishops can say: This is what the Catholic Church believes. We theologians can't tell people what the Catholic Church believes. We can tell them what we think we should believe and our reasons for thinking that. But only the Pope and Bishops are judges of the faith. Therefore, you should listen to our arguments and become informed about the issues on which your judgment is needed. That's all I'm asking you to do.

BISHOP: Dr. Grisez, I'm one of those bishops appointed before the good bishops were appointed.

(Laughter.)

So I don't know where that leaves me.

A postulate of your paper is that the Church is divided and you said in your comments, the Magisterium is divided. In reference to the teaching church, I find no division because of the status of the Magisterium itself. My understanding of Magisterium is that it is the Pope and bishops in agreement with him and I think in doctrinal agreement with him. My view of the current picture is of the Magisterium on one side and a few well-publicized dissenting theologians and other dissenters on the other side.

DR. GRISEZ: Well, I'm not going to give you a list of bishops' names or describe occasions, but I'm not talking through my hat. That's number one. Number two, the premise that the Magisterium is the Pope and Bishops in communion with the Pope is correct, but we mustn't define communion in a way that begs the whole question. Being in communion with the Pope essentially means this: that you're in good standing with the Pope. So the bishops who disagree, whom I could name, are in communion with the Pope. There's no question that they are. He can celebrate Mass with them, be in juridical and Eucharistic communion with them, and yet they disagree with him on these matters. That's the problem.

DR. HAAS: Just to address this briefly, I would point out that my wife and I are both converts to the Roman Catholic Church. We came into the Church while all of this controversy and division was going on.

We came into the Church to a large degree because of the consistency and the clarity and the force with which the Roman Catholic Church has taught everything that Dr. Grisez teaches or has articulated for us, if you will. We were aware that there was division but there was no shadow of a doubt in our minds, my wife's and my mind, as to what the Catholic position was. I have never read anything in print by a member of the U.S. hierarchy that would disagree with the Holy Father on this and, certainly, the U.S. hierarchy has never said anything corporately contrary to the teaching of the Pope. It has been totally consistent with what the Holy See has taught.

So I just want to say that a motivating factor for our conversion apart from grace and faith, was the consistency with which the teaching of the Catholic Church had been presented.

Now just the other day, I got a call from Channel 6 T.V. News because they were doing a special, if you will, on the 30th Anniversary of the pill—such a thing to celebrate—but they wanted somebody to present the "Catholic" position. They called the Archdiocese which recommended that they come talk to me. The interviewer gave me all of fifteen seconds to present the Catholic Church's position on contraception and the pill. You all know what that is like, to deal with the media today.

But the thing here is that everybody knows what the Catholic Church's position on contraception is.

BISHOP: Dr. Grisez, what is your opinion on the development of the Universal catechism that is going on now? Is that at least in part an answer to your problem?

DR. GRISEZ: Apparently, no. I think the catechism project has its merits and I hope it will come out well, but I don't think it's going to resolve the problem.

One can see the conflict I've been talking about in the remarks that have been publicly made about the catechism draft by various groups in this country. One also can see, if one reads the draft of the catechism, certain vestiges of what's been going on. So, you should examine the draft of the catechism very carefully. Of course, I don't expect you to do it all by yourself. You can use theologians, whether they agree or disagree with me, and get them to tell you what they think about it. However, don't believe them.

(Laughter.)

Never believe a theologian, starting with me. Don't believe anything I say. Theologians are not to be believed. What do you do with them, then? Look at what they say and ask yourself: Do I think this passage is right? Do I think it makes sense? In other words, you get theologians to propose questions for you to ask yourself. Look at the text and ask yourself: What does my faith require that this catechism say? That's what you need to do. You're the judges of the faith. You're the teachers responsible for the faith. Take up that cross and carry it.

Chapter 11

THE MEDICAL ASPECTS OF ADDICTION

Sister Marysia Weber, R.S.M., D.O.

The problem of "addictive" or compulsive disorders is one of increasing complexity, manifest frequency, and publicity. Pedophilia in particular has resulted in many legal, financial, and religious concerns. "Addiction" is now being addressed by many who have a diverse understanding of the medical and psychiatric concepts of the topic. This has promoted the treatment of "addictive" and compulsive disorders, but this has also created a need for accurate diagnoses of these disorders in order to provide the most effective treatment.

The goal of this paper is to present the pathological use of alcohol and drugs from the medical and psychiatric perspective and to address pedophilia as distinct from substance-use disorders. The specific objectives are to clarify the medical-psychiatric use of terms referring to substance-use disorders and sexual disorders. A second objective is to explore the literature in the field and identify possible early indicators of pedophilia in general and specifically related to the ministerial priesthood.

SUBSTANCE-USE DISORDERS

The term "addiction" has become so popularized that it is used by some professionals and non-professionals in a variety of contexts. Colloquially, addiction refers, not only to the abuse of alcohol, drugs and sexual behaviors, but also to any activity performed excessively such as watching television or playing bingo, for example. Such inclusive use of the term "addiction" is misleading in that it implies a similar pathological process in the abuse of chemicals, sexual disorders, or the excessive performance of any activity. In 1964, the World Health Organization concluded that the term 'addiction', is no longer a scientific term and recommended substituting the term 'drug dependence'" (Kaplan, 1988). This term will be described in more detail in the paragraphs to follow.

Drug or psychoactive substances are those substances which affect the brain. One can become psychologically or physiologically dependent on psychoactive substances. Psychological symptoms of dependence would include: the perceived need to use a psychoactive substance to function day to day, behavioral changes after using psychoactive substance(s), and defensiveness about using these agents. The physiological characteristics of dependence include tolerance and withdrawal. Tolerance is the need for markedly increased amounts of a substance in order to achieve intoxication or desired effect; or alternatively, a diminished effect with continued use of the same amount of a substance. Withdrawal is a substance specific syndrome that follows the cessation of, or reduction in the use of a psychoactive substance. The withdrawal symptoms can vary depending on the substance used by a particular individual. Common physiological symptoms include increased blood pressure, pulse, respirations, anxiousness, restlessness, irritability, insomnia, impaired attention, and possibly tremulousness, profuse sweating, and even convulsions. Substances which evidence dependence-inducing properties: include 1) legal although

164

controlled or taxed substances, such as alcohol, 2) legal substances and those prescribed by a physician, such as sleeping pills or tranquilizers including benzodiazepines (e.g., Valium, Xanax or Ativan) and barbiturates (e.g., Nembutol, and Seconal), or 3) illegal substances, such as cocaine, heroin, or marijuana among others.

Since some psychoactive substance-use disorders stem from a composite of causative factors, it seems appropriate to orient a therapeutic approach to all identifiable contributing aspects of these disorders, whether physiological, psychological or sociological. Although it is apparent that the most pressing problems demand attention first, therapeutic endeavors should be broad enough to cover these three aspects simultaneously whenever possible.

Treatment programs for clergy such as "Guest House" report at least 85% sobriety several years after treatment. Good prognosis is associated with a 90 day length of treatment course and long-term maintenance after-care which can include formal psychotherapy, support groups such as AA, or deterrent agents such as Antabuse for those recovering from alcohol dependence.

The term "addictive personality" has been used colloquially by some to refer to individuals who are "addicted" to some substance or behavior. Since it is not possible to predict who is an alcoholic, drug user, or sex offender simply by personality style, it would be more useful diagnostically to refer to a specific disorder and underlying psychopathology, as appropriate. In addition, the term "addiction" is not a diagnostic term for reasons already discussed.

SEXUAL DISORDERS

Paraphilias are defined by DSM III-R as "characterized by arousal in response to sexual objects or situations that are not part of normative arousal activity patterns and that in varying degrees, may interfere with the capacity for reciprocal affectionate sexual activity" (DSM-III-R p. 279). The essential feature of disorders in this subclass is that unusual or bizarre imagery or acts are necessary for sexual excitement. Such imagery or acts tend to be consistently and involuntarily repetitive. Only pedophilia will be addressed in this paper.

Pedophilia has been described as a complex of symptoms in a variety of ways in the literature (Finkelhor and Araji, 1986; Mohr, Turner and Jery, 1964). The standard psychiatric reference, DSM-III-R, describes pedophilic behavior as recurrent urges and sexual arousal through fantasies and sexual activity on the part of an adult or adolescent above the age of 16 years whereby the sexual urges and arousal involve a child or children that have not reached puberty (usually 13 years of age or younger). Pedophilia as a complex of symptoms will later be addressed in greater detail.

The term "sexual addiction" is used by some to refer to sexual disorders. There are several arguments against the use of the term "addiction" when referring to deviant sexual activity with a child, as in pedophilia. The diagnostically accepted use of the colloquial term "addiction" as already described by the American Psychiatric Association is defined as a strong dependence both physiologic and emotional upon alcohol or some other drug. As already discussed, this often involves an abstinence syndrome if the drug is withdrawn or if tolerance develops, the need for markedly increased amounts of a substance in order to achieve the desired effect. In considering pedophilia, it becomes evident that it is not possible to become physiologically or psychologically dependent on deviant sexual activity with a child. The withdrawal symptoms of increased pulse, pressure, respirations, diaphoresis, tremulousness, and possible seizures if sexual activity with a child ceases, is not feasible. In addition, pedophiles do not develop tolerance to sexual activity with a child requiring increasing numbers of contacts for the same effect.

Also, those who are alcohol or substance dependent strive for complete abstinence from use of the chemical as these agents are not essential or inherent to human life. In the case of the individual who suffers from pedophilia, the deviant sexual activity must cease. But to consider the focus as primarily abstaining from deviant sexual behavior, would be a symptomatic approach to the problem. The ultimate goal is to address the underlying psychopathology hindering an individual from healthy, mature expressions of human sexuality. What is meant by healthy "mature" expressions of human intimacy is the capacity to value an individual for who he or she is, independent of any need-satisfying function that an individual may serve. Such a focus of relationship transcends the limits of need-gratifying attachments, including the genital level of relationship to a level of interpersonal affirmation and commitment.

Another argument against comparably linking pedophilia and psychoactive substance-use disorders through the use or the term "addiction" is that unlike substance-use disorders, pedophilia always involves a victim. Even if the pedophiliac may be generous and very attentive to the child's needs in all respects other than sexual victimization, this is done "in order to gain the child's affection, interest and loyalty and to prevent the child from reporting the sexual activity" (DSM-III-R p. 285–286).

The term compulsion has alternatively been used to refer to some sexual disorders. This term more accurately lends itself to the recurrent deviant sexual urges and behaviors described in paraphilias. That is, the repetitive often stereotyped urge to perform a behavior which insistently forces itself into consciousness even though the subject may not wish to perform the action. Performing the action may generate increasing anxiety while completion of the action temporarily decreases tension. Temporary decrease of tension is thought to reinforce these behaviors such that they become compulsive. The sexual response cycle can also evoke many neuroendocrine changes with pleasurable or analgesic type qualities. Sexually deviant compulsions toward children then, can be thought of as a behavior for pedophiliacs to temporarily relieve themselves of psychological pain, physiological discomfort, loneliness or frustration.

Different forms of pedophilic behaviors have been described (Howells, 1981; Langevin, 1983; Finkelhor et al., 1986; and Groth et al., 1982). Groth refers to the "fixated" child molester, as a pedophile who is developmentally arrested, and to the "regressed" child molester, as a pedophile who despite a more or less normal psychosexual course of development, regresses under stress to an earlier developmental level and to pedophilic behavior. "Fixated" pedophilic behavior is said to become evident during adolescence. Groth cited the age of 14 as the modal age of onset of sexual molestation in some 2000 incarcerated pedophiles he has worked with. The pedophile's behaviors involve compulsive, pre-meditated, and pre-planned offenses. In addition, characterologic immaturity and poor sociosexual peer relationships, are often present. Most

167

problematic, however, is the finding that the offender does not view his behavior as inappropriate. The "regressed" pedophile is said to molest children episodically as compared with the "fixated" type and the child molestation is often precipitated by stress and is thought to emerge in early adult life. Substance abuse is also more common in the "regressed" type of pedophilic behavior. Primary targets are usually opposite sex victims and such behavior exists along with traditional but underdeveloped peer relationships. In both types, the defense mechanisms of denial and rationalization are quite prominent. Denial is a strong defense mechanism which refers to "the refusal to acknowledge the presence or existence of a situation or problem" (Hinsie 1970). Also known as negation, denial is a primitive defense, consisting of an attempt to disavow the existence of an unpleasant reality. Denial is such a strong defense mechanism that even in those individuals who have been charged with sexual molestation, eight to twelve months of intensive therapy is not uncommonly necessary before denial remits enough to effectively begin to address the psychodynamics underlying pedophilic behavior. Rationalization is "a justification of attitudes, beliefs, or behaviors that might otherwise be unacceptable by an incorrect application of justifying reasons or intervention of a convincing fallacy" (Kaplan et al., 1985). According to Groth (1982), pedophilic behavior may be considered to exist on a continuum between poles describing exclusively "fixated" and "regressed" behavior styles. Similar behaviorally oriented references for pedophilia include the use of the terms "preference" and "situational" molesters (Howells, 1981).

Many authors cite findings that pedophiles have some degree of social difficulty (Johnston, 1986; Groth, 1978; Lanyon, 1986). Howells (1981) and Lanyon (1986) also state that because those molesters studied are those who have been "caught", that those who are more socially skilled go undetected (Howells, 1981; Lanyon, 1986); many pedophiles are said to be otherwise respectable and law-abiding citizens. Pedophiles are often the victims of childhood molestation themselves; this is substantiated by clinical findings which indicate that molesters report having been victimized with greater frequency than non-molesters (Groth, 1979; Berlin, 1986; Lanyon 1986). It has been suggested that approximately 30% of those pedophiles who were victimized later become offenders (Kaufman, 1988). This number actually may be underestimated.

Biological studies relating to child molesters are limited and of those studies completed, the findings are quite diverse and nonspecific. Plasma testosterone levels have been usually found to be within normal limits (Rada, Laws and Kellner, 1976). But elevated testosterone levels have been reported (Berlin 1983b). Most often these individuals are reported to be relatively free of psychosis or of gross mental defect (Burgess, et. al. 1978; Lanyon, 1986).

In view of these findings, there appear to be multifarious factors contributing to the development and expression of pedophilia. Immaturity in emotional, psychological, social, and sexual development, in addition to the utilization of the defense mechanisms of denial and rationalization seriously effect the pedophile's capacity to make conscious, responsible choices. Also, the habitual nature of the pathological behaviors and repetitive cycles of primitive and premature resolution of internal tension, based on low frustration tolerance and poor impulse control, contribute to the lack of development of conscious and personal decision-making skills on the part of the pedophile. Such repetitive cycles of immediate, primitive and self-gratifying behaviors ultimately result in a decreased capacity to make mature, adaptive choices in life.

Prognosis for pedophilia is dependent upon many factors, including motivation, habitual patterns of response, situational factors, in addition to external and internal resources available to the individual. Since the "fixated" pedophile most often does not view his behavior as inappropriate, it is very difficult to have such an individual willingly participate in therapy. The possible effectiveness of treatment, therefore, can be tremendously hindered in these individuals. Groth (1982) reports that he believes that the "regressed" pedophile has a better prognosis than the "fixated" pedophile, because of pre-existing higher levels of maturity and to the situational stress related, and episodic nature of the "regressive" type. Other factors that can complicate the treatment of both the "regressed" and "fixated" types of pedophilia are characterologic disturbances unrelated to pedophilia itself.

The literature reports that the incidence of relapse for same sex pedophilia preference is twice that of opposite sex pedophilia preference (DSM-III-R). Rattenbury (1986) looked at the incidence of relapse in treated versus incarcerated (non-treated) pedophiles, rapists and incest offenders and found that in one to nine years following relapse of those individuals who had been incarcerated, the proportions of relapse in the treated and imprisoned groups did not differ. Groth et. al. (1982) indicate that the pedophilic behavior "is something the offender will need to work with every day of this life" (p. 143). They also state that it "would be misleading to suggest that we have reached a state of clinical knowledge that insures successful rehabilitation of adults who sexually molest children" (Ibid, p. 140).

Regarding the treatment of pedophilia, experience indicates that a multimodal approach to therapy is the most effective and that relapse is very often the case if such therapy is not continuous. Modes of therapy include: psychotherapy, behavior modification, use of synthetic female hormones, and surgery. Psychotherapy focuses on gaining insight into current dynamics of the pedophile's feelings, thought patterns, and behaviors. Some pedophiles act out of frustration and depression. The underlying dynamics of these would need to be explored and addressed. The individual who is engaged in pedophilic behavior often has a very restricted understanding of himself as a sexual being. Education about human sexuality is indicated for such individuals so as to make the pedophile more self-aware. In addition, some pedophiles, were themselves sexually molested, and would benefit from therapeutically addressing these issues. Not infrequently, those who were molested turn to molestation as the only form of nurturing they know, or alternatively identify with the aggressor and are now in a position of power because they are the adult and no longer the child victim.

Biological therapies include the use of synthetic female hormones, surgical castration and neurosurgical ablation. The synthetic female hormone used in the United States is medroxyprogesterone acetate (Depo-Provera). This agent is administered intramuscularly every one to two weeks and decreases the secretion of testosterone by the testes several fold. Elevated testosterone level of itself, however, does not result in pedophilic behavior. In fact, only in some pedophiles is the level of testosterone elevated. In both normal and sexually deviant oriented behavior patterns, the reduction in testosterone levels result in decreased sexual drive and erotic fantasies and can potentially also inhibit penile erection and ejaculation. Stated another way, Depo-Provera decreases both normal and pathological sexual drive and often results in chemically induced impotence. Depo-Provera, however, does *not* of itself result in normal healthy expressions of human sexuality. Many recommend that the testosterone level be maintained at a level equivalent to that which exists before the onset of male puberty to be most effective (Hucher). There are some studies in which pedophiles have been treated with Depo-Provera for periods ranging from three months to five years (John Hopkins group). The major side-effects of Depo-Provera include: a higher proportion of circulating sperm with broken tails, weight gain, lethargy, cold sweats, nightmares, shortness of breath, increased blood pressure, leg cramps and hypofunctional testes. High doses of Depo-Provera has resulted in breast cancer in female dogs, but there has been no reported case of Depo-Provera related cancer in humans. In addition, the longterm psychological and physical effects of Depo-Provera induced pre-pubertal levels of testosterone and sperm, as well as abnormal sperm forms, and attenuated but not necessarily healthy adult socio-sexual responses, are not yet known. Within three weeks after the cessation of the medication, sexual arousal, whether deviant or non-deviant, returns. Berlin (1986) states that Depo-Provera will hopefully "make it easier" for the pedophile "to successfully resist unwanted temptations"; yet he adds that the "drug cannot change the nature of his sexual orientation" (p. 25).

Another potential side effect which is not addressed in the literature is that of Depo-Provera on the offspring of men who have been treated with this drug. There are reports of normal appearing offspring of men who had been taking Depo-Provera at the time these offspring were conceived; however, these children will need to be more thoroughly evaluated as they mature physically, intellectually, and emotionally. Needless to say, the cited effects of Depo-Provera render its use medically controversial. The moral issue regarding the use of this agent also needs to be addressed.

Oral cyproterone acetate is another synthetic derivative of the female hormone, progesterone, used to treat pedophilia. This agent is currently being used in Canada and Europe but is not available in the United States. As with Depo-Provera, response to treatment includes a reduction in sexual urges, erotic fantasies, and ability to achieve an erection. Common side effects include fatigue, decreased appetite, and mild depression after a few weeks of treatment. Also, in 20% of 300 men studied by Laschet and Laschet, breast enlargement during the course of administering cyproterone acetate was noted in the men after six months of treatment. As with Depo-Provera, the effects of cyproterone acetate remit within one month of discontinuing the agent. Again, the longterm effects of administering this agent are not yet known.

Surgical treatment involves either the surgical removal of the testicles or the ablation of brain pathways associated with sexual desire. The former is no longer used as a treatment option. The latter involves the ablation of the hypothalamus, an area of the brain thought to be associated with sexual desire, and has been used for violent sex offenders. This approach has been met with only limited success.

Review of treatment highlights the difficulty in treating pedophilia. Intervention to prevent further sexual abuse from occurring is just the initial phase of addressing the problem of pedophilia. Other essential phases involve educating offenders about integral mature expression of sexuality, interpersonal skills, and healthier coping skills. Despite these additional phases of treatment, however, "the effectiveness of this approach is largely untested" (Barnard et al, 1989, p. 94).

Therefore, although the existing knowledge used to treat pedophiliacs is imperfect, the fact remains that child sexual abuse is an enormous multidimensional problem. Clinicians need to become familiar with intervention strategies to help patients control their deviant behaviors, impulsiveness, and preoccupations. Many of the above treatment modalities appear promising, but have not been systematically tested over an adequate period of time to determine the efficacy or permanence of their effects. To date, treatment is at best palliative, that is, there is no known cure for pedophilia. "Until systematic research confirms the effectiveness of attempts to change molesters' sexual preferences for children, clinicians must be satisfied with helping these people manage their deviant and socially unacceptable urges" (Barnard, 1989, p. 94–95).

Treatment of those individuals who are victims of pedophilic behavior also needs to be addressed. The effects of sexual involvement with an adult on a child seems to depend, in part, on the child's attitude regarding such activity. In particular, if the child holds himself responsible for the encounter, or if the child is pressured to conceal the sexual activity, or if the response from family or friends is negative and judgmental, the child will more likely be negatively affected. If the adult was seen as warm and loving and the child is able to speak freely about the sexual involvement, it is thought that the child will be less seriously traumatized. This, however, is not always the case and should be addressed on an individual basis.

As with the offender, a victim of sexual molestation and the victim's family members need careful psychiatric evaluation and the child himself or herself should also have a thorough physical exam to rule out any physical problems as a consequence of the sexual abuse. Family therapy can be very useful in helping distraught parents, in particular, learn how to most therapeutically address the trauma their child may have incurred as a consequence of being sexually molested. The offender's family may also need psychological support including education about the sexual disorder and the therapeutic processing of the psychological traumatization that such news may have evoked.

THE MINISTERIAL PRIESTHOOD AND PEDOPHILIA

If pedophilic tendencies and/or behaviors have been expressed in the priest-candidate prior to ordination, the capacity to make free and conscious choices at the time of ordination should be brought into question. For example, if an individual is not capable of discriminating the pedophilic behaviors are deviant, as in the "fixated" pedophile, this indicates a lack of understanding of the existence of a significant problem. Alternatively, if the individual recognizes the deviancy of his behaviors but denies or rationalizes them, as in the case of the "regressed" pedophile, then this indicates an incapacity to seek assistance for his existing problem. The first example addresses the very capacity to understand that a problem exists. The second addresses the capacity to make a conscious choice regarding an existing problem.

Let us consider three means of identifying possible indications of pedophilia in a priest-candidate: 1. the interview 2. observation 3. testing.

1. The interview
   In an initial interview or in a series of interviews, it might be helpful to ask questions regarding:
   a. self-esteem.
   b. emotional needs; are they child-like?
   c. dominant/passive behaviors.
   d. the prevalence of particular sexual fantasies, e.g., of molesting children.
   e. whether or not the individual has ever been sexually molested.
   f. past experiences of shame, humiliation, or powerlessness as a child and at the hands of an adult.
   g. whether the individual finds himself more comfortable with children or with adults.
   h. the need to control children.
   i. whether the individual has emotional needs which be believes can only be met by children.
2. Observation
   Observation would best occur in various settings, such as on an individual basis, in group settings, with peers and with children. Behaviors or tendencies to be observed might include the following:
   a. childish emotional needs.
   b. "pseudo-adult behavior" when with adults, yet the individual appears to be more comfortable when with children than with peers.
   c. low self-esteem.
   d. timid, unassertive, awkward behavior and poor social skills.
   e. others have the sense that they do not develop a peer relationship with the individual.
   f. immature responses during participation in peer group settings.
   g. maturity of relationships with peers of like sex, peers of opposite sex and with children.

174

3. Tests

Although not diagnostic in themselves, various psychological tests may be utilized in conjunction with observation and interview techniques, to help develop a comprehensive clinical picture of each priest-pedophile's level of functioning and underlying psychopathology.

A potential problem with priestly formation as it currently exists is the many hours of unsupervised and unstructured time. Such periods could trigger sexually deviant behavior or chemical abuse in individuals with such a propensity. Even those individuals who have relatively healthy developing personalities would benefit from a community environment which facilitates personal growth through healthy peer interactions. The milieu of many seminaries in which much time is unstructured and spent alone, does not foster healthy psychosocial development of seminarians in general. Loneliness, frustration, and other forms of psychological discomfort or pain are common to the human condition and if not addressed, foster further isolation and hinder personal growth. A healthy "sense of self" evolves through daily human interactions and confrontations in which self-awareness and personal growth evolve in the context of the duality of the awareness of another. The development of this "sense of self" determines, to a significant degree, the extent to which an individual is capable of interacting maturely and cooperatively with others. It is critical that the daily seminary schedule lend itself to the practical aspects of community life necessary for interpersonal growth and dialogue with hope of obviating isolation and self-absorption. The call to priesthood involves the spiritual enrichment of the lives of others and this generative objective cannot be achieved without self-awareness. That is, a self-awareness which has the capacity for intimate celibate relationships which integrally value other human lives.

SUMMARY AND CONCLUSIONS

In summary, we have described both medically and psychiatrically the pathological use of alcohol, benzodiazepines, and barbiturates, and have reviewed why diagnostically the term drug dependence is preferred to the term addiction. The concern regarding the use of the term addiction with respect to pedophilia was also discussed suggesting instead the term compulsion. Various theoretical approaches regarding the etiology of pedophilia were reviewed, as was the wide range of related terminology and differing treatment results.

Regarding pedophilia, a multimodal approach to therapy is considered most effective. Several years after intensive treatment, however, relapse is often the case. Given this fact, caregivers need to ask themselves if treatment truly is effective. More accurately then, treatment is palliative. That is, multimodal therapy as it is presently available does not in any way relieve the underlying psychopathology of pedophilia. Psychotherapy reduces the rate and effects of the illness, but it does not eradicate the disorder. Depo-Provera attenuates some aspects of the deviant urges to sexually molest children but the side effects of this medication results in other problems including abnormal sperm forms and possible exacerbation of psychological immaturity secondary to the pre-pubertal testosterone levels. These facts are a tremendous burden for caregivers. The tremendous suffering the pedophile endures by being so obsessed with deviant urges are often so intense that they color the pedophile's participation and performance in many activities and functions. The pain and suffering inflicted onto the child-victim well into his or her adult life also needs to be seriously considered and addressed.

Once a priest is recognized as having pedophilia his caregivers and religious superiors have the obligation to relieve such an individual from the responsibilities and obligations which the pedophile is not capable of assuming. A proposed approach to the problem of pedophilia within the priesthood is restricted ministry, in which there is no contact with children. The viability of such a proposal, however, needs to be critically evaluated. Restricted ministry would entail no work involving families at which children or adolescents might be present. But the administration of any sacrament will potentially involve the presence of children. One possible group that these priests could minister to is religious. But again, this would need to be in a setting in which there are no children. Each case of pedophilia would need to be carefully considered.

It seems that an individual who is recognized as having pedophilia does not have the capacity for functioning as an ordained ministerial priest since this psychopathology and ordination are mutually exclusive. Stated alternatively, pedophilia entails psychological defects which are known to habitually impair an individual's capacity to make reasonable conscious choices. Such irregularity would seem to affect the pedophile's capacity to receive orders. Any therapy that ignores this will be less than complete and will actually cause greater pain and suffering for these individuals.

It needs to be made clear that laicization is not a punishment. Rather, laicization frees priests who suffer with pedophilia from the obligation of living the sacerdotal life, the obligations of which they do not have the capacity to fulfill. We as caregivers or spiritual authorities have the responsibility for these men and their victims. We are culpable if we are negligent in providing compassionate preventative care to the fullest degree possible given that treatment is most often known to be palliative.

Pedophilia is a disorder with multifarious underlying psychodynamic issues. This fact underscores the need for careful and thorough psychiatric evaluation of seminary candidates. If psychological deficiencies emerge regarding human sexuality, they need to be appropriately addressed including the consideration that a potential priest candidate does not have the capacity for priesthood. Sound psychosexual development needs to be fostered in the form of education and participation in seminary community life. Fostering the development of healthy, integrally intimate celibate relationships facilitate the capacity for the unfolding of the fullness of the call to the ministerial priesthood.

References

American Psychiatric Association (1984) *Diagnostic and Statistical Manual of Mental Disorders* (III-R), Washington, D.C.

Barnard, George W., Fuller, A. Kenneth, Robbins, Lynn, and Shaw, Theodore (1989) *The Child Molester: an integrated approach to evaluation and treatment*, Brunner/Mazel Publisher, New York.

Berlin, Fred S., and Meinecke, Carl F., (1981) "Treatment of Sex Offenders with Antiandrogenic Medication: Conceptualization, Review of Treatment Modalities, and Preliminary Findings", *American Journal of Psychiatry,* 138 (5): 601–607

Berlin, Fred S. (1983) "Ethical use of Psychiatric Diagnosis", *Psychiatric Annals,* 13: 231–331.

Berlin, Fred S. (1983) "Sex Offenders: A biochemical perspective and a status report on biochemical treatment", in *The Sexual Aggressor: current perspectives on treatment.* Greer, J. C. and Stuart, I. R. (Eds.),. Van Nostran Reinhold Company, New York.

Berlin, Fred S. (1986) "Pedophilia: diagnostic concepts treatment, and ethical considerations." *American Journal of Forensic Psychiatry Interfacing Issues of Psychiatry and Law,* 1, Vol. 7: 13–30.

Burgess, A. W., Groth, A. N., Holstrom, L. L. and Sgroi, S. S. (1978) *Sexual Assault of Children and Adolescents.* Lexington, MA: Heath Publishing Company.

Coleman, Eli (1986) "Sexual Compulsion vs. Sexual Addiction: the debate continues", *SIECUS Report,* July: 7–11.

Coleman, Eli (1987) "Sexual Compulsivity: definition, etiology, and treatment considerations", *Chemical Dependency and Intimacy Dysfunction,* pp. 184–204.

Coriden, James A., Green, Thomas J., Heintschel, Donald E. (1985) *The Code of Canon Law: a text and commentary,* pp. 729–730.

Friedrich, W. N. (1988) "Child Abuse and Sexual Abuse", in *The MMPI: use with specific populations,* ed. R. L. Green, pp. 246–258. Grune & Stratton.

Finkelhor, D. (1984) *Child Sexual Abuse—New Theory and Research.* New York: Free Press.

Finkelhor, D. and Araji, S. (1986) "Explanations of pedophilia: a four factor model", *The Journal of Sex Research.* 22: 145–161.

Frisbie, L. V., and Dondis, E. H. (1965) "Recidivism Among Treated Sex Offenders", *Research Monograph* (no. 5). Sacramento California Department of Mental Hygiene.

Gaffney, Gary R. and Berlin, Fred S. (1984) "Is There Familial Transmission of Pedophilia?". *Journal of Nervous and Mental Disease,* 172 (no. 9): 546–548.

Gaffney, Gary R. and Berlin, Fred S. (1984) "Is There Hypothalamic-Pituitary-Gonadal Dysfunction in Paedophilia?", *British Journal of Psychiatry,* 145: 657–660.

Giarretto, H. (1982) "A Comprehensive Child Sexual Abuse Treatment Program", *Child Abuse and Neglect,* 6: 263–278.

Groth, A. N. and Birnbaum, H. J. (1978) "Adult Sexual Orientation and Attraction to Underage Persons", *Archives of Sexual Behaviors,* 7: 175–181.

Groth, A. N., Hobson, W. F., and Gary, T. S. (1982) "The Child Molester: clinical observations", in *Social Work and Child Sexual Abuse,* J. Conte and D. A. Shore (eds.), pp. 129–144. New York: Haworth.

Hinsie, Leland E. and Campbell, Robert J. *Psychiatric Dictionary, 4th edition,* Oxford University Press, London, Toronto 1970.

Howells, D. (1978) "Some Meanings of Children for Pedophiles" in *Love and Attraction,* M. Cook and G. Wilson (eds.), pp. 57–82. London: Pergamon Press.

Howells, K. (1981) "Adult Sexual Interest in Children: considerations relevant to theories of etiology", in *Adult Sexual Interest in Children,* M. Cook and K. Howells (eds.), pp. 55–94. London: Academic Press.

Hucker, S., Langevin, R., Wortzman, G., Bain, J., Hardy, L., Chambers, J. and Wright, S. (1986) "Neuropsychological Impairment in Pedophiles", *Canad J of Behav Sci/Rev Canad Sci Comp,* 18 (4).

Johnston, F. A., Johnston, S. A. (1986) "Differences Between Human Figure Drawings of Child Molesters and Control Groups", *Journal of Clinical Psychology,* 42 (4).

Kaplan, Harold and Sadock, Benjamin (1985) *Comprehensive Textbook of Psychiatry,* 4th edition.

Kaplan, Harold and Sadock, Benjamin (1988) *Synopsis of Psychiatry Behavioral Sciences Clinical Psychiatry,* 5th edition.

Kaufman, Joan (1987) *Los Angeles Daily Journal,* September-October p. 15.

Lanyon, R. I. (1986) "Theory and Treatment in Child Molestation", *Journal of Consulting and Clinical Psychology*, 54 (2): 176–182.

Langevin, R. (1983) *Sexual Strands*. Hillsdale, N.J.: Erlbaum.

Langevin, R. (1985) *Erotic Preference, Gender Identity, and Aggression in Men*. Hillsdale, N.J.: Erlbaum

Mohr, J. W., Turner, R. W., and Jerry, M. B. (1964) *Pedophilia and Exhibitionism*. Toronto: University of Toronto Press.

Mrazek, F. J. (1984) "Sexual Abuse of Children", in *Advances in Child Clinical Psychology*, B. Lakey and A. E. Kazdin (eds.), 6: 199–215. New York: Plenum Press.

Neuman, G. G. (ed.) (1987) *Origins of Human Aggression—Dynamics and Etiology*. New York: Human Sciences Press.

Paulson, Rev. Jerome E. (1988) "The Clinical and Canonical Considerations in Cases of Pedophilia: the Bishop's role", *Studia Canonica*, 22: 77–124.

Rada, R., Lewis, Al, and Kellner, R. (1976) "Plasma Testosterone Levels in the Rapist", *Psychosomatic Medicine*, 38: 257–268.

Rada, R. T. (1978) "Sexual Psychopathology: historical survey and basic concepts", in *Clinical Aspects of the Rapist*, R. T. Rada (ed.), pp. 1–19. New York: Grune and Stratton.

Sturup, G. K. (1972) "Castration: the total treatment", in *Sexual Behaviors: social, clinical and legal aspects*, Resnick, H. P. L. and Wolfgang, M.D., (eds.). Boston: Little Brown.

Travin, S., Bulestone, H., Coleman, E., Cullens, K., Melella, J. (1985) "Pedophilia: an update on theory and practice", *Psychiatric Quarterly*, 57 (2).

Chapter 12

THE MORAL ASPECTS OF ADDICTION

The Reverend John F. Harvey, O.S.F.S., S.T.D.

Introduction

In accepting the invitation to speak on this subject I realized that I would be addressing a very complex and sensitive issue with no easy answers. Our understanding of addiction in general and of the addictive process is the result of many years of study concerning alcohol and other drugs, but our very imperfect knowledge of sexual addiction, and particularly of pedophilia, is not even ten years old. Yet it is in this area that the Church in America is faced with serious problems. For this reason I decided that I would limit my discourse to sexual addiction, and specifically to pedophilia among religious and clergy. Lawsuits against clergy accused of pedophilic actions have made sensational headlines in our newspapers and TV talk shows. Accusations of neglect against bishops and religious order superiors abound. Ordinary people ask whether we take care of the victim of pedophilic action, and some want to know what do we do for the priest pedophile himself. What provisions does canon law make for situations like these? Is there any hope that such a priest can be restored to some kind of priestly ministry within the Church? I do not expect to answer all these questions, but perhaps I can make some helpful suggestions. I shall divide my reflections into three parts: (1) psychological considerations; (2) moral evaluations of sexual addictive behavior; and (3) pastoral perspectives and approaches based upon my own experiences and those of others. I shall conclude my paper with a few suggestions.

1. Psychological Considerations.

The moral aspects of addiction cannot be properly understood unless one considers the available psychological data on the nature of addiction and the addictive process, as well as the specific forms of addiction. Such a study will raise questions concerning the degree of responsibility which the addict has for his behavior in the past, and his present and future responsibility. Since we are still learning, however, about addictions, particularly sexual addictions, we need to approach the subject with docile readiness to change our views as more data becomes available.

A. Definitions of Addiction

I understand compulsion or addiction as modes of behavior either within the thought and feeling patterns of the individual or in his relationships with others or with the culture which clearly show that the individual concerned is out of control, and this despite the fact that he has consciously tried to rid himself of this behavior with little or no success. Step One of A.A. refers to addiction when it says: "I am an alcoholic, and I am powerless over this condition." One can adapt Step One to the pedophile who seeks help for his condition: "I am a pedophile, and I am powerless over this condition," or to another man who never acts our his fantasies, but spends a fortune on pornographic videotapes. The least common denominator, then in all addictions or compulsions is that one has consciously tried to overcome the behavior over a considerable period of time, but has failed to do so, and now possesses a sense of despair because serious elements of his life are threatened with destruction. He is powerless in this regard. With this working definition of addiction in general terms I should like to consider some specific forms of addiction and to reflect upon the interconnection of addictions, and the underlying addictive process.

B. The Different Forms of Addiction: Process and Substance Addictions

In *Escape From Intimacy* Anne Wilson Schaef expands our understanding of addictions by pointing out that addictions do not exist in isolation, and that "since we live in an addictive society, we have all been exposed to and trained into an addictive process.... It is of the utmost importance to be aware that this underlying addictive process is culturally based and learned. It functions under rules of its own, rules that could be compared to flowing water finding its own course. We all know that when a stream is blocked, it will find its own way ... It is not that the water goes away when its path is changed; it just finds another ... way to express itself. The addictive process is much the same. If one path for its expression is cut off, it finds another."[1]

Both Schaef and Patrick Carnes observe that as one begins to get control over one addiction, another emerges.[2] Thus, the recovering person moves from one addiction to another for two basic reasons: (1) failure to recognize and treat the underlying addictive process; and (2) failure to accurately isolate and focus upon the specific addictions. "When we only deal with the specific addiction, we tend to switch from one addiction to another, or to have 'cross-addictions.' ... We must face each of the specific addictions and the underlying addictive process *together and separately* for recovery to succeed."[3]

Schaef distinguishes the chemical or ingestive addictions from the process addictions in which one is addicted to a **process**. Examples of such are addictions to work, money, sex, relationships, and romance. In all these there is no ingestion of a chemical or other substance. Dr. Gerald May gives a similar broad definition of addiction: "Addiction exists wherever persons are internally compelled to give energy to things that are not their true desires. To define it directly, addiction is a *state* of compulsion, obsession or preoccupation that enslaves a person's will or desire. Addiction sidetracks the eclipses the energy of our deepest, truest desire for love and goodness. We succumb because the energy of our desire becomes attached, nailed to specific behaviors, objects or people. *Attachment* ... is the process that enslaves desire and creates the state of addiction."[4]

Process addictions can be just as destructive and fatal to individuals, families, institutions and societies as substance addictions. We need to treat multiple addictions, understanding each individually, and trying to see how it interacts and supports the others. Ultimately, we need to study the relationship of each specific addiction to the underlying addictive process in **this one person**.[5]

It is only lately that we have begun to recognize process addictions, and prominent among these are pseudo-relationships. There is a growing literature on relationship addiction, loving too much, loving too little, and the like. Addictions that play themselves out in pseudo-relationships affect many people in our society, and cause much pain.[6]

It should be noted, however, that sex, love, and relationship addictions are separate addictions, and that all three can find expression in addictive relationships. To move toward recovery one must look at the dynamics of the addictive relationship, and at the specific addictions leading into addictive relationships. It is important to keep in mind that the "acting out" addictions, like alcoholism and pedophilia, are more interesting to the public, but the less sensational sexual addictions, like voyeurism and romance junkies, also cause a great deal of destruction and pain.[7]

Shaef, moreover, does not believe our research into addictions has adequately addressed the ways in which our contemporary culture has contributed to the various forms of addiction,—to see how our families, schools, churches and political system have contributed to our condition. It is not enough to stop with the family.[8]

C. Characteristics of Sexual Addiction

Patrick Carnes says that "the addict substitutes a sick relationship to an event or process for a healthy relationship with others.

The addict's relationship with a mood altering 'experience' becomes central to his life."[9] Sexual Addiction is an illness with a definite set of treatable symptoms. Yet it is difficult to communicate the seriousness of the illness to the popular and professional public. Carnes stresses that people tend to confuse sexual addiction with pleasurable or frequent sexual activity. But ordinary persons can learn to moderate their sexual behavior, while the addict cannot do so.[10]

The addict has lost the ability to say no, because his behavior is part of a cycle of thinking, feeling, and acting which he cannot control. Instead of enjoying sex as a self-affirming source of pleasure in marriage, the sex addict uses it as a relief from pain, or from stress, similar to the way an alcoholic relies on alcohol. Contrary to love, the obsessional illness transforms sex into the primary need, for which all else may be sacrificed, including family, friends, health, safety and work. As time goes on, the sex addict finds himself helplessly trapped in a cycle of degradation and shame.[11]

Sexual addiction has also been described as a spiritual breakdown, as a state of mind and a set of beliefs that can exist separately from other people. It becomes a relationship with oneself.[12]

Sexual addiction is also mood-altering, affecting the individual like any other mood altering drug. The obsession becomes a 'fix', and the addict seeks a 'high' from the sexual fix. It will be profitable to trace the development of this obsession which leads to compulsive behavior.

D. Development of an Addictive System According to Carnes

1. Initiation Phase

It is very difficult to distinguish the initial stages of addiction from normal sexual behavior. Many youngsters become involved in sexual experimentation, but the future addict puts far more energy into such activity. Self-stimulation was more than experimentation; it was a way to banish pain. Sex became a way to get through life's difficulties and pressures. As the young addict moves into adult years his sexual acting out becomes a ritualized pattern, whereas in the case of the non-addict, despite some lapses even into promiscuity for a time, he/she is able to move on to an existence where one is in control of one's sexual desires. But not all addicts have this kind of developmental history.

Given an extraordinary period of stress concomitant with intensely pleasurable sexual experiences, they will begin to forge a potent pattern of sex as relief from stress, which becomes a pattern for life. Carnes sees two different kinds of catalysts for these patterns: (1) catalytic environments and (2) catalytic events.

(1) Catalytic environments are characterized by extremes, situations, for example, with high performance expectations and a low degree of structure, such as in professional training schools, medical schools, law institutes, seminaries, and graduate schools. Usually there is a great deal of unscheduled time and only periodic accountability. In all these extreme environments there is also progressive self-doubt. *"Anxiety* and *control* are common aspects of these experiences."[13] The addict experiences uncertainty whether he will master his environment, and so he turns to his addiction for temporary relief from anxiety, but in the long run it will only make things worse.

(2) Then there are the catalytic events, which are the two kinds: abandonment events and sexual events. **Abandonment** events involve a perceived significant loss. A child who loses his parents at a very tender age may feel abandoned. Divorce, separation, and death can all be seen by the child as abandonment, and the child feels worthless. These feelings are carried into adulthood, and they can be taken away only when the addict repudiates his faulty belief system, which can come with therapy. This brings us to the damage done by **sexual events**.

Sexual events can be thrust upon a young man, like a father taking his son out, and purchasing prostitutes for them both. The young man thought he was doomed to live like his father. Usually addicts can remember the first sexual incident that started them on the way to addiction like the eleven year old girl who was seduced by her father and became a prostitute at sixteen. Once a pattern of behavior is developed, the addict enters the **establishment** phase of the sexual addiction.

Second Phase: Establishment Phase.

By this time the sexual addict has entrenched himself in a pattern of activity, which is carefully planned and executed in a way in which the addict feels will remain secret. As Patrick Carnes points out, the way one knows that a given person has moved into this phase is the predictable quality of their **regular behavior**. From study of such behavior one notes the emergence of a cycle with four distinct and sequential components:

1. **Preoccupation**: The addicts's thoughts become focused on the behavior. By anticipating the pleasure of the next encounter, or remembering the previous episode the addict can go through a mood-altering experience, a "high", and at the same time he can blot out the current events of real life. This leads to little attention to one's daily duties, and an unconcern for responsibilities of work or home. He will seek out an environment which is provocative (cruising). In short, he has already lost control. This preoccupation naturally leads to ritualization,

2. **Ritualization**: The addict regularly follows a method which prepares him for sexual activity. Examples are multiple. The incest parent makes elaborate preparations to be alone with the child; the compulsive masturbator browses in adult book stores; another goes to a homosexual porno-theatre at noon each day. Rituals involve contexts, such as city parks, public restrooms, and bars. One's work pattern in which one regularly overextends himself to the point of exhaustion, and then feels the need for reward through sexual behavior. At this point the person comes to believe that he needs the sexual gratification to survive. "Sexual obsession is pursued to its peak regardless of risk, harm, or other consequences. There is only one kind of control that matters now—control of source of sexual pleasure."[14] This leads to the next stage of the cycle: sexual acting out.

3. **Sexual compulsivity**: Since I use terms compulsion and addiction interchangeably, I understand sexual compulsivity as the inability to control one's sexual behavior, and the behavior is the cornerstone of the addiction. Without the acting out the addiction is not established, because the behavior is still under control[15]. But it is difficult to determine loss of control in sexual addiction because of the wide variety of behaviors possible. The sexual behavior becomes the most important aspect of the addicts life, it is now a mood altering behavior in which family, work, other people become secondary. A helpful clue to knowing that the person has reached the establishment phase is that the person despairs of changing his behavior. This brings us to the fourth phase, shame and despair.

186

4. **Shame and Despair**: Following the climax experience of pleasure, the addict plummets into shame and despair more deeply with each repetition of the cycle. He also becomes more isolated. But these very moods create the need to begin the cycle again. It does not make any difference whether the focus is food, drugs, alcohol, or sex. The addict relieves the feelings of pain and guilt by getting high again. One reenters the preoccupation phase, and the cycle begins all over again. The cycle is the way the addict keeps pain at bay.

Carnes holds that there are two kinds of mistakes that clinicians often make about the addict's despair: "The first is to diagnose the depression as simply depression and not tie it directly to the addiction. For example, one common error is to view the sexual behavior as symptomatic of the depression. Another error of this kind would be to assess the despair as excessive guilt, masking the depressed state.... To help the sex addict, the therapists must carefully assess whether the despair is that which is an integral element of the addictive cycle, or whether clinical depression is present as well. The other mistake is to dismiss the possibility of an addictive cycle, if there is not despair."[16] This addictive cycle, moreover, is part of a still larger addictive system, which supports the cycle; there are three other elements: **belief system; impaired thinking; and unmanageability**. The driving force of the addictive system is the **belief system**, which is a mosaic of beliefs held by the addict that influences all his practical decisions in daily living.

Flowing out of the faulty belief system is **impaired thinking**. A female addict may rationalize her affairs with married men with the argument that it makes her own marriage endurable. But despite all the denial and distortion the addict gets deeper and deeper in a hole. In short, his life becomes **unmanageable**. The consequences of his behavior make the addicts's life unmanageable, eating away at his sense of self.[17]

II. The Moral Evaluation of Addictions, particularly Sexual Addictions

Since Father Russell Smith has adequately treated the distinction between the objective morality of a pedophilic act (as seriously immoral and criminal) and the subjective responsibility of the pedophile priest[18] I will concentrate on the latter question of personal responsibility. There is no question that first of all the diocese or religious order should take care of the victim of sexual abuse, but that having been done, one calls the priest to accountability.

A. Distinction Between Past Behavior and the Present

One must make a distinction between the moral responsibility of the addict for his past actions, and his current responsibility for the future. From our growing, but still incomplete, understanding of addiction we realize how difficult, if not humanly impossible, it is to make an accurate **moral** evaluation of the past behavior of the addict. We have no way of categorizing the kinds and degrees ofcompulsive sexual behavior, or for that matter of any other sort of compulsive behavior. Each person reveals a different degree of compulsion in a different pattern of personality traits and life circumstances. As we have already seen, one needs to look at many factors. As authors, including Rudolph Allers, note: "We cannot know anything about the nature of the alleged irresistible impulses unless we know all we can found out about the total personality."[19]

A person who acts freely one day may act compulsively the next, and others would not be the wiser.[20] Often the compulsive person seems perfectly free in what he does despite the fact that he is under the influence of one dominant purpose which shuts out all other thoughts from his mind, and eliminates any chance that counteracting motives will have any efficacy. His mind is filled with one big image: a pornographic book shop, a child, a teenager. While his actions seem deliberate and free, they are result of the narrowing of consciousness to only one idea. This is compulsion in the full sense. Pedophilia in the **strict sense** of acts "insistently and involuntarily repetitive" with prepubertal children is a form of such compulsion.[21]

There is another form of compulsion in which one becomes immersed in the object of his desire, feeling that he must give into the impulse to get some physical relief or he will suffer great pain. He has to have a quick "fix" at a truckstop restroom, or he will masturbate. Here the person is aware that he can resist, and that there is another option. Yet the pull of the flesh is strong.

This brings us to what I would like to call the **moment of truth theory**, which Allers developed years ago. What Carnes refers to as the phenomena of preoccupation is described by Allers as the first stage. But these impulses become irresistible even before they are **fully** developed. The person has the feeling that something is going to happen. He knows he should turn away, but he does not. There is a certain fascination in the danger, and a desire to find fulfillment for one's sexual desires, at least on the unconscious level. "This action may, therefore, not carry any responsibility, and nevertheless not be excusable, because in fact the person has assented to its development."[22]

Actually, as the result of practicing the Twelve Steps, sexual addicts come to realize that there was a latent insincerity and a desire for sexual satisfaction in their previous protestations that they really "didn't want it to happen." These addicts are now honest about their motivations. For this reason I do no see much wisdom in any attempt to evaluate the moral responsibility of addicts for their past actions. Since we moralists have much empiric evidence that the addict lacks the degree of advertence and the full consent of the will necessary for serious sin, we should question the application of ecclesiastical penalties to priest-addicts, particularly priests involved in sexual acts with teenagers or with those below the age of puberty.[23] In this regard there is a presumption that pedophiles, whether in the strict (below the age of puberty) or broad sense (ephebophiles), are addicts, and therefore presumptively lacking in full advertence and freedom.[24] If such is the case, it diminishes imputability for pedophilic behavior, but it leaves the pedophile with the fundamental responsibility to use the clinical, psychological, and spiritual means to control such behavior.

Now it can be argued that priest-addicts are not guilty of serious sin, because of the nature of their addiction, but at the same time they are incapable of continuation in sacerdotal ministry, because their addiction will lead to relapses. This argument will be considered in the pastoral section of the paper.

For this reason I hold that the principal moral question with regard to addiction of any kind is not how responsible was the addict in his past actions, but whether the addict will use the known means to control his addiction, whatever its nature. Then I must ask in a given situation whether there are programs developed to help the addict control his particular addiction. In more recent years programs have been developed on the basis of A.A. wisdom to help addicts in many different areas: overeaters, gamblers, drugs and various sexual addictions. I prefer to concentrate on clerical pedophiles as a form of addiction and to consider whether professional programs in conjunction with spiritual direction and pastoral supervision offer any reasonable hopes that these men can be restored to restricted ministry in the Church. Be it noted that I use the term pedophile in the broad sense, namely, anyone involved in a genital act, or obsessed with the desire for such, with persons below the age of eighteen. In popular and legal usage, as contrasted with the professional description in DSM, III, the term is so understood, and it is in this broad sense that I use the term in my proposal for a pastoral program. I have worked with priests who are pedophilic in the broad sense. Obviously, I rely upon accurate diagnosis of each person by professional therapists, and I have not worked with any priest who could be classified as a pedophile in the strict sense.

III. Pastoral Insights: Dealing with the Priest-Pedophile

It goes without saying that the spiritual guide of a pedophile priest must work closely with a residential rehabilitation program. The spiritual guide of such a person must thoroughly acquaint himself with the background of the pedophile, including constant consultation with the pedophile's therapist. Instead of speculating about the degree of freedom the pedophile possessed, one must analyze the meaning of many incidents in his past with a spiritual plan for the future. From attentive listening, from reading the person;s autobiography one can see in the life of this person most, if not all, of the elements described by Patrick Carnes in *Contrary to Love*. In addition, one listens to the experience of other pedophiles, and continues to read the pertinent literature. One should keep in mind that there are disagreements among therapists concerning the capacity of the pedophile to overcome his addiction/compulsion.

In general terms one school of thought sees the condition as so rooted in the individual that it is very improbable that he will ever be able to understand his sexuality in an adult way, consequently remaining in a state of mind where relapse is very probable. This seems to be the position of Sister Marysia Weber in this volume. Another school of thought, typified by Patrick Carnes, sees the possibility of individuals by therapy and spiritual support systems moving away from the condition of pedophilia into a mature exercise of their priesthood. The first school of thought would hold that there is very little one can do for the pedophile priest, because he is not able to change; and hence he should not be allowed to exercise his priesthood; the second school believes that he can grow up spiritually and psychologically through the kind of program I advocate in this paper.

If the priest has become acquainted with the signs of sexual addiction, he will probably acknowledge that he is one in writing his autobiography. I know this from reading such accounts. But in some instances the priest may avoid the admission that he is a pedophile in need of help. Usually at this point he is engaged in **DENIAL**. Such a one will need more therapy, spiritual direction and group support before he is willing to admit, let alone accept, what is already painfully obvious to therapist and spiritual director. Very probably in such an instance he has not been caught in any sexual act, and has not been subjected to scrutiny by religious or civil authorities. There is also the priest who has reason to believe that he has pedophilic inclinations, but is afraid to seek help, because he believes his superior will throw him out of ministry.

Practically all the priest-pedophiles I have worked with during the last five years, however, have no hesitation in admitting their condition. Wanting to get over their addiction, they come to a spiritual director for guidance. They are willing to do whatever is required of them in the hope that they will be restored to some kind of priestly ministry in the Church.

A Pastoral Program for the Pedophile-Priest

If the priest has not been to a residential program, like St. Luke's Institute in suburban Washington, he should be sent to such a place as soon as possible. The program treats the whole person: physical, psychological social, and spiritual aspects are considered. Not only do different therapists deal with diverse aspects of the total person, but the individual is introduced to the value of group spiritual support systems. When the priest is judged ready to return to his diocese or religious order, a careful report is given to his Provincial or ordinary, and there is full consultation concerning what kind of work this priest can do. Before going into details concerning the post-residence era of the pedophile-priest it would be well to point out that such residency programs require that for a number of years the priest return for a period of aftercare every six months.

Suggestions for the Post Residency Period

Before considering the properly pastoral aspects of guidance during this time I should like to advert to the use of Depo-Provera by some psychiatrists in helping the pedophile to maintain control over obsessional sexual desires. Since the time I treated this question in my book, **The Homosexual Person**, I have had reason to take a more cautious opinion about the morality of administering Depo-Provera to the pedophile. I still believe it is moral to administer this drug as a means of freeing the person from obsessive sexual temptations, provided the attending psychiatrist has monitored the side-effects upon the individual over a given period of time, and provided the patient is aware that there may be serious side-effects of the drug and freely consents to take the drug. At this writing we have no double blind studies on the side effects of the drug.[25]

Dr. Fred Berlin of John Hopkins Medical Center advises that, besides the use of Depo-Provera, individual counseling the group support interaction are necessary. He adds that the pedophile must be able to trust his counselor or counselors completely.[26]

Post Residency Care

I should like to describe four aspects of a recovery program for the priest-pedophile after he comes home from a rehabilitation center: (a) the spiritual; (b) the psychological; (c) pastoral supervision; and (d) regular attendance at spiritual support group meetings.

192

(a) **The Spiritual**: Unless the priest-pedophile has accepted on a deep level of personality his powerlessness, and his need for direction of various sorts, together with a willingness to enter into a spiritual support system, he is in danger of future relapse. He must find a spiritual director, and see him regularly, just as he sees the clinical psychologist or the psychiatrist.[27] Furthermore, the spiritual director should be in touch with the therapist, and should be given permission by the priest-patient to speak to the therapist, and the therapist should be given a similar permission by the priest to speak to the spiritual director. If the therapist asks for such a permission in writing, it should be given. It is necessary for the spiritual director and the therapist to integrate their knowledge of the priest so that both can help him more effectively.

Not only should the spiritual director be concerned with co-operation with the priest's therapist; he should also monitor his regular attendance at spiritual support meetings during every week. Regular practice of mental prayer is part of every such system, and it cannot be neglected by the priest. The spiritual director must guide the priest in all aspects of the spiritual life, and this is not realistically possible unless he sees the priest at least every other week, or at least keeps in touch with him when it is not possible to visit with him. Oftentimes the priest-pedophile will raise questions, which, on the surface, seem more psychological than spiritual, but upon reflection he will see that such questions have a spiritual aspect which ought to be treated by the spiritual director as well as the psychiatrist or clinical psychologist.

(b) **The Psychological**: It would be a mistake to think that in treating the psychological aspects one can neglect the medical problems of the priest-pedophile. I have already adverted to the question of Depo-Provera, but there are also other medical conditions which are strictly the province of medical doctors. Having made that distinction, there remains a whole area of the priest's personality which needs attention from both the clinical psychologist and the psychiatrist. The best example is depression, which can have such destructive effects on the person.

The principal phenomena which I have encountered in the psychological area during the post residency period of the priest pedophile are depression and the temptation to masturbation. Depression seems to be directly related to the fear that one will not be reinstated in any kind of ministry, or that one will be put on the shelf for the rest of his life. The temptation to masturbation is not unusual in persons believing that all opportunities for meaningful priestly ministry have been closed. Conversely, in my experience priest-pedophiles who have been given the opportunity for some form of ministry find it easier to overcome depression and any tendency towards masturbation or other forms of acting-out. The most important gift which God gives these priests-pedophiles is **HOPE**. Beyond the detailed treatment of sexual addiction through patient and faithful adherence to Twelve Step Programs, both the psychologist and the spiritual director should impart to the priest-pedophile a sense of dignity and hope. This brings me to the next element in a post-residency program for such priests.

(c) **Pastoral Supervision**: After a priest has completed a residency period in a rehabilitation center, and a positive recommendation is sent to his superiors, the priest should enter a supervised after-care program, which should be carefully spelled out, and made the object of a written contract between the diocese/religious congregation and the priest. One archdiocese has published a policy, stating clearly the conditions under which the priest who has completed a residency may work in a vocational rehabilitation program of up to four years in non-parish ministry. Each priest will have a supervisor. Only four or five years after successful aftercare will the priest be eligible for consideration to a permanent contractual assignment, excluding ministry to minors and others at risk. If he does not fulfill the elements in the aftercare contract, he will be removed from active ministry. This supervision is strict, as it should be, but at least it gives the priest hope.

When all concerned judge that their priest-client is ready to return to **restricted** ministry he should be given that opportunity by the religious order provincial or the ordinary of the diocese. It is noted that I speak of **restricted** ministry. The pedophile-priest should not be allowed to minister to young male persons twenty one years and younger, and, above all, not to males below the age of puberty.

From working with such priests during the last five years I have noted that whenever they have been faithful to the four conditions mentioned above, spiritual direction, regular therapy, con-

194

stant pastoral supervision, and attendance at spiritual support system meetings there have not been any relapses into any pedophilic activity. (As a matter of fact, in working with nine priests over the last several years, all of whom receive professional therapy, I have no record of any relapses. One other has not had a relapse since he joined a support group and received spiritual direction.) Admittedly, we all have more to learn about pedophilia, and I mean the sum total of knowledge we have from professionals in the field, but my experience of the past five years in which I have followed the progress of nine men closely, and several others at a distance, gives me reason to believe that such men deserve the opportunity to minister as priests in the Church, albeit in a restricted way.

While I have tried to get information from various centers for the rehabilitation of clergy I have received statistics from only one, and this despite a guarantee of anonymity and confidentiality.

One center sent me the following information as of September, 1989. "In the last five years we have treated 68 men whose primary problem has been sexual attraction to minors. Thus far 55 have completed treatment. Of these 55, 33 have returned to ministry. Sixteen are not in ministry on an involuntary basis. Two are voluntarily not in ministry, and four others have situations including jail." The director of this institute goes on to say that up to September, 1989 "there has been no known recurrence of sexual acting out with a minor for those treated priests we have in active follow-up. In fiscal 1989 96% of those eligible for aftercare workshops attended them."

The author of this report is not saying that no one will ever fall again: "Obviously at some point some individual will get in trouble gain, but how much certainty is reasonable and by extension legally defensible."[28]

(4) **Regular Attendance at Spiritual-Support Meetings**: No point is more stressed by those institutes dealing with pedophiles than regular attendance at group-support meetings.[29] It is also my personal experience in conducting such meetings for priests, as well as in receiving positive reports from clergy who regularly attend Sexaholic Anonymous or Sex Addicts and Love Anonymous meetings in our large cities. Important as individual spiritual direction may be, or individual contact with a professional

therapist, or external supervision of restricted ministry, the most important element in recovery remains The Twelve Steps.[30] In preparation for this presentation I have sought autobiographies from priest pedophiles, and no other element is more important than what these priests have gained from belonging to a group who share not only their helplessness, but also share their fellowship and hope. Before I submit my own suggestions, however, I would like to address some anticipated objections to the position that under certain conditions the priest pedophile ought to be restored to restricted ministry.[31]

Some Anticipated Objections To Restricted Ministry for Priests Who Have Gone Through Rehabilitation Programs:

1. If a bishop reassigns a priest who has gone through such a program, he is risking the financial patrimony of his diocese, because the bishop has no absolute guarantee that the priest will not relapse with dire financial consequences for the diocese. True, one can give no such guarantee in this situation anymore than one could give if the priest were an alcoholic, a drug addict, or a womanizer. But the risk can be reduced through the programs and means already proposed, and, furthermore, as one Attorney points out, returning the priest to the lay status would not insulate the Ordinary from suit in the event of future wrong doing. "My judgment is that the Ordinary is just as well protected if a program of no coverup, full disclosure, clergy and laity reporting, counseling, change of assignment following therapy, proper supervision, and continued therapy were implemented. Each case must be settled on its own facts."[32]

Already many lawsuits have been pursued, and many financial rewards given to families of victims. But the fact that so many bishops have taken necessary steps with regard to both the victim and the accused, that there is no coverup, and that the faithful know that the priest is sent to a program with the hope that he can still exercise his priesthood away from male youth will help the laity to understand that the Church is dealing with the situation in a just manner. It mist be admitted, however, that in the present climate of opinion, the hysteria of the media, the greediness of unscrupulous lawyers,and the fact that juries can be swayed to grant huge sums of money to victims of sexual abuse by a priest are sources of worry for every ordinary and religious order provincial.

196

2. **All persons who have sexual contact with children are true pedophiles**. We turn to the Diagnostic and Statistical Manual of Mental Disorders (DSM III) which describes pedophilia as follows: "The essential feature is the act or fantasy of engaging in sexual activity with prepubertal children as a repeatedly preferred or exclusive method of achieving sexual excitement. The difference in age between the adult with this disorder and the prepubertal child is arbitrarily set at ten years or more. For late adolescents with this disorder no precise age difference is specified."[33] In the strict sense pedophilia is a condition in which an adult has an enduring and at times almost exclusive sexual interest in children. But many individuals who have had sexual acts with children also have sexual acts with adults, or with teenagers, and it is very difficult to classify these persons. The growing literature on the subject indicates that there are many different views about the nature of pedophilia. For this reason one must be careful concerning the kind of therapy given, and the prognosis one makes to ecclesiastical superiors concerning a priest who has had sex with a child. We may not be dealing with pedophilia in the strict sense.

3. **Once a person acts out with children, he will continue to do so**. In responding to the above objection I have partially responded to number 3. But suppose a given priest were a true pedophile, I know of several priests who are such and who have not acted out since therapy in 1980 and 1981. One is engaged in many forms of ministry, but not with children or adolescents. The other has no ministry in his diocese, but hopes to be reinstated in some form of restricted ministry when his situation is considered by the appropriate authorities. Both have been faithful to a rigorous spiritual program.

4. **The disorder cannot be controlled**. Again, I make a distinction. Most of the "pedophile" priests I have worked with have had trouble with teenagers and not with persons under the age of puberty. It seems that such persons have less difficulty in controlling sexual impulses, but even with the strict case of pedophilia I have witnessed two priests leading chaste lives, and actively engaged in therapy, ministry, and 12 Step Programs.

Some Suggestions to Ecclesiastical Superiors

1. It is wise for a diocese to formulate in writing a policy to handle accusations of clerical misbehavior in regard to children, so

that the rights of all parties concerned are protected. Some dioceses have done that. One published it in the diocesan newspaper.

2. The canonical rights of accused religious and priests should be observed. It is very important that the pertinent canons be applied with due consideration of recent psychological knowledge which strongly indicates that in very many cases of pedophilia or of ephebophilia we are dealing with reduced imputability.

3. Where a cleric is accused of sexual contact with children it is necessary that professional psychiatric or psychological opinion be available. The evidence of clinicians and of institutes shows that generally in these situations the priest or cleric had a seriously diminished ability to control his actions. Certainly, the cleric should accept whatever professional help is offered by the diocese.

4. There are situations where the scandal was so great that it would be advisable for the cleric to petition for laicization. But most situations which I have encountered in several dioceses are not of this kind. Then the issue is whether the priest should be given a second chance to serve the diocese in restricted ministry. In the present climate of the Church forced laicization is not approved by Roman congregations, and the chances of a canonical trial bringing about laicization of the priest accused of pedophilia are indeed slim, if we apply canons 1322, 1323, and 1324.[34] It would seem best, then, that such a priest be restored to restricted ministry under the qualifications already mentioned. This policy, moreover, should be made known to the faithful, so that no one can accuse the bishop of "coverup."

5. I have had individuals say to me that when it comes to the situation of a priest involved with children or adolescents we should throw them in prison and lose the key. Will it not cause scandal, then, if we give such a priest a second chance? My response is that in the Christian understanding of life the greater scandal is to discard them as useless. Why do we apply standards of mercy and leniency to priests involved with alcohol, drugs, or women, and at the same time apply all kinds of pressure to persuade priests involved with children or adolescents to seek laicization? Are we not dealing with the same phenomena of compulsion in all these situation? Should we not try to help any priest who is willing to follow out a rigorous program of rehabilitation in order to be restored to priestly ministry? Yes, it is a challenge to all mem-

bers of the Church to encourage such priests not to give up. If this is our attitude, we need not fear scandal, except pharisaic. I remember the mother of a teen age boy who had accused a religious order brother of questionable conduct, not sexual molestation. The religious order sent the brother to a rehabilitation center. The mother, however, asked: "What will you do with him when he comes home?" I said he will be put to work again in a carefully supervised program. "Good," she said, "if I thought you were going to discard him, I would make trouble. After all, he is human."

One may ask what are the alternatives to giving such a priest another chance under qualified conditions. Persuade him to seek laicization? And if he refuses to do so, inform him that the bishop has no assignment for him, and therefore he should move out of clerical residence and find secular employment? What will this rejection do to his spirit? Does it make it more likely that he will not have a relapse when he feels that he is a total failure? Studies on sexual addiction indicate that a person's sense of being worthless is a primary ingredient in the continuation of the addiction. We have no certitude, moreover, that the laicization of a priest, or his removal from priestly ministry will give the diocese legal immunity in the event of future relapse, which in my judgment, is rendered more likely by such policies.

On the other hand, those who have been given another chance have been faithful to their programs, and have regained a sense to self-worth. Such is my pastoral experience. As I finish this paper I came across the opinion of the president and chief executive officer of St. Luke Institute in Suitland, Md.: "Physicians, psychiatrists, psychologists, and therapists all agree that treatment can make a difference. All of us who work from time to time with pedophiles believe this, too. Since we began treating some pedophiles four years ago, none has relapsed as far as we know. And with our after-care program we are in contact with most of them. We do believe the pedophile can manage his addiction. We do believe that risk can be reduced to the level of any situation where free will is involved. We do believe that people are redeemable."[35] Indeed I know priests who are faithful to the program, partly because they hope that they will be given another chance in the future. But even if that chance does not become actual, they want to remain chaste.

Conclusion: There are no easy answers to these problems made more complicated by new factors every day. It is so recent that the question of sexual addictions, including pedophilia, have been subject to scientific study. We need to seek more information on the progress of pastoral programs for priests who are recovering from these weaknesses. These priests need a seed of hope. They need our support and prayers.

As Father Keller put it: "Finally, it is the hallmark of the Christian to extend compassion and support to all those who are struggling or who are in need. The pedophiles in today's church are often the most despised, but also in the greatest need."[36]

Notes

1. Harper and Row, San Francisco, 1989, p. 1.

2. *Escape From Intimacy*, p. 1; *Out of the Shadows*, Compcare Publications, 1984, Minneapolis, Minn. p. 19.

3. Schaef, *op.cit.*, 1–2.

4. Gerald G. May, *Addiction and Grace*, New York, Harper and Row, 1988, p. 14.

5. As Rudolph Allers points out, "We cannot know anything about the nature of alleged irresistible impulses unless we know all we can find out about the total personality." Irresistible Impulses: A Question of Moral Psychology, *American Ecclesiastical Review* 100, 1939, 219.

6. Schaef, p. 3.

7. Shaef, p.5.

8. Shaef, p.6.

9. *Out of the Shadows*, p.4.

10. Carnes, *Contrary to Love*, 1989, 4–5.

11. Carnes, *Contrary to Love*, Compcare Publications, 2415 Annapolis Lane, Minneapolis, Mn., 55441, 4–7.

12. Charlotte Eliza Kasl, *Women and Sexual Addiction*, Minneapolis, Mn., 1984, pp. 5, 7, 8 quoted in Shaef, p.10.

13. Carnes, *op.cit.*, p. 52–55 at 55.

14. Carnes, *Contrary to Love*, p. 64.

15. Carnes, *ibid*, 65.

16. Carnes, *ibid*, p. 67–69.

17. Carnes, *ibid*, pp. 69–73.

18. Russell Smith, "Pedophilia" *Ethics and Medics*, Feb., 1990, vol. 15, no. 2., 3–4.

19. "Irresistible Impulses: A Question of Moral Psychology," *American Ecclesiastical Review 100* (1939), p. 219.

20. John Ford and Gerald Kelly, *Contemporary Moral Theology*, vol. 1, *Questions in Fundamental Moral Theology* (Westminster, Md., Newman Press, 1958) p. 230.

21. *The Diagnostic and Statistical Manual of Mental Disorders*, Third Edition (DSM III) p. 266.

22. Allers, *art. cit.*, pp. 216–217.

23. In an unpublished manuscript, "The Clergy in Court. Recent Developments Concerning Canonical Rights" Thomas P. Doyle, O.P., J.C.D., the author stresses the point that one may have sex with someone below the age of puberty, and not be a pedophile. One must repeat the distinction between the **condition** of pedophilia and a pedophilic **act**. Doyle believes that ecclesiastical authorities should consider that pedophiles have reduced ability for self control before residential therapy, and for this reason it would seem that such a disorder would significantly reduce imputability for a canonical crime.

24. Although 30 years old, *Contemporary Moral Theology*, vol. I, (John C. Ford, S.J. and Gerald Kelly, S.J.) Newman Press, Westminster, Md., 1959, contains much wisdom on the question of compulsion in its various degrees, and it has direct reference to addictions despite the fact that no one talked about sexual addictions then. Read chapter 11. "Freedom and Imputability Under Stress", pp. 201–247. The concluding observations ring a bell in my mind: "... Given the traditional conceptions of sufficient deliberation and sufficient consent, and given the psychological knowledge we now have as to emotional and instinctive obstacles to human acts, we are staying well within the bounds of theological requirements in concluding that we should judge much more leniently than we have in the past a great many individual cases of human misconduct and frailty." (247)

25. A prominent psychiatrist refuses to prescribe Depo-Provera, because of the lack of research on the short-term and long-term effects of the drug. He is of the opinion that the doctor prescribing D-P can be liable to suit in the future. Perhaps a written consent form should be used.

26. John F. Harvey, *The Homosexual Person*, Ignatius Press, 1987, chapter nine, "Psychological and Pastoral Reflections on Pedophilia" pp. 215–227 at 225.

27. Gerald May describes the spiritual growth of the addict and our threefold participation of prayer, meditation, and action in responding to God's grace. He also presents his own images of the mystery of grace. *Addiction and Grace*, pp. 91–139: *"The power of grace flows most fully when human will chooses to act in harmony with divine will"* (139) Italics author's.

28. Confidential Communication, October 3, 1989.

29. Patrick Carnes in *Contrary to Love*, pp. 151–186, shows how the sexual addict reclaims reality through the practice of the Twelve Step Program. Each step counters elements of the addictive system. He also explains the kind of spirituality found in the Steps. Ann Wilson Schaef, *Escape from Intimacy*, 143–149, adds other insights found in the Steps for the sexual addict.

30. In *The Priest*, "Some Thoughts on Priests and Pedophilia" February, 1990, Msgr. Robert Bacher stresses the importance of Group Support systems in the recovery process from sexual addictions: "Of greatest importance is the community of other priests who have the same problems, or at least other addictions, and the necessary interaction which takes place in small and large group activity." (49–51 at 51)

31. Eric Griffin Shelley, "The Clergy and Compulsive Sexual Behavior", *The Priest*, May, 1989, 40–45, gives an account of a priest-patient who has recovered from his sexual addiction and has been restored to priestly ministry. He continues to work with such priests.

32. Francis Mulligan, Civil Attorney, Reading, Pa., April 13, 1989, Memo Regarding Civil and Criminal Liability, p.3.

33. DSM III, p. 266.

34. Thomas Doyle, *op. cit.* The author cites other canons as well.

35. *Ibid.* p. 51.

36. Rev. G. Martin Keller, "The Pastoral Care of Pedophiles", *House of Affirmation Newsletter*, Spring, 1989, p.2.

Selective References

Robert Bacher, "Some Thoughts of Priests and Pedophilia" *The Priest*, February, 1990, 49–51.

John Bradshaw, Incest and Sexual Addiction, Three Tapes, Bradshaw Cassettes, Houston, TX 77098.

Patrick Carnes, *The Sexual Addiction*, Compcare Publications, 2415 Annapolis Lane, Minneapolis, MN., 1989.

——— *Contrary to Love*, Compcare Publications, 1989.

John C. Ford, and Gerald Kelly, *Contemporary Moral Theology*, vol. 1, Questions in Fundamental Moral Theology, Newman Press, Westminster, Md., 1959. Ch. 11 "Freedom and Imputability Under Stress" 201–247; and Ch. 12:1 "Juridical Aspects of Subjective Responsibility", 248–276.

Eric Griffin-Shelley, "The Clergy and Compulsive Sexual Behavior", *The Priest*, May, 1989, 40–45.

Benedict Groeschel, "Homosexuality and Pedophilia", Pope John Center Proceedings, 1989.

John F. Harvey, OSFS, *The Homosexual Person*, Ignatius Press, 1987, ch. 9. "Psychological and Pastoral Reflections on Pedophilia" 215–227.

Gerald G. May, *Addiction and Grace*, New York, Harper and Row, 1988.

Anne Wilson Shaef, *Escape From Intimacy*, Harper and Row, 1989.

Brenda Schaeffer, *Is it Love, or Is it Addiction?* Hazelden Publications, Pleasant Valley Road, PO Box 176, Center City, MN. 55012.

Russell Smith, "Pedophilia" *Ethics and Medics*, Feb., 1990, vol. 15, no. 2, pp. 3–4.

Unpublished Manuscript: Thomas P. Doyle, "The Clergy in Court: Recent Developments Concerning Canonical Rights."

John F. Harvey, OSFS, DIRECTOR OF COURAGE
ST. MICHAEL'S RECTORY, 424 W. 34 ST., N.Y., 10001, N.Y.
Tel: 212–421–0426

Chapter 13

PASTORAL CONCERNS ADDICTIONS

BISHOP: I would think that detection of a potential pedophile is horrendously important before ordination, Sister.

And I wonder, are there any salient personality features of a potential pedophile? If you were just talking with someone in your office, would you be able to detect that this person is a pedophile? A fellow who's drunk can't walk a straight line. Are there external lines of pedophilia?

SISTER WEBER: That is a very good and difficult question. If we refer back to some of the signs and symptoms that might be used as indicators, I would first point out that these men are much more comfortable with young children. They will try to look for opportunities to be with young children. They will be less comfortable with adults. Try to observe social interactions amongst seminarians in the refectory or classroom.

Seminarians should be encouraged to speak about sexual issues, as well as about their fears and their life desires. In the seminary setting, this could help promote a healthy sociosexual development. In the process, other content may surface that would provide initial indicators about those who may be troubled with urges to molest children. A seminarian's reluctance or inability to discuss human sexuality in a mature fashion, or a preoccupation with children should be explored further.

In addition, it might be helpful to take notice of how seminarians respond to assignments or requests made of them. Their response or lack of it may be an authority problem or it may be suggestive of other developmental issues that might need to be addressed. What are they doing with their free time? How much unstructured time are they given during seminary formation and what is to be gained from unstructured time? Is it productive for their development or do they use it to sneak off and molest children? Today, these are questions and issues that have to be addressed.

BISHOP: There's no instant way to tell.

SISTER WEBER: Unfortunately, no. Direct questioning is not often fruitful but we have to become more comfortable with questions regarding sexual deviancy in order to begin to screen for these problems. You could start out by asking, "do you ever have fantasies of being molested?" "Have you ever had fantasies of molesting another?" If they respond in the positive to either question, a supportive, nonjudgmental response could encourage further self-disclosure. Other questions might include: "Have you ever acted out your urges to fondle children" "Do you feel as if there is no one to speak to about this? Do you have to keep this in hiding?"

Sometimes, direct questioning is too threatening and asking questions in the third person is more comfortable. For example, "Do you know of anyone who was sexually molested? What was their story? What happened to them? What seemed to be that individual's fear about this?" Our goal is not to punish or threaten, but to help these individuals receive proper treatment.

FATHER HARVEY: I certainly agree with Sister on the need for some kind of good sex education in seminary. I've done workshops in seminaries and I find that if you present the material in a certain way then some people who have trouble may come forth and seek help. What I've noticed in many seminaries is that they're afraid to talk about the issue of sexuality because they're afraid that if this gets to those in charge of the seminary, they will be thrown out. They're terribly afraid and they have to have some way in which they're encouraged to talk to someone about their difficulties.

There is a woman, Dr. Maria Valdez, who is in the New York area who has been to seminars on several occasions and has given workshops together with myself. The result has been that people will go and talk with her further about their own sexual situations. They have to be encouraged to seek help without having external authority come down and say, "look, if you had to see someone like Dr. Maria Valdez, a clinical psychologist, you'd better leave because there must be something wrong with you." I think we handle it best by a workshop in which we really discuss sexuality, heterosexuality, homosexuality, the meaning of celibacy.

And in regard to my own work with Courage, I'm working with people over the age of twenty-five and at the present moment I don't have anyone whom I would classify as a pedophile in either the strict sense or the sense of the regressed pedophile.

The priests I work with present a different situation. Of the five I work with regularly, four out of five have difficulties with teenagers. One did have difficulties with those below the age of twelve and I was convinced that he was a pedophile in the strict sense and I sent him to a psychiatrist. The psychiatrist also said he was a pedophile. He had been involved in pedophilic acts. But other elements such as the motivation for fixated pedophilia in the sense of the constant compulsion and fantasies and recurrent activity, were not present. What he really needed was to learn better how to relate to adults which he has been doing and he has not had any failures in eight years.

That's what I'm driving at there.

You might say I'm getting people in the "postpartum" situation. You're talking about a potential situation when you asked Sister that question, Bishop.

BISHOP: Sister, you mentioned Depo Provera. I know it as a contraceptive. It is medically forbidden in the States but it is often sent and sold in third world countries like ours. Is that the same substance?

SISTER WEBER: I do believe that some third world countries use progesterone as a contraceptive. Yes, Depo-Provera is a synthetically produced progesterone.

BISHOP: Sister, on the question of interviewing young men who might be interested in the priesthood, it seems to me we've got to be sneakier than they are.

In any kind of an interview, if they have even the slightest suspicion that something that happened to them in their childhood or even fantasies, may exclude them they'll do their best to conceal it.

Some of these people really feel called to the priesthood and they're going to protect that call. They think, "I know it's not going to happen again and I know that God's grace is sufficient and all that kind of denial and rationalization. I think to get involved in a direct or even an indirect interview would be fruitless in 99 percent of the cases.

SISTER WEBER: We have to start somewhere. Unless the issue is directly addressed, we will find ourselves falling into the same pattern of avoidance of the topic that we are struggling with today. Responses of denial and rationalization will be given by some individuals whether the question of pedophilia is addressed directly or indirectly. By asking the questions openly, it is best communicated to the seminarians that this is an area of concern which requires clarification in order that they continue in their priestly formation. If a seminarian hides information which is later disclosed, this places the Church in a very different position of responsibility than if the issue was never directly approached.

Over time, one becomes more easeful with asking questions regarding sexuality and with discovering the cues of sexually deviant behavior. This will allow for earlier intervention and treatment if necessary. Earlier detection will hopefully also facilitate earlier determination of whether or not a man has the emotional capacity to become an ordained priest.

True pedophiles, whether fixated or regressed type, suffer from immature and obsessive thought patterns in which they psychologically align themselves with a child object as if the child is an extension of themselves. They desire to be nurtured by that object. This bespeaks a woundedness of a psychological arrest. Even though such a man may say he feels a call to the priesthood, he has to be asked and tested about what motivates him to seek the priesthood. The priesthood could be a respected and opportunistic position in which to molest children. It is critical to ask questions regarding sexuality in hope of bringing the issues to the surface. If an individual responds defensively, this is something to watch. If someone avoids answering questions regarding sexual deviancy and appears threatened by such questions, this could be another clue to underlying pathology. You will then have to evaluate such an individual more extensively. If he is a pedophile, he is suffering deeply and needs professional help.

As described earlier, pedophiles do not have the capacity to make a conscious free will choice. Obsessive urges to molest children pervade their thought processes. Such thoughts are present as they perform their day to day activities. A fixated pedophile has no insight into the inappropriateness of his behavior; a regressed pedophile can alternate between urges to molest children and guilty feelings about his behavior. Even with some insight, however, fear of the ramifications of such behavior, if discovered, often results in the regressed pedophile's not seeking treatment of his own free will.

FATHER HARVEY: I agree with Sister and I think that what the Bishop says about the interview being tricky, I quite agree with that too. The person will be on the defensive so I feel that while we have to help them get at the root of where they are that the better method has to be an unthreatening method such as a workshop in which we talk about human sexuality in all its phases and then point out to them that there are people available to help them if they want to talk about their own specific difficulties. This would be a matter of confidence between them and the particular therapist.

Even that approach has its drawbacks in many respects in that there are some individuals who are bound and determined they're going to move toward the priesthood and they may not reveal to the therapist all of the truth that they should. In fact, in many instances, they are not even aware of it at this particular time. For some of the priests I've worked with, the seminary days were a kind of peaceful period when they didn't seem to be aware of their own difficulty. What Sister said about their proclivity to be with children, if that had been noticed that would certainly be something which the superior or rector or the teacher could take note of and ask questions about. But oftentimes, it's not noticed. An individual is not aware of himself and then he's ordained to the priesthood and this suddenly begins to come up.

BISHOP: Sister, you mentioned that 30 percent of pedophiles say that they were molested as children. Is that part of the denial or part of blaming or would that percentage be true of the rest of the population?

SISTER WEBER: It is a rough estimate. The estimate was extrapolated from the studies that have been done on individuals who were themselves physically abused and who then became physical abusers. It is very hard to get accurate numbers.

With some pedophiles, if they were molested as children, and the experience was not overtly perceived as traumatic, they might assess the sexual fondling as having been a way of being nurtured or loved. If the experience was frightening or negative, the experience might still have been used by the child victim as an effective way to at least receive some attention from a parental figure. In the latter case, when that victim child becomes the "powerful" adult and no longer has to tolerate being a victim, he tries to retaliate by becoming the aggressive child molester. This is called, "identification with the aggressor". Retaliatory maneuvers bespeak the emotional immaturity of someone who has pedophilia.

BISHOP: Well, 30 percent say that they were molested as children. Have we any kind of a "guesstimate" what percentage of the population in general were molested?

SISTER WEBER: The studies at this time vary so much that good statistics are not readily available.

BISHOP: Father, in your long work with priests with homosexual problems, have you seen a difference in the profile of priests who are homosexual and acting out and priests who are acting out with adolescent men, boys? Is there a difference in the profile of those two groups?

FATHER HARVEY: Yes, there is. But before I get into that, I'd like to mention a very useful set of tapes by John Bradshaw of Houston, Texas which deals with sexual addiction and incest and he gives a figure—talking about incest in America, he gives statistics that about 34 million American women have suffered some type of sexual abuse as children. He claims that this kind of sexual abuse is much more prevalent than people are willing to admit because the individual who goes through this, as Sister has pointed out earlier, tends to deny that it ever happened so that probably the figure is higher.

Now with regard to your question, yes, I would say there is a difference in profiles I've worked with homosexual priests for about eleven years in northern Virginia at Missionhurst, 250 priests and brothers. I would say that the difference in the profile that the ordinary homosexual priest who had acted out, acted out with adults, and definitely did not or only very rarely had anything to do with a teenager. Now, I'm working with a small group of people. I'm talking about nine people. The chief characteristic has been acting out with teenagers. Are there any pronounced differences in personality traits as I observed them in the various meetings that they have attended? I would have to say no, I don't see, except for the behavior itself. But what I do notice in one, particularly, who I felt was a pedophile but I was told by the psychiatrist he was not. I felt he had to learn how to relate to other adults much better than he had in the past.

So I don't see much difference at the present moment between the two groups except that one was engaged principally with teenagers, the other principally with adults.

SISTER WEBER: I would like to comment on Father Harvey's distinction between a pedophile and somebody who predominantly molests teenagers. One who predominantly molests teenagers is not a pedophile and the dynamics of this type of individual are different than that of a true pedophile. Also, the treatment of these individuals would be different. We have to be very careful not to equate the two. Otherwise, we are lumping all the sexual deviancies together which compromises appropriate intervention and treatment.

When I recommended laicization, I was recommending this for individuals who have true pedophilia. I would not recommend this for someone who is predominantly acting out with adolescent girls, for example. In this latter case, the acting out might be an unresolved issue regarding his masculinity; unresolved authority issues, and so forth. A man who is solely active with adolescent girls would have a better prognosis with appropriate intervention as he would not typically have the regressed obsessive thoughts that drive pedophiles. The importance of an accurate diagnosis is critical because the diagnosis will determine the most effective treatment, and ultimately, it will determine the best placement for the individual in question.

I have a concern that unless we can overcome our hesitancy to discuss with the seminarians, their sexual concerns, that we will allow fear to be a prime motivation leading to avoidance of addressing potential problems of sexual deviancy. Our goal should be to dispel fear regarding sexuality and its potential deviancies. If someone truly has pedophilia and this is discovered, then I think something needs to be done. We have an obligation for the Salvation of these men. We must compassionately move them out of a situation where they cannot function as ministerial priests.

By comparison, take the example of someone who has a psychotic disorder and who wants to become a priest, but is bothered by delusional thoughts which hinder his capacity to concentrate even when he is trying very hard to function normally. To leave such an individual in the setting where he has difficulty functioning is not a service to anyone concerned.

BISHOP: My limited experience with priests who have been guilty of sexual abuse leads me to ask this question: Have you noticed among priests who have this difficulty a gift for manipulation? They seem to be able to control a situation, to control even their fellow priests or lay people, to always seem to be kind of popular because they do things that always result to their advantage.

FATHER HARVEY: First of all, before I answer your question, I'm very, very grateful for Sister bringing out that point about activity with teenagers not being pedophilia in the strict sense. The difficulty, the confusion arises because under the law in most of our states, any kind of an activity with someone under the age of eighteen is considered pedophilia and there's all kinds of liability so some bishops are in real trouble. That's why, perhaps, I'm having good success with the people I'm working with because they are not truly pedophiles. I think that helps lessen the differences between Sister and myself with regard to some of those issues.

But now to pick up the question about manipulation, I agree thoroughly that there's a great deal of manipulation that goes on. As a matter of fact, one of them used to tell me how he would ingratiate himself with the family and, usually, the acts take place with religious families, see. They manipulate themselves into the good graces of the family and then something begins to happen.

SISTER WEBER: Your Excellency, what you describe is inherent to what is called a maladaptive personality trait. The maladaptive behaviors of such an individual are often more bothersome to the public at large or to those who live with him than these traits are bothersome to the individual himself. What bothers the individual is not his own behavior, rather, the fact that others are complaining about his behavior. To avoid this, the individual develops more patterns of deviousness similar to what you are describing. This is experienced by us as manipulation, denial, and rationalization.

What you are astutely picking up, Bishop, is a mental attitude that is inherent to pedophilia which is very difficult to deal with. By themselves, pedophiles often do not understand the inappropriateness of their behavior.

This is why I recommend that being very direct with these people is the safest way to communicate the fact that in considering the priesthood, they have to be responsible for their actions. If an individual has the potential to begin to change his behaviors, he first has to understand the inappropriateness of his behavior and have the capacity to responsibly address his actions.

BISHOP: It had seemed to me that the big divergence between the two presentations this afternoon reside in the hope for successful therapy in the matter of pedophilia. Father, I'm not too sure now if you were speaking of real pedophilia in your very sanguine approach. I thought, Sister, you were very direct and excluded any possibility, any real hope for a real pedophile to return to ministry. It seemed that there was a great difference on that whole question of a priest returning after being convicted and our risk of liability.

SISTER WEBER: I do not believe that someone who has true pedophilia can truly function within a restricted ministry. If that individual is a fixated pedophile, he is obsessed with the desire to molest a child. He is constantly thinking about this whether or not he is in the presence of a child. If he is of the regressed type, guilt, shame, and self-doubt prevail in a ruminative fashion.

The restrictive ministry for a pedophile would be similar to placing a toddler in a room by himself in which we would constantly have to watch what he is doing so as to keep him from inadvertently hurting himself because he is ruled primarily by his desires. His interests would lead him to pull on an electric cord or knock down the coffeemaker. How soon before the brass lamp comes crashing down on his interested head? Similarly, restricted ministry would be psychically stressful for a pedophile due to the constant need for vigilant monitoring. Continuing with our analogy, if alternatively, we move the toddler out of an environment which had to be restricted, for example, we stripped the room of everything that could harm him, and then placed him in there with professional help so that he could potentially begin to explore and discover who he is and what he is about in a more free and healthy manner. This would be a much more therapeutic and compassionate intervention for someone who suffers with pedophilia. This could not happen for the pedophile while remaining the priesthood. There are too many situations in which he would need to be monitored and restricted to protect him and others from his deviant sexual urges. He could never come to the freedom of his own self-control.

Perhaps one more example would help. If an individual is a pilot and he develops a seizure disorder, he will no longer be able to fly the plane himself. He has completed his training and proved himself as a pilot, but the seizure disorder was not discovered or disclosed until after he completed the program. For his sake and certainly, for his passengers sake, you would not allow him to continue to fly. He has to find another profession that is appropriate to his skills and takes into account his disability. In likeness, a priest-pedophile should not be returned to ministry which he does not have the capacity to fulfill with a level of obligation inherent to the sacramental priesthood.

FATHER HARVEY: I think that several members of St. Luke's Hospital in Washington would disagree with Sister with regard to these matters from their particular work with the pedophiles. There is a controversy going on here and different opinions. I also think that there are very different degrees of pedophilia and a whole lot more we need to know about it. I certainly agree that the lower the age of the child the poorer the prognosis.

I think Father Benedict Groeschel made that point here last year and I wonder do we really have a full and clear picture of a true pedophile now. Why is it that some of the individuals who seem to be in that category seem to be able to overcome it? I'm puzzled by the situation of a a priest in one of the religious orders. This

212

particular priest was accused of taking two ten-year old boys to some hotel and photographing them in the nude and he had this proclivity towards children of that age. Apparently that was his one act.

This particular priest was put back in ministry after being at John Hopkins and he has done well for the last eight years. He had all the signs of pedophilia it seems in the sense of the proclivity toward children, yet, he's doing well. I'm puzzled by that. If it's not possible, how come he's able to do it. That's my particular dilemma at this particular moment. It may be that many others are not able to do it.

I also think that in so many instances, we're too quick to categorize persons as pedophiles and maybe that has been part of my difficulty in understanding this whole subject. But it seems to me that where there has been activity with a teenager which is pedophilia in either the broad or loose sense according to Sister's definitions. But she did say that with regard to the regressed pedophile that there was more hope than there was for the fixated pedophile. But I feel, Sister, that after having made that distinction earlier in your talk, you never returned to that distinction again, so that throughout the rest of the talk it seems that you were talking almost exclusively about the fixated pedophile rather than the regressed pedophile who from my understanding, because of the stress performs an action with a child below the age of puberty. But if that's only occasional, it would seem that with therapy, he might have a better chance.

SISTER WEBER: I would like to clarify again the fact that both the regressed and the fixated pedophile are always going to have a propensity to act out according to their deviant sexual desires. Statistically, there is more hope for the regressed pedophile because he has a higher level of functioning. But statistically, it has been shown that the regressed pedophile will eventually relapse if he is not in continuous treatment.

The studies have shown that relapse is almost to be expected. However, thorough evaluation of an individual who seems to have been involved in one isolated "pedophilic act", as cited by Father Harvey, is critical, because some like that may not be a pedophile. It would be a tragedy to label somebody as having pedophilia when they do not have this disorder which has no known cure.

FATHER HARVEY: You seem to make the point that the pedophile, as such, lacks the capacity for the priesthood which would mean that this ordination would be invalid. Is that what you were saying?

SISTER WEBER: What I said is that they lack the capacity to make a conscious, free will choice. Their capacity is hindered. There is a demonstrable psychic defect in their capacity to reason.

FATHER HARVEY: Is that capacity to reason so pervasive it affects all the areas of life? I mean, for example, you made the point that there have been no studies of priests pedophiles so far. As far as therapeutic programs are concerned for priests, there are no studies so far made. Could it not be that the priest, the so-called pedophile, that he has a kind of motivation which makes a difference? And could not one say that a person could not be free in certain of his actions, but free in the decision to become a priest?

SISTER WEBER: I do not recall saying that there are no studies on priest-pedophiles, I do know that formal studies are scarce in relation to the priesthood.

Regarding free choice, there is such pervasiveness of the pedophile's deviant sexual desires over his psyche that those same desires also invade the control of his behavior and his capacity to reason in a multidimensional fashion. That is by definition what these men suffer with. Canon 1401 speaks of a psychic defect and a hindered capacity to reason. If an individual cannot reflect on his behavior and its appropriateness or inappropriateness, then this demonstrates a psychic defect. The fixated pedophile feels that he had done nothing wrong. The regressed pedophile is reluctant to admit the deviancy of his behavior and battles with intense denial and rationalization responses. This intense, inner battle can drive him into a state of stress which is alleviated for him by a repetition of the pedophilic behavior.

FATHER HARVEY: Well, I still have my difficulty, Sister. Some of these individuals who are pedophiles seem to have some degree of freedom and some psychologists feel they do. So that's where I am. I can't go any further.

BISHOP: I have sent seminarians as candidates to various seminaries, John XXXIII in Boston for adults. We send seminiarians to the seminary, the Grand Seminary in Montreal for those who speak sufficient French and are able, therefore, in the future to serve in

214

two languages. We've sent them to St. Peter London, Ontario. I also have them in St. Paul in Ottawa.

All these seminaries insist on their own testing, psychological testing. They have their own battery of tests and, usually, when they report back to the bishop to find out what their discoveries have been concerning these various individuals, none of the seminaries so far have indicated anything that might touch on sex identification, whether they're homosexuals or not or whether they have ever been involved in any devious sexual activities. And they, certainly, have never indicated that a candidate might be a pedophile. So we're at a little bit at a loss.

My own experience with professional psychiatrists or clinical psychologists regarding candidates to the priesthood or potential candidates, is that they've not divulged anything that they might have come across in their testing relative to sexual identity or anything dealing with sex actions. So we've always been a little bit at a loss when it comes time to decide whether a candidate should be accepted. If we accept it on the basis of the reports, well, obviously, they always emphasize the positive.

Father Harvey, if you were a bishop and you had clear evidence that the candidate or potential candidate was a homosexual, would you accept him as a candidate to the seminary?

FATHER HARVEY: The first question I would want to ask is how did I get this evidence that he's homosexual. If the evidence that I had was that he had been acting out, I would not accept him for the seminary.

Now, I suppose the other kind of evidence would be if the man himself told you, if he came out and said, you know, I have homosexual proclivities and I've had to struggle against them and I've been working hard on them. I'm talking to a psychologist or a psychiatrist about this. I want to be a priest and I've led a chaste life not only externally but he's free of the habit of masturbation. I think in the second case I would want to know more I'd ask him to give his therapist permission to discuss the matter with me to see what the therapist thinks in terms of a prognosis about this particular man. If he were not willing to do that, then I would not accept him.

I think the seminary has a right to knowledge in those particular instances and if you have that kind of evidence and have hesitation, you have the right to decide that you're not going to accept a homosexual into your seminary. Others may take a different view of that, but my point is that you have a right to knowledge and oftentimes if he's seeing a therapist, what might be involved here are other factors in that person's life which would constitute a poor prognosis for studying for the priesthood. I know there's great controversy here. There's a whole group of bishops in one part of the country who will not accept anyone with a homosexual orientation in the United States. Others take a different view.

SISTER WEBER: Regarding your comment, Your Excellency, that those who have professionally assisted you in providing psychological testing, did not reveal the resultant information to you— this saddens me, as it defeats the purpose of their professional intervention. This places you and the pedophile back to square one. There has to be a professional understanding that is established ahead of the testing, regarding what you expect as a result of the testing and evaluation. The information has to be shared otherwise it is not going to be useful to the priest-candidate nor to those who would have ultimate obligation for him if he entered the seminary and was ordained.

It is true that there is no one test that will reveal pedophilia. Dr. Freidrich of Mayo Clinic tested known pedophiles with the MMPI. 60% of those tested, showed a normal MMPI profile. One test does not currently provide the desired clarifications. However, because the disorder is complex, a series of tests and a commitment to monitoring will be necessary to unravel its signs and symptoms. At this time, we know that part of the unraveling can occur thorough directed questioning and psychological interviews, observations, followed up by appropriate sharing of the information with those in a position to help these men. Any suspicion must be followed up with further evaluations and interventions.

BISHOP: I want to go back to the question, about receiving back a man into active ministry who has been under therapy for pedophilia or some other sexual difficulty. It seems to me, Father Harvey, that counselors and therapists like yourself who do such admirable work are very concerned about rehabilitating the person, restoring them to a good self image and good mental and emotional health so that they can return, that your objective centers around the good of the individual whereas, a bishop or religious

216

superior has to take it from a different point of view. While we're certainly concerned with the good of the individual, we also have to be concerned with the common good and the way in which our people and the public at large view a priest who has been convicted of pedophilia or some other sexual problem. And, also, we have to consider our own presbyterate.

Although they have much love and compassion for a brother who has a problem, the presbyterate will feel that we should not take that person back because that person continues to give our presbyterate a bad name.

It is also harmful to the priesthood itself and to recruiting good vocations into the priesthood.

So Bishops have to view the possibility of receiving this priest back, I think, from a different perspective than you would have and that could often lead us to a very different conclusion than you would make.

FATHER HARVEY: I realize the position in which you are as a bishop and that restoration of a man who has gone through a program and has practiced virtue for a number of years remains a calculated risk, I recognize, too, that the other priests have their view of things, but I, also, know from talking to other priests in one diocese where several people are out of the service at the present moment that the other priests would like to see them back in some kind of ministry.

Scandal is certainly a factor which would have to be handled. In one diocese where they have a policy of allowing a priest to come back under restricted conditions, they make it known that he's coming back. There's no coverup with regard to the public or the other priests. So it's a judgment call, and certainly, you have to make that kind of a call. Some bishops may feel that they could take the man back. Others feel that under the circumstances they may not and I'm not making any judgment about that. I respect your point of view. I know the terrible financial liabilities that dioceses can be threatened with and I understand the other factors too.

But the question of scandal cuts both ways. If you take a man who is willing to come back and has done everything he can and you put him on the sidelines completely when he could do some restricted ministry, then people may feel that you're not giving them the opportunity which people may feel they ought to have. I remember in one case of a brother in a religious order, not a priest, who was accused of sexual indiscretion. There was no action. But he was accused by a teenager and when he was sent to his superiors they decided to send him down to St. Luke's. I saw the sixteen-year-old and I saw the parents as I sometimes do. I do some troubleshooting. And after we had been in there a while, the mother came to see me again and she says, "what's going to happen to brother so and so?" I say, "When he comes out we'll give him some kind work, a supervised ministry and work within the Order, the congregation where he happens to be." And she said, "Good. I thought if you were going to discard him, I'll make a public issue of it." So, the whole question does cut both ways.

SISTER WEBER: From the medical and psychiatric information that we currently have, we know that these individuals suffer tremendously. Their obsessiveness and the guilt that is so pervasive in their personality style, drives them to try to isolate out that part of themselves. They often deny this part of themselves to themselves and to others. The capacity for self-reflection is diminished. They have to rely upon us, to see them as they are and to respond to their lack of self-control in a compassionate professional manner.

If a priest truly has pedophilia, it is not accurate to consider the difficulty he has with his free will when confronted with obsessive compulsive urges to molest children as being analogous to whether he is free to walk across a street, for example. A free will decision of an adult, as I am referring to it, has to do with consciousness at a higher level of awareness than such "freedom" to perform basic tasks.

At this time, there is no known cure for either the regressed or the fixated pedophile. Treatment in either case is palliative and statistics predict that a pedophile who leaves intensive treatment will likely relapse.

With that risk in mind, we cannot forget the victims. We have to remind ourselves of the effect to the child victim. Not only is the child a victim to sexual molestation, but when such victimization is performed by a ministerial priest, the psychological and spiritual trauma incurred are potentially greater and therefore, potentially more difficult to treat. Such potential risks might better be the focus of any consideration of scandal.

BISHOP: And at the present time, I guess you could say, the public media is doing a very good snowjob on the Church because we are completely absorbed in this issue. So I was very happy today to hear expressions like our addictive society, a society that generates addictive processes in us.

And in that respect, manipulation, addiction, compulsion marks economic activity, political activity, family activity, even our relationship with the environment is marked with a certain addictiveness.

Maybe it's time for us as leaders in the Church, in light of the Gospel, to get the searchlight going in the other direction. At the present time, we're being demolished by society. We should be putting the searchlight on society with regard to things. So I'd like you to give us some suggestions out of your experience on how we may turn this thing around from a PR standpoint as far as the Church is concerned.

FATHER HARVEY: There's a book which I read recently by a psychiatrist name Gerald May called "Grace and Addiction". He makes the points which you just made, Your Excellency, and he goes on to point out that we can begin to change our own lifestyle individually, change family lifestyle. He talks about the need to bring the whole notion of God's Love and Redemption into family life and teaching people—this is the principal theme of his book—teaching people how to freely love. He sees addiction as attachment to desire and that attachment to desire makes you a slave to whatever that object is and reduces your whole area of freedom.

He's using his theory in his therapy in the Washington, D.C. area, to get people to begin to truly become free in light of the Gospel message and to have a deeper understanding of Supernatural Grace working in their life.

We oftentimes say, "there goes the media again and the media has perverted or distorted the message of the Gospel and they make us look "silly" and all this sort of thing.

We need to change our very lifestyles and get down to the practice of virtue and learn the true meaning of Christian detachment. That would be a little help but it's not going to change the world around.

SISTER WEBER: I think that we as Catholics need to be a model for a world that is very troubled today. We need to be very clear and consistent in our convictions. Our actions must be consistent with our convictions. We need to clearly delineate between what we are going to accept as being who we are as priests and religious and we need to be clear about what we will and will not accept.

Rather than fear society's response to laicization of those priests who suffer with pedophilia, or the scandal or liability this presents for the Church, our focus would better be directed toward fear of the Lord which seeks to preserve the dignity of the grace of the sacramental priesthood and the obligation for the Salvation of those men who suffer with pedophilia as well as for the Salvation of their victims.

PART III

"CHRISTIAN" ETHICS AND SOCIETY

Chapter 14

THE NATURAL MORAL LAW AND FAITH

John Finnis, D.Phil.

I. What norms, if any, does revelation teach?

Did the divine public revelation in Jesus Christ include any definitive moral teaching?

Thesis A. Revelation does definitively propose both moral principles and specific moral norms, not merely as positive laws of the ecclesiastical community but as permanent truths about human good, human destiny and human moral responsibilities.

Thesis B. Revelation was never concerned to teach, whether by confirmation or introduction, any truths about the content of specific moral principles and norms. It leaves intact the role of unaided reason in identifying which moral principles and norms (of the natural moral law) are true for each stage of human history.

Some influential theologians propose thesis B, as follows.

Revelation's role *de moribus* is to provide new motivation.[1] Accordingly, the Church's moral mission is to reaffirm those "transcendental" or "formal" principles—love of God and neighbor, justice, mercy—which orient us towards God and our human brothers and sisters, articulating the essentially Christian motivations for all other moral judgments and behavior. *These* general principles the Church can teach definitively, but they settle no specific moral questions in today's complex societies. There are no infallibly proposed moral teachings, because even solemn definitions *de moribus* could not definitively settle the truth about any concrete moral *quaestio disputata*.

True, the Church teaches specific moral norms about e.g. killing, sexual activity, etc. But such teachings can never be definitive. They only reinforce, for each era, the norms and policies which, in the prevailing conditions, seem likely to promote the humanization required by morality's general principles. As human experience grows, the Church changes the specifics of her moral teachings (retaining always the vision of love of God and neighbor). The Church today admits this of her "social teaching", and should admit it of her (other) specific moral teachings: they are the Church's current judgment of what is humanly practically reasonable, not truths of faith.

Critically understood, the divine word proposes no specific evaluations as permanently valid. What behavior contributes to human advancement must be evaluated by human *ratio* in, or for, specific contexts. This practical reasoning yields generalizations which can be called norms of natural law, valid *as generalizations*, for (and only for) *similar contexts*.

Such, then, is thesis B. I shall argue that it does justice neither to revelation nor to reason. Part II indicates thesis A's theological sources, and part III offers some explanatory reflections on them. Part IV takes up the arguments for thesis B, and part V considers its appeal to many Catholics.

II. Revelation's own testimony

The contents of the divine revelation completed in Jesus are settled not by unaided reason, but by God's choice to disclose himself and his wise intentions for humankind.[2]

224

"By this revelation the invisible God, out of the fullness of his love, speaks to men as his friends and dwells with them, in order to invite and receive them into society with him." (*Dei Verbum* 2). Every true practical implication of that convenantal *societas* with God in Christ is a moral norm: indeed, that is what a Christian moral norm precisely is. For this reason, too, revelation's content must be settled by God's initiative.

What, then, is proposed to us in revelation about revelation's relationship to reason *de moribus?*

As *Romans* says, God's eternal power and deity are knowable from "created things" (1:19-20), amongst which are human hearts inscribed with moral requirements known in conscience — so that Gentiles who do not have God's revealed law "do by nature what the Law requires" (2:14-15). In other words, moral truths which the Gentiles know, truths of natural law, are included in God's revealed law. *Romans* later (13:8-10) makes it clear that the law which Christian love fulfills centers on the Commandments.

Jesus identified observance of the Commandments as a condition for eternal life (*Matt.* 19:16-20; *Mk.* 10:17-19; *Lk.* 18:18-21). He articulated no rounded moral system, but strategic and exemplary moral truths[3] to be drawn out by the Church, just as she "develops" his other teachings.[4] His moral teaching was at its most specific in defining true marriage's indissolubility, by reference to the commandment, the specific moral absolute, against adultery; and it is precisely here that Jesus stated his moral teaching's grounding in the order of creation.[5]

So the earliest Christian philosophers and systematic theologians had solid grounds for calling the Decalogue's precepts (at least its second table) natural moral law.[6] These revealed norms are also rational, available to any conscience not blinded by sin.[7] And they guide us towards human fulfillment, by disclosing God's plan for our sharing in his glorious kingdom.[8]

Aquinas comments on *Hebrews* 5:12 ("You need someone to teach you again the rudiments of the oracles of God"): "the rudiments, the first principles and elements of the oracles of God are the *articula fidei et praecepta decalogi.*"[9] In the generation before Trent, John Driedo of Louvain sums up the common teaching:

The teachings of natural and moral philosophy, just insofar as they are entertained by philosophers or by peoples, have nothing to do with faith. Yet, many of those teachings are *de necessitate fidei,* insofar as they are demonstrable from sacred scripture, either expressly or by tacit implication.... Thus, for example, it is heresy persistently to assert that adultery, or theft, or false testimony are not wrongful.[10]

Trent itself forcefully recalled Christian faith's bearing on Christian life, i.e. Christian morals. Conversion's last stage is the resolve to "keep the divine commandments" (D-S 1526); Christ charged his apostles with teaching those commandments (D-S 1527). Keeping them is essential if faith is not to be dead and fruitless (D-S 1531); no one is exempt (D-S 1536, 1570) and it is heresy to call their observance impossible (D-S 1536, 1568).[11]

There are moral dogmas (*pace* many theologians today):[12] in a definitive mode, Trent anathematized certain moral teachings.[13]

Vatican II reaffirms all Vatican I's relevant teachings, along with all Trent's teachings on the relationship between revelation and natural law. A summary, using Vatican II's terms:

Those eternal decrees of God's will (*DV* 6) which are our supreme norm (*DH* 3) include requirements *per se* accessible to human understanding (i.e. natural law) (*DH* 3)[14] but, in the fallen human condition, known with firm certitude and uncorrupted accuracy only from revelation (*DV* 6 and 7; *DH* 3; citing Vat. I, D-S 3004-5).[15] This revelation, completed in Christ, is the source of *all* moral teaching and includes everything conducive to the holiness of life of God's people (*DV* 8; citing Trent, D-S 1501). It can be taught definitively, whether by definitions or by the universal ordinary magisterium (*LG* 25, citing Vat. I, D-S 3011, 3074).[16]

III. On the necessity and appropriateness of moral revelation.

Why has the Church authority to identify truths of *natural* moral law? And how can human nature, which we seem to know only as fallen, ground moral truth? The ultimate answer is Vatican II's: revelation's very heart is Jesus Christ who "fully reveals man to man himself" (*GS* 22).[17] In Jesus, human nature is revealed as it ought to be.[18]

"Christ, the new Adam, in the very revelation of the mystery of the Father and His love, fully reveals man to man himself *and brings to light his most high calling*" (*GS* 22). Revelation is strictly necessary because humankind's supreme calling is to a supernatural fulfillment.[19] Moral norms are the requirements of an appropriate human response to that calling.

And humankind, having in Adam rejected the divine gift promised in that calling, needs redemption. True moral humanism demands that our humanity be understood as it really is: fallen, redeemed, called to glory. Our choices and actions should be attentive to the realities of our situation and our true opportunities, only fully disclosed by revelation.

So: (1) Ways of acting unappealing to unaided reason become attractive to a reason enlightened by Christian faith and hope. For example, a non-reciprocal and vulnerable love (going beyond respect) of enemies: this demand's rational force emerges only when we learn our calling to cooperate with Christ, and learn mercy's healing power in cooperation with his grace.[20]

And (2) The reasonableness of some specific moral norms is obscured by worldly horizons and limited hopes which can be displaced only by the true horizon: Christ's kingdom, a community in this world but not of it.

This second point can be put more philosophically. Natural moral law includes norms absolutely excluding choices to destroy, damage or impede a basic human good (a basic aspect of human fulfillment, a good intrinsic to human persons and their communion), such as bodily life and health, or knowledge of truth. For, practical reason's first principles direct one towards these basic human goods, so that one always has a reason not to choose to destroy, damage or impede any instantiation of any such good. And this reason to exclude every such choice cannot be outweighed. For, the intrinsic, basic, personal human goods involved in any option available to rational and morally significant free choice cannot (prior to moral judgment) be aggregated and commensurated so as to guide moral judgment by identifying a net overall "greater good" or "lesser evil". But people often treat these moral absolutes as overridden whenever that seems to promise greater good or lesser evil, for commensuration of the costs and benefits of alternative options seems possible when the "forseeable" fate of some community—some person or set of persons—is treated as a single, quasi-technical goal. Selecting a community as the reference-point for this artificial commensuration is necessarily the work of feelings rather than reason. But a technological model of practical reasoning readily encourages and camouflages the rationalizations involved. They can be dissolved only by faith in and hope for the one truly criterial community, the kingdom being built up here on earth, in mystery, and completed only in heaven.[21]

IV. The main arguments for Thesis B.

Thesis B is supported by (i) a "proportionalist" ethical theory, (ii) a protest against legalism, and (iii) inferences from certain texts of Vatican II.

(i) *Proportionalism.*[22]

What is proportionalism? A straightforward, rather unsophisticated version of proportionalist moral method is offered in an influential textbook (promoting thesis B):

> What ought we to do? We ought to do that action which maximizes the good and minimizes the evil. How do we discover the right thing to do? We discover it by balancing the various 'goods' and 'bads' that are part of the situation and by trying to *achieve the greatest proportion of goods to bads.* What constitutes right action? It is *the action which contains the proportionally greatest maximization of good and minimization of evil.*[23]

Judgments of right and wrong, then, can only be made by a comparative evaluation, identifying which, among alternative norms or actions, promises the greatest proportion of pre-moral human good and/or the least proportion of pre-moral evils (harm). All the circumstances must be taken into account. And circumstances change. So there can be no permanently true specific norms.[24] Christian tradition's specific norms are only generalizations, really true only in some times and cultures.[25]

Why did theologians never entertain such a method until, say 1965? Because, despite its plausible appearance it is in fact irrational. For no one can commensurate goods and bads (to direct moral choice) without presupposing the very moral judgments proportionalist method is meant to justify.[26] Thesis B's appeal to reason encounters insuperable philosophical objections.[27] Its proponents now commonly concede that the "commensurating" by which they hope to guide moral judgment is done by culturally formed "emotions" (or "intuitions"), or by *choices*.[28]

Moreover, when combined with the doctrine of Providence, proportionalism has (contrary to its proponents' *intentions*) an absurd consequence: that those in doubt about what to do could rightly choose *anything* they felt inclined to. For proportionalism tells us to choose the option promising greatest overall, long-run, net good. But, *whatever we choose to do* — even if we merely follow our whim — we can be certain that, if we accomplish what we attempt, our chosen action tended toward overall, long-run net good (since God's providence permitted it), while if we fail to accomplish what we attempt, our failure tended toward overall, long-run net good (since God's providence excluded the success of our effort). So: choosing according to whim fulfills one's supreme moral duty as defined by proportionalism — a *reductio ad absurdum* which shows that proportionalism confuses human responsibility with divine providence.

Proportionalists overlook a key distinction. No particular act can be adjudged *right* without considering all relevant circumstances: *bonum ex integra causa*. But one can judge an option/act *wrong* as soon as one sees a moral defect in relation to its ultimate purpose (end, motive) *or* the circumstances *or* the means (precise object): *malum ex quocumque defectu.*[29]

(ii) *Protest against legalism*
Thesis B protests against presenting morality (and moral revelation) as divine decrees, to be obeyed in order to merit the salvation established as reward by a further divine decree.[30]

Some such protest is appropriate.[31] Christian morality, even including its claim to include the natural law, has often been presented legalistically. But, properly understood,[32] revelation does not disclose God as choosing morality's content, or as choosing to reward conformity to morality, or as threatening to punish disobedience to it. Rather, revelation (in elements of the Old Testament, and plainly in the New) discloses a God who wills only what truly will fulfill us, a God who, given that he has chosen our human nature, has no choice about morality's content. Moral principles and norms are obligatory by their intelligible relation to the goods towards which they direct action, and not by any extra force from divine decree. Revelation helps identify the requirements of a rational love of human good, in the actual human situation of original sin and divine redemption to life in a heavenly community to whose unsurpassable human fulfillments all are summoned.

There is no *threat* of hell, only the *warning* about the intrinsic and inevitable implications of unreversed choices which disrupt friendship with God because instrinsically opposed to the human good he lovingly creates. True, heaven (unlike hell) depends on a gratuitous divine choice to promise and enable a relationship surpassing human nature's capacities and the intrinsic meaning of human choices. But that promise having been made, the relation between morally good human choices and the building up of the heavenly kingdom is far tighter than that between human desert and human reward. As Vatican II summarizes the tradition's reflection on the data of revelation:

> ... after we have obeyed the Lord, and in his Spirit nurtured on earth ... all the good fruits of our nature and enterprise, we shall *find them again,* but freed of stain, burnished and transfigured, when Christ hands over to the Father ... 'a kingdom of truth and life, holiness and grace, justice, love and peace'. On this earth that kingdom is already present in mystery. (*GS* 39)

These goods of the kingdom — truth and life, holiness, justice, love and peace — are divine blessings but also are fulfillments of what human beings can be; they are human nature in its flourishing. The moral principles and norms definitively proposed in Christian tradition are nothing other than articulations of what is required to be and remain open, in all one's free choices, to a human flourishing (the flourishing of all human persons and communities) which is not cut down by emotion's fettering of rational service of those goods of persons.

Proponents of thesis B typically remain within the toils of legalism. They see moral teachings, e.g. on adultery, or killing innocents, precisely as if they were positive laws laid down by the Church for the "greater good".[33] They propose that the Church teach these norms *as laws* (and so with exceptions based on *epikeia*, and timely revision or repeal). They obscure, to the point of suppressing, all connection between specific types of moral choice and the building up of the heavenly kingdom.[34] Their work thus fails to meet Vatican II's challenge to moral theologians: to show the nobility of the calling of Christians,[35] the shaping of Christian life to a heavenly-earthly end, morality's *intrinsic* relation (given God's promises) to eternal fulfillment.[36]

(iii) *Fallacious inferences from Vatican II*

Thesis B's proponents appeal especially to *GS* 33: "The Church... does not always have a ready answer to particular questions."[37] But this true proposition in no way implies that the magisterium can never authoritatively answer any specific moral question.[38] "Not all" does not entail "none".

Other arguments for thesis B exhibit a similar slide from "some" to "all". E.g.: It does not follow that, because some modern moral problems are complex, revelation contains no specific moral norms decisive for any modern moral problem.[39]

Vatican II warns us against separating "social" from "moral" teaching, not by assimilating the latter to a "social teaching" conceived of as *all* relative to time and place, but by recalling that *some* of the strategic norms of *social* morality are exceptionless moral absolutes (*GS* 27, 80).

V. Why Thesis B appeals

If the arguments for thesis B are so weak, why does it appeal to many Catholics? Essentially, its appeal is twofold.

1. As Vatican II makes clear,[40] pre-conciliar Moral had serious deficiencies: failure to incorporate scriptural doctrine, to elucidate the faithful's heavenly calling, and to link that with the obligation to bring forth fruit in charity (*OT* 16). I have mentioned the resulting legalism, and some of the resources provided by Vatican II for a more adequate *Christian humanism*. The old Moral, moreover, isolated by the seminary curriculum from Philosophy as from Dogma, suffered serious philosophical weaknesses. But thesis B's own deficiencies only make it a new — and worse — problem, not the solution desired by Vatican II.[41]

2. Our culture is shaped by the Enlightenment's ideological successors, liberal and liberationist[42] secular humanisms, and is dominated by technological successes.

Thesis B's methodology was articulated by enlightened secularists (Bentham, Mill, Marx...) who projected a this-worldly kingdom of God, without God, and relocated heaven at the end of earthly progress. Their new morality knew no absolutes save: Pursue the net greatest earthly happiness. As determinists, they ignored free choice's reflexive implications for the chooser's own character.[43] As secularists, they could not acknowledge that the personal goods nurtured by refusal to kill the innocent, lie, or fornicate, are not extinguished in the earthly ruin which may result, but are goods to be "found again, transfigured" in the kingdom (*GS* 39). So, for them, the goods at stake in choice cannot have the (incalculable!) significance always known to the martyrs for moral truth.

And all the while, technology's successes lend glamour to cost-benefit modes of reasoning, a glamour which overshadows sober philosophical demonstrations that aggregative reasoning can resolve no *moral* problem.

The economics and politics of whole cultures, socialist and capitalist, now support a secularist lifestyle and penalize alternatives.[44] So some theologians feel that the costs of Christian moral life (as taught by the Church) are too high, and so seek to lighten the burden on the faithful by dissolving all the specific moral absolutes of Christian tradition.

But their warm-hearted effort lacks grounds in either reason or faith. Pastorally its failure seems manifest. And that should be no surprise, for its pastoral motivations seem merely sentimental.

Would not a sound pastoral sense, rather than seeking to lower the cost of discipleship, instead adopt the strategy of Christ: to insist upon and highlight the cost — "If any man would come after me, let him deny himself and take up his cross and follow me" (*Matt.* 16:24 & par.) — but at the same time to relativize that immense cost, and make it seem a light burden, by doing everything to arouse and intensify hope for everlasting life in heaven? That was the strategy adopted by St. Paul, too, when he relativized the sufferings of this life by comparing them with the glory of the resurrection — something he was not afraid to do even when he is addressing the sophisticates of Athens.[45] That, in a word, is the strategy abandoned by those many Catholic theologians and teachers who recall heaven only at funerals — and about hell seem to have total amnesia.

Notes

1. Josef Fuchs SJ, *Christian Morality: The Word Becomes Flesh* (Georgetown U.P., Washington DC; Gill and Macmillan, Dublin, n.d. [1987] 12-13 elaborates: a new "intentionality", new "readiness to live seriously", new orientation, attitudes, self-awareness, even the attitudinal and theoretical (anthropological) bases for a new facility in discovering natural law's concrete moral content. (The title of the leading paper in this new collection of Fuchs's papers sums up thesis B: "Christian Morality: Biblical Orientation and Human Evaluation" (originally in *Gregorianum* 67 (1986) 745 63).

2. Reason has a significant role in revelation and its reception. By our intelligence, we identify our responsibility to seek truth about the more-than-human source of existence, meaning and value. By following our intelligence, we can judge that there is indeed such a source, and that our own intelligence and free will are somehow images of that source's personal nature. By our practical understanding, we can judge that human fulfillment is only possible in some harmony with that creative personal being, source of all fulfillments. All these judgments can reasonably be made without divine revelation, and they all dispose us to seek, hear, and accept that revelation as preached by those who announce the gospel.

3. This is denied, without serious argumentation, by proponents of view B: e.g. Josef Fuchs, *Christian Morality*, 6, 109-110; Gerard J. Hughes, *Authority in Morals* (1978). 17-18, 24, 95.

4. On this developing understanding of revelation, see *DV* 8.

5. Moses because of the hardness of hearts allowed divorce, but *from the beginning of creation* it was not so; And I [Jesus] say that whoever puts away his wife and marries another commits adultery; and she, if she marries another, commits adultery, too: cf. Matt. 19: 4-9; Mk. 10:4-12; Lk. 16:18.

6. In Irenaeus' phrases: *naturalia legis . . . , naturalia praecepta quae ab initio infixa dedit hominibus . . . , naturalia et liberalia et communia omnium: Adv. Haer.* IV, 13,1; 15,1; 16.5. On the whole matter of the importance of the Decalogue in the apostolic and early patristic eras, see Guy Bourgeault, *Decalogue et morale chretienne:enquete patristique sur l'utilisation et l' interpretation chretienne du decalogue de c.60 a c.220* (Paris, 1971).

7. As Justin Martyr had earlier noted: *Dialogue with Trypho* c.93, 1.

8. For Irenaeus links the Decalogue tightly to his theology of human fulfillment: the glory of God is living man, but the life of man is the vision of God; and God has no need of our love or service; it is we who have need of God's glory, which can in no way be attained save through service of God; and to prepare us for this life of friendship with God and concord with neighbor, the Lord articulated the Decalogue which Jesus reaffirmed, amplified and perfected (*Adv Haer.* IV. 20, 7; 16, 3 & 4; 12, 5; 13, 1 & 3). See also John Bligh, *Galations* (St. Paul,London, 1969) 292-299.

9. So, at the outset of his fundamental treatise on justification, St. Thomas speaks of the two aspects of the Gospel law: (i) the grace of the Holy Spirit, and (ii) the "documenta *fidei et praecepta* ordinantia affectuum humanum et humanos actus", precepts which he immediately specifies as "moral precepts, such as those found in the Gospel", and which he promptly shows include the commandments of the Decalogue (which he teaches are also precepts of natural law): *S.T.* I-II q.106 a. 2c; q.107 a 2c; q.100 aa.1 & 3. For his use of the phrase *fides et mores,* or its cognates, in contexts which make clear that *mores* refers to teachings such as wrongfulness of adultery, see also his commentary on *Titus* 3:8-9 and on 1 *Cor.* 14:23. On the meaning of that phrase in Trent, see Finnis, " 'Faith and Morals': A Note" *The Month* 21 (1988) 563 at 564-5.

10. Driedo, *de Ecclesiasticis Scripturis et Dogmatibus* ([1533] in his *Opera Omnia* I, 212).

11. Likewise, Trent anathematizes the claims that the only Gospel command is faith (D-S 1569), and that the Decalogue is irrelevant to Christians (D-S 1569)

12. In dealing with this question, these theologians very frequently confuse the question whether there are Christian moral dogmas with the question whether the Church's moral doctrine is specifically Christian (i.e. *adds* to the *content* of natural moral law), or with the question whether the Church infallibly teaches propositions of natural law which are *not* also revealed. For a characteristic mixing together of questions, see Josef Fuchs SJ, *Personal Responsibility and Christian Morality* (Georgetown U.P., Washington DC; Gill & Macmillan, Dublin, 1983) 124, especially the sentence: " ... it is noteworthy that in the Church's two thousand years, seemingly no definitive doctrinal decision on moral questions has been made, at least insofar as these would be related to natural law, without being at the same time revealed."

13. Viz. that it is licit to have several wives at a time, and not forbidden by the divine law repromulgated by Christ (D-S 1802); that a marriage can be dissolved for heresy, domestic incompatibility, or willful desertion (D-S 1805); that the Church errs in teaching anyone who remarries after dismissing his or her spouse for adultery is guilty of adultery (D-S 1807).

14. See footnote 1, citing Aquinas, *S.T.* I-II q.93 a.2. On Vatican II's teaching on natural moral law, see further Finnis, "The Natural Law, Objective Morality, and Vatican II" in William E. May (ed.), *Principles of Catholic Moral Life* (Franciscan Herald Press, Chicago, 1980) 113-151.

15. Vatican I, *Dei Filius,* cap. 2 *de revelatione.* Hence the hallowed "definition" of natural law given by Gratian: "jus naturale est quod in Lege et in Evangelio continetur". *Decretum* I, 1. The classic contrast is not between natural and revealed law, but between *natural* and *positive* (man-made, *humana lex*): see e.g. Aquinas, *S.T.* I-II qq. 94, 95; *Codex Iuris Canonici* (1983) can. 199; (1917) can. 27.

16. *Vat. I. Dei Filius* cap. 3: "Porro fide divina et catholica ea omni credenda sunt, quae in verbo Dei scripto vel tradito continentur et ab Ecclesia sive solemni iudicio *sive ordinario et universali magisterio* tamquam divinitus revelata credenda proponuntur"; *Pastor aeternus* cap. 4: "Romanum Pontificem, cum ... *doctrinam de* fide vel *moribus* ab uni-

versa Ecclesia tenendam definit . . .ea infallibilitate pollere, qua divinus Redemptor Ecclesiam suam in definiendam doctrina de fide vel moribus instructam esse voluit . . . " Vatican II also adds: "For by the will of Christ the Church is teacher of the truth, and it is her responsibility to preach and authentically teach the Truth which is Christ, and at the same time by her authority to declare and confirm the principles of the moral order, which flow from human nature itself": *DH* 41.

17. Correspondingly, "Whoever follows Christ, the perfect man, becomes himself more of a man": *GS* 14.

18. Moreover, as I have noted above, Jesus' self-disclosure includes a moral catechesis referring us, in a Hebraic idiom, to that nature as a principle of specific moral norms.

19. " . . . revelatio absolute necessaria dicenda est . . . quia Deus ex infinita bonitate sua ordinavit hominem ad finem supernaturalem, ad participanda scilicet bona divina, quae humanae mentis intelligentiam omnino superant . . . ": Vat. I, *De revelatione* cap. 2, D-S 3005. Vatican II reaffirms this, quoting the last eleven words: *DV* 6.

20. Hence it seems right to affirm that there is a specifically Christian ethic, not proposing any new moral *principles,* but proposing new, specifically Christian moral norms as the true implications of natural law principles in a world fallen and redeemed, as the moral implications of a strategy of dealing with evil in such a world and in cooperation with Jesus. See Grisez, *The Way of the Lord Jesus,* vol. I, *Christian Moral Principles* 606-607.

21. The concepts and arguments deployed in this paragraph are more adequately expounded in, e.g., Grisez, Boyle and Finnis, "Practical Principles, Moral Truth, and Ultimate Ends" *Am. J. Jurisprudence* 32 (1987) 99-151; Finnis, Boyle and Grisez, *Nuclear Deterrence, Morality and Realism* (Oxford U.P., Oxford and New York, 1987), 238-319.

22. This is a label which many proponents of such a principle are happy to apply to their principle and method: e.g. Fuchs, *Christian Morality* 16; Edward V. Vacek SJ, "Proportionalism: One View of the Debate" *Theol. St.* 46 (1985) 287. On the relationship between the labels "proportionalist", "teleological", "consequentialist" (and "utilitarian"), see Finnis, *Fundamentals of Ethics* 80-86. There are, of course, differences among proportionalists about the meaning, content, and application of their method; the struggles of Richard McCormick SJ to articulate a viable version have resulted in a particularly instructive melange. NB: references to "proportionality" in e.g. expositions of "the principle of double effect" need not, and should not, be understood as proposing proportionalism, i.e. a weighing of overall net pre-moral goods and bads. Instead they require that choices comply with other moral norms such as fairness. See Grisez, *Christian Moral Principles* 147-71; Grisez, "Moral Absolutes: A Critique of the View of Josef Fuchs, S.J." *Anthropos [Anthropotes]* 1985, 2, 155 at 177-86; Finnis, Boyle and Grisez, *Nuclear Deterrence, Morality and Realism* 261-7.

23. Timothy E. O'Connell, *Principles for a Catholic Morality* (Seabury Press, New York, 1978) 153 (emphasis added). Fr O'Connell's goes on to explain (155-164) that the goods and bads to be maximized and minimized are the "pre-moral" goods and bads. (His definition is unsophisticated e.g. in speaking of actions "containing" maximization etc, and in its assumption that no methodological choice need be made between maximizing good and minimizing evil.)

24. This *a priori* argument against revelation of specific moral norms is relied upon particularly by Francis A. Sullivan SJ, *Magisterium: Teaching Authority in the Catholic Church* (Paulist Press, New York, 1983) 149-152. Sullivan believes that "the majority of Catholic theologians today" subscribe to it: 149. He cites eighteen theologians, starting the list with Franz Boeckle (principal author of the Declaration of Cologne of 25 January 1989) and Charles Curran, and proceeding through other public dissenters from the Church's most insistently taught moral teachings: J. David, Josef Fuchs, Bernard Haering;, Louis Janssens, Daniel Maguire, Richard McCormick, Bruno Schueller, Gregory Baum, et al.. Sullivan cites no

theologian among the many who have written in support of the Church's moral magisterium today. Although the relevant chapter of Sullivan's book was explicitly written as a reply to an article by John C. Ford SJ and Germain Grisez, Sullivan has not replied to Grisez's refutation of the chapter: Grisez, "Infallibility and Specific Moral Norms: A Review Discussion" *The Thomist* 49 (1985) 248-287.

25. Thus Paul and Jesus wished only to give the answers appropriate "for precisely the questions posed by the people of their time and culture", and "this fact obviously can relativize the lasting significance of their answers to particular questions for other times, cultures and worldviews": Josef Fuchs, *Christian Morality* 6. In the context, Fuchs plainly means that their answers to *all* particular questions are of only relative and temporary significance.

26. More philosophically sophisticated proportionalist theologians sometimes admit this: e.g. Vacek, "Proportionalism: One View of the Debate" at 303; Richard McCormick, in McCormick and Ramsey (eds.) *Doing Evil to Achieve Good* (Loyola U.P., 1978) 250; see also Bernard Hoose, *Proportionalism: the American Debate and its European roots* (Georgetown U.P., 1987) 89. The proportionalist supposition that it is possible to guide moral judgment and choice by identifying the pre-moral greatest net good (or lesser evil) ignores the incommensurability of the basic human goods, *and* of their possible realizations in the particular persons affected by morally significant choices (including the agent). (This last-mentioned source of incommensurability is well brought out in Bartholomew M. Kiely, S.J., "The Impracticability of Consequentialism", *Gregorianum* 66 (1985) 655-86). The diversity of goods and of persons entails that comparisons can be made only by some standard of evaluation; but if a standard is not moral its application will yield only a non-moral comparison and a technical maxim of action; if the standard, however, is moral it can indicate that some choices — e.g. of adultery, or killing the innocent, etc. — are always worse evils than any which must be suffered as a result of refusing to make such choices (cf. GS 27, 3). Indeed, if the supposed overall long-run net "greater good" or "lesser evil" were discoverable, morally significant choice be impossible: see Finnis, Boyle and Grisez, *Nuclear Deterrence, Morality and Realism* 254-60. St. Thomas notices the incommensurability of the goods at stake in options for morally significant free choice: *S.T.* I q.82 a.2 ad 1; I-II q.13 a.6 obj.3; *de Malo* q.6 a.un. c. Note also that in every context in which a moral issue is to be resolved, Aquinas refuses the invitation to solve the issue by identifying "the lesser evil": see *in Sent.* IV d.6 q.1 a.1 qa.1 obj.4 & ad 4 (killing); d.9 q.1 a.5 qa.1 obj.3 & ad 3; *Summa Theol.* II-II q.110 a.3 obj.4 & ad 4; III q.68 a.11 obj.3 & ad 3 (killing); q.80 a.6 obj.2 & ad 2.

27. Still perhaps the best compendium of these philosophical objections is Grisez, "Against Consequentialism" *American Journal of Jurisprudence* 23 (1978) 21-72; see also Finnis, Boyle and Grisez, *Nuclear Deterrence, Morality and Realism* 238-272. These give many references to the secular philosophical literature.

28. See e.g. McCormick, in McCormick and Ramsey, *Doing Evil to Achieve Good* 227, 229, 250-252. See also McCormick, *Notes on Moral Theology 1981 through 1984* 16: "actions where we sense very strongly (sense of profanation, outrage, intuition) that the actions are counterproductive [in general and in the long run]."

29. The specific negative moral absolutes are to be understood, not as contained in irreducible intuitions, as if they were first principles of practical reason and natural law (as they were sometimes presented in neo-scholastic tradition: e.g. Josef Fuchs SJ, *de Castitate et de Ordine Sexuali* (Rome, 1963); John Courtney Murray SJ, *We Hold These Truths* (Sheed and Ward, New York, 1960) 328-330), but precisely as specifications of (the implication of) love of God and of every human person made in his image.

30. See e.g. Fuchs, *Christian Ethics in a Secular Arena* 53; Mahoney, *The Making of Moral Theology* 315.

31. See Grisez, *Christian Moral Principles* index s.v. "Legalism"

32. As in St. Thomas's treatise on law (natural and — human or divine — positive): *S.T.* I-II qq. 90-96.

33. Thus Richard McCormick SJ, discussing the norm excluding direct attack on innocents, suggests that "where we view norms as 'virtually exceptionless' we do so or ought to do so because of the prudential validity of what we refer to technically as *lex lata in praesumptione periculi communis* (a law established on the presumption of common and universal danger)": in McCormick and Ramsey, *Doing Evil for the Sake of Good* 44. He describes the Church's identification of moral norms as a "norming" (i.e. a norm-*making*): ibid. 200, 232. Again (ibid. 251) he says: "I would grant that the basic goods are incommensurable. One cannot measure one against the other if they are indeed basic. But perhaps we can *adopt* a hierarchy of values, either personally or societally. ... the conclusions of traditional Christian ethics here ... are the community's adoption of a hierarchy of values.... ".

34. See Grisez, "Moral Absolutes: A Critique of the View of Josef Fuchs, S.J.", *Anthropos [Anthropotes]* 1985, 2, 155 at 163-168. Typical expositions of view B, such as Timothy O'Connell, *Principles for a Catholic Morality* (Seabury Press, New York, 1978) ignore the whole question of humankind's last end.

35. *celsitudo vocationis fidelium in Christo: OT* 16.

36. *GS* 22, 38-39; *LG* 48.

37. "The Church, which guards the deposit of God's word, drawing from it principles of the religious and moral order, though she does not always have a ready answer to particular questions, desires to join the light of revelation with everyone's experience, so that the path mankind has recently taken may be illuminated." This is quoted, with intent to promote view B, or some similar view, or to premise the argument in the text, in Sullivan, *Magisterium* 151; Mahoney, *The Making of Moral Theology* (OUP 1987) 303. A particularly vivid expression of the fallacy is Fuchs, *Christian Ethics in a Secular Arena* (Georgetown UP, Washington DC, Gill & Macmillan, Dublin, 1984) 60, arguing that *no* matter of natural law could belong to the indirect or secondary object of infallibility, *because* "it does not seem conceivable that *the unlimited number* of concrete questions regarding the moral rightness of 'horizontal' acting have such a [n inner] relationship [to explicitly revealed truths] and therefore belong to the competence of the magisterium in the same full sense as revealed truths do" (emphasis added). Not all the many ... therefore none.

38. See, e.g. Sullivan, *Magisterium* 151.

39. As Sullivan *Magisterium* 150-151 fallaciously supposes. Some modern-moral problems are complex; some modern moral problems were moral problems 2,000 years ago; some ancient moral problems which are still moral problems were complex then, as now. There are some manifestly revealed moral requirements manifestly relevant to some perennially complex moral problems, e.g. as to the dissolubility of true marriage. Consider also:

> One cannot reasonably acknowledge a divine public revelation without some individual, prior and independent moral understanding and judgment(s). Therefore, the interpretation of each part of revelation's contents can and must be controlled by ethical judgments generated independently of revelation.

(See, e.g., Fuchs, *Christian Morality* 6-7; Hughes, *Authority in Morals* (1978) i-vii, 1-25, on which cf. Finnis, "Reflections on an Essay in Christian Ethics ..." *Clergy Rev* 65 (1980) 51-57.) *Non sequitur.* The premise is acknowledged and taught explicitly by Vatican II in *DH* 2, and implicitly by Vatican I (D-S 3004, 3005). The conclusion simply denies the authority of Scripture, magisterium and tradition, and is gratuitous. On the decisive authority of the magisterium in interpreting Scripture, see *DV* 10. Or again:

> Revelation cannot override or supersede all our prior moral judgments. Therefore revelation can neither authoritatively confirm nor correct any of our moral

judgments (provided that these are based on some coherent ethical methodology consistent with common moral opinion). Hughes, loc. cit.

Non sequitur. Again the premise is the tradition's implicit position, to which the same sources in Vatican I and Vatican II testify. The conclusion simply denies the authority of revelation, on the basis of the fallacious inference from "not all" to "none". Consider also:

> *The magisterium cannot always readily answer every moral question. Therefore there are at least some questions on which revelation cannot give the moral guidance which conscience needs.*

This too is a *non sequitur.* In relation to one's many affirmative responsibilities ("Honor your father and your mother ... ", "Feed your children", "Pay your taxes" ...), one will always have to make prudent and conscientious judgments more specific than any which could be taught either by revelation or by a philosophical articulation of the natural law. But there is no reason to suppose that revelation, taken with all its resources, lacks any element of the guidance which conscience *needs* in order to make such judgments. In relation to one's negative responsibilities (e.g. not to be killing the innocent, or committing adultery, or lying), conscience can be sufficiently guided by revelation to exclude, absolutely, certain options. The development of doctrine can be expected to unfold further implications of revelation taken as a whole (as occurred e.g. in relation to slavery, baby-making, etc.).

40. By calling "specially" for its improvement (*Theologiae morali perficiendae*): *OT* 16.

41. It did not adequately articulate the links between the first principles of practical reason, the basic forms of human good, and specifically moral principles and norms. Its analysis of action failed to distinguish systematically between the intentional and the conventional and the physical. It offered no clear critique of the ethical and meta-ethical philosophies emanating from the Enlightenment.

42. It is important not to forget that view B's attack on the moral absolutes of Christian tradition is sponsored not only by theologians in the consumer societies of the West but also by many "liberation" theologians in the Third World, where Marxising ideologies may be expected to long outlive their collapse in Europe. For a clear example, see Juan Luis Segundo, *Liberation of Theology* Orbis Books, Maryknoll, N.Y., 1876) 154-75.

43. Such changes in the character of choosers render the calculus of the consequences of actions quite senseless, as I have noted in n. 26 above.

44. Whole national and international cultures form around the acceptance of the nuclear deterrent's standing proposal to massacre non-combatants, of abortion and infanticide, of serial polygamy and other forms of sensibly moderated adultery, of contraception and of contracepted and other forms of masturbatory sexual intercourse.

45. Whom he did not shrink from urging to repentance and warning of the coming judgment in righteousness: *Acts* 17:30-31. Cf. 2 *Cor.* 4:17-5:11. See also *Gal.* 5:19-21 (and 6:8) with the accompanying reading from St. Leo the Great in the Office of Readings for today, 8 February 1990 (Thursday of Week 5).

Chapter 15

THE RETURN TO VIRTUE ETHICS

Alasdair MacIntyre

Any attempt to give a brief account of recent changes in English-speaking moral philosophy is going to suffer from three defects. It will be highly selective. It will oversimplify even in respect of that to which it attends. And it will incur the dangers involved in trying to write the history of events to which we are still too close in time. Twenty years from now a retrospective account might well present these same changes somewhat differently.

I begin by asking: what were the salient features of English-speaking moral philosophy in the years 1950-80, against which a good deal of recent work in virtue-ethics may be accounted a reaction? A first such feature was a largely exclusive focus upon *moral rules* and an attempt to identify the distinctive features both of moral as contrasted with other types of rule and of the reasoning appropriately used to justify claims about the content, form and application of such rules. Such rules were generally held to be impersonal, that is, to embody a standard distinct from and independent of any particular set of interests. Secondly they were generally taken to be universal in form, binding any rational person whatsoever and regulating the conduct of anyone to anyone. Their content was correspondingly highly general; what was enjoined or prohibited by such rules was intended to capture what held in *every* human situation of some particular recurrent type. Thirdly the compelling grounds for giving one's allegiance to these rules, formulated in some particular way, were to be grounds equally available to and equally compelling, in principle at least, to any rational person whatsoever, whatever his or her initial standpoint, circumstances or interests might be.

Such rules collectively were taken to define *right* action. And on this dominant view *the right* was, and indeed for those who still embrace this type of view is, sharply distinguished from *the good*. On questions about the right rational agreement, so it was held, is not only possible, but required. By contrast on questions about the good disagreement is extensive and probably ineliminable. What is right is what any rational person may require of any other; what is good is a question about which each individual is and ought to be free to make up his or her mind in his or her own way in accordance with his or her private preferences, provided that in acting upon the view which he or she adopts, he or she does not infringe the freedom of any other individual.

Moral rules where thus, on this account, to be formulated in independence of any particular determinate conception of good, let alone of *the* good for human beings. Some moral philosophers held and hold that such rules could and should be formulated without any reference at all to the goods which individuals might be choosing to pursue. Others, influenced by and intent on improving upon classical utilitarianism, held that moral rules should be devised and corrected by some method which gave equal weight to the preferences of every individual who would be affected by the relevant types of action. Both groups agree in holding that moral rules are to be formulated in a way that is somehow neutral and impartial between rival and alternative conceptions of

240

human good. The good was thus to be rendered irrelevant to our shared public morality.

This account of morality had and has four other outstanding characteristics. First it makes morality independent of all human and institutional attachments: our loyalties to and dependences upon family and friends, school and political community, let alone to church or synagogue, are to be subordinated to and judged in terms of the dictates of morality. They are not themselves, any of them, to be understood as primary sources of moral insight. Secondly there is no place for *authority* on specifically moral issues. Each individual is *qua* rational person to be considered autonomous in uttering to him or herself the prescriptions of morality. Thirdly, in the course of specifying the types of protection for that autonomy of the individual which morality, thus understood, prescribes, greater and greater emphasis came to be laid upon the *rights* of individuals, *rights* to lead their lives in whatever way they might choose, provided equal rights were accorded to other such individuals. A continuous multiplication of types of claims about rights ensued. And fourthly this account tended to generate problems about cases in which rules so formulated turn out to conflict with one another, so that attention was focused increasingly on those types of occasion on which the prescriptions of morality become in some way problematic, because conflicting considerations are involved. College courses with titles like 'Moral Problems' became increasingly frequent. Dilemmas and decisions about dilemmas were presented as pervasive features of the moral life. And of course in all four respects this then dominant tendency within academic moral philosophy reflected and was reflected by a wider society in which to a considerable extent communal attachments were denigrated, authority was denied, claims to rights were multiplied and morality was understood as pervasively problematic.

Those within academic moral philosophy who shared this for so long dominant standpoint tended to view themselves as the heirs of Kant or Mill or both. They had of course moved away from, and presumably in their own view improved upon, Kant and Mill on a variety of issues. And they did not on many matters, some of them both philosophically and morally central, agree among themselves. Topics of disagreement included and still include both the

241

precise content of moral rules and the appropriate modes of argument by which their content is to be identified and from which their binding force for rational persons is to be derived. Disagreement among philosophers is so familiar and so endemic a phenomenon that the special significance of these particular disagreements needs to be remarked. For if it were the case that moral rules are those rules about which, both in respect of content and of type of argumentative support, all rational persons whatsoever can and must agree, then the inability of philosophers who uphold this type of account of moral rules to agree among themselves on central questions provides an initial ground for skepticism about the type of account which they are defending. And the range, the depth and the *de facto* ineliminability of these disagreements have themselves provided one good reason why an increasing number of moral philosophers came to reject this particular point of view.

Yet even when that point of view was most dominant within academic moral philosophy and seemed to be most successful, it had already been seriously challenged on at least three other different issues. First it was suggested that its moral vocabulary was an impoverished one, in which the highly abstract concepts employed in framing moral rules could not provide adequately rich descriptions of the salient features of certain kinds of morally important situation. The idiom of the philosophical moralist was compared to its disadvantage with the idiom of the morally perceptive novelist or dramatist. What this latter type of idiom can describe in a way that the former cannot is perhaps twofold: on the one hand the particularities of the traps and pitfalls of the moral life, set by or arising from various kinds of misunderstanding, deception and self-deception, and on the other the particularities of, the detailed virtues of persons who can function as models of moral aspiration, saints and heroes. From the point of view which I have described as dominant there appeared to be little or no place or function within morality for historical and biographical portraits of saints and heroes, and hence also little need to attend to the virtues.

Secondly it was urged against the dominant view that it greatly exaggerated the extent to which the moral life is a life of problems, of situations which confront moral agents with dilemmas. Against this it was pointed out that moral agents characteristically encounter such situations with an already well formed character, and that the resources which they are able to bring to bear upon such situations vary with how their *character* has been formed, and with what has been learned in the course of their past character formation. But character becomes well formed, moral agents acquire set dispositions to act well, that is, virtues, primarily insofar as they learn how much of the moral life is unproblematic, how much of it is constituted by a daily round of duties, determined by the fixed points of life in some community within which authoritative moral teachers have been able to inculcate the relevant types of virtue.

Another very different critique of what I have called the dominant view rested on the contention that the allegedly distinctive and distinctively binding character of moral rules was unintelligible except by giving them the force of a moral law and that to give them this force without understanding them in the context of the virtues only seemed plausible because the moral rules in question are an unrecognized residue, a survival from an older theological view of ethics. "To have a law conception of ethics", wrote G. E. M. Anscombe in a justly famous article, "is to hold that what is needed for conformity to the virtues, failure in which is the mark of being bad *qua* man (and not merely, say, *qua* craftsman or logician)-that what is needed for *this,* is required by divine law. Naturally it is not possible to have such a conception unless you believe in God as a law-giver; like Jews, Stoics and Christians". Moral injunctions, that is to say, in general derive their peculiar binding force only from whatever it is that gives point and purpose to obedience to them. And the force that they will have if what gives point and purpose to them are divine commands will be very different from what it will be on the type of view which Professor Anscombe was criticizing.

Notice that Professor Anscombe in this passage spoke of the moral law as specifying what the virtues require and thus the argument had already, as in the two other types of criticism, moved beyond rules to virtues. Indeed it became clear to a number of moral philosophers that, if they were to give their due to the variety of considerations advanced in criticism of what I have called the dominant view, it would have to be by providing some rival and alternative account of the moral life, in which some well worked out conception of the virtues played a central part, not of course to the exclusion of moral rules, but in such a way as to

243

provide, in part at least, a context for a different understanding of the nature and status of moral rules.

What virtues someone judges that he or she needs to acquire will depend both upon what it is in life which that person takes him or herself to be attempting to achieve and upon what obstacles have to be overcome to ensure that this attempt is not frustrated. Hence what virtues such a person comes to value will depend upon what it is that he or she supposes to be his or her good. And since it will be impossible for a rational person to reach conclusions about his or her own good, without considering in some detail how his or her good is related to the good of others, it will be equally impossible for such a person to avoid giving some account to him or herself of how the virtues in his or her life are related to what is good and best for human beings in general.

Some strong connection of this sort between conceptions and catalogues of the virtues and conceptions of the human good has been recognized by a number of the philosophers whose writings have contributed to recent virtue ethics and to a sustained challenge to the earlier view. Hence in trying to elucidate the nature of the relationship between virtues and rules, it has proved impossible any longer to consider the nature, function and binding force of moral rules in detachment from considerations about the nature of the human good. Where the adherents of the previously dominant view had argued in favor of a conception of moral rules as neutral and impartial between rival conceptions of the human good, and a consequent exclusion of any conception of the human good from our shared public morality, their more recent critics have argued that only by reference to some determinate conception of human good can moral rules be adequately specified, and that failure to understand moral rules in the light of such a determinate conception will necessarily result in just the kind of inability to agree about what the content of moral rules is and why they are to be obeyed which is encountered in conflicting statements of the earlier view.

Adequately specified and genuinely shared rational moral rules will thus require to some significant degree at least a shared understanding of human good. Hence another topic which has become more important in recent moral philosophy has been that of the common good, understood not just or at all as some kind of summing of individual preferences, but rather as the good of that form of community, within which individuals have to learn what their own good is, and through the relationships of which they have to live out the life in which each individual tries to achieve his or her good. The virtues then are appropriately conceived as those dispositional qualities which individuals must possess, if they are both to sustain the shared life of this type of community and to achieve their own good. Moral rules thus become understood as the norms governing both social relationships and individual actions within the type of community, whose life sustains and is sustained by the virtues. Rules articulate those inviolabilities required for the life of such a community.

Much of the philosophical work done to elaborate such conceptions of the virtues and their place within the nexus of morality has been done either on particular virtues or on topics highly relevant to the elucidation of such virtues. So, for example, the place of virtues in the life of communities has been discussed both in connection with justice and with such virtues as friendship and patriotism. Out of such work a point of view has emerged according to which the standards of morality are to be understood not as standards independent of the life of community, to which appeal may be made against the community, but rather as standards informing the life of communities in good order, only to be learned in and from a community, modified and reformulated through the experience of that community and thus functioning as standards which are *ours* rather than *mine* or *yours.* Since it is only through the moral education afforded by such a community that individuals acquire the virtues, which enable them to participate in and to carry forward the tasks involved in understanding what such standards require in the face of new situations and, if and when necessary, extending or reformulating them, a corresponding conception of the moral agent emerges.

He or she can no longer be thought of as an independent, individual rational calculator, weighing his or her own interests and preferences against those of others, or else finding good reasons for adopting a moral stance of neutrality in respect of rival interests, but will instead be from the beginning someone trying to understand his or her own good in the light of what he or she has learned from others in the community about that shared conception of goods, and more especially of the common good, which already informs their common life. And to achieve this understanding such a person will need to acquire both moral and intellectual virtues.

This has led not to a dismissal of, but to a radical revision of the ways in which the autonomy of a moral agent is conceived. Different types of dependence upon others have been distinguished, so that thinking for oneself in moral matters is no longer confused with trying to find the resources for adequate moral judgment entirely within oneself. Among the types of dependence necessary for growth in independence, that whereby one learns from others, more advanced than oneself, how to deliberate practically and how to to acquire the virtue of practical rationality is crucial. We need, so it has come to be recognized, moral teachers. Unsurprisingly therefore in recent virtue-ethics Aristotle has assumed the kind of importance which in the earlier dominant view was assigned to Kant and Mill. It has thus been recognized that virtue ethics to-day is a return to a set of earlier modes and stances in moral philosophy. And this is nowhere more so than in discussions of the nature of practical reasoning and that virtue which Aristotle called *'phronēsis'* and Aquinas *'prudentia'*. This has been an area of extensive enquiry, both in the exegesis of what Aristotle wrote- and to a lesser, but not insignificant degree of Aquina's interpretation of and extension of Aristotle-and in attempts to draw upon Aristotle in formulating some account of the relationship of reason to desire more adequate than those which were derived from Kant and Mill. So the ways in which reasoning about ends, both proximate and ultimate, is possible, and the ways in which such reasoning can inform, redirect and transform desires- and thus provide an education in the virtues- have received a good deal of attention.

An inescapable question which arises at this point concerns the nature of moral creativity and the type of character from which creative judgment and action emerges. So conceptions of the saint or hero as role model become practically relevant in learning what more is demanded of us than what rules prescribe and what virtues are necessary to us if we are able to learn from saints and heroes what more that is. It is an important conceptual point that we cannot adequately specify what courage or generosity or indeed any virtue may require of those who practice it only in terms of rules or maxims. Moreover there is that to every virtue which enables those who possess it to go beyond the rules in specific situations in ways not provided for and not providable for in advance. Since this is so, the elucidation of a particular virtue has to proceed by combining what can to be said in terms of rules or maxims with concrete descriptions of particular persons who who exemplify that particular virtue. Novels can of course be illuminating in this regard, but real life examples of saints and heroes clearly have an advantage over any fiction.

Studies of particular virtues other than *phronēsis*- and also of vices- most of article length, but some of book length, are increasingly frequent in the philosophical literature. Justice, courage and friendship have been studied at book length. Virtues of which there are article-length studies include generosity, compassion, modesty and temperateness, and topics such as the relationship between vice and lack of self-knowledge have assumed a new importance. So naturally enough has the question of the unity of the virtues. Together with these enquiries others arise: how are the virtues to be classified and catalogued? What is the significance of the fact that in different cultures different classifications and catalogues of the virtues are to be found? Are there standards independent of any particular cultural and social order by which rival claims about the virtues arising within different cultural and social orders can be adjudicated? And if there are not such standards, is there any other way in which rational agreement about the virtues can be reached by those beginning from very different and incompatible starting-points? On these latter questions some of the most relevant work has been done by those at home in both classical and contemporary Chinese moral philosophy, especially Confucianism.

The raising of this whole new range of questions has of course had implications for the discussion of theses and issues central to the older dominant view. From within recent virtue ethics the concept of a right has received relatively little attention. But it is clear that from the standpoint of a virtue ethics, rights would not primarily provide grounds for claims made by individuals *against* other individuals or groups. They would instead have to be conceived primarily as enabling provisions, whereby individuals could claim a due place within the life of some particular community, and the question of what rights individuals have or should have would be answerable only in terms of the answers to a prior set of questions about what sort of community this is, directed towards the achievement of what sort of common good, and inculcating what kinds of virtues. So as the enquiries of virtue ethics advance an increasingly wide range of disagreements with the earlier dominant stand point becomes increasingly clear. Yet now three caveats have to be entered.

The first is this: I have systematically contrasted certain aspects of recent virtue ethics with what I have characterized as an earlier dominant standpoint; but many moral philosophers would insist that virtue ethics is still a minority interest, even a somewhat deviant minority interest, and that what I have described as an earlier dominant point of view is *still* the dominant point of view. And in terms of counting heads, especially within some of the most prestigious philosophy departments, they have a strong case.

Secondly there continue to be trenchant criticisms, both of virtue ethics overall and of particular theses within virtue ethics, by those who still uphold the earlier positions. Among these criticisms one perhaps deserves special attention. I have suggested that an inability to secure rational agreement on moral rules was damaging to the earlier position. To this it has been retorted that disagreements within recent virtue ethics have been quite as multifarious and as radical. Yet if the central theses of a specifically Artistotelian type of ethics of the virtues are true, then agreement can be expected to emerge not from untramelled philosophical debate, within which every substantive point of view on or even against the virtues is to be heard, but only from debate within particular communities seeking to embody in their own shared life some conception of the common good sufficiently strong as to place constraints upon a rational understanding of the virtues. It will be in terms of the concrete agreements of social life and the debates which arise from these, and not in the theoretical debates of academic philosophers, that in the end any particular account of the virtues will have to succeed or fail. The philosophy of the virtues has to be transformed into a politics of the virtues.

Yet to this it may well be said in turn that, given the state of continuing debate and large disagreement within contemporary virtue ethics, this may be to beg the question. For it is undeniably the case that within academic philosophy rival conceptions of the virtues are still very much in contention, some of them not at all Aristotelian. So there have been recent influential restatements of Hume's view of the virtues and of Nietzche's, both of them fundamentally at odds with any Aristotelian, let alone Thomistic view. Nonetheless it is clear that the focus of debate has to a significant degree altered within moral philosophy and that recent work in virtue ethics has been influential in so changing it. If that change has been as yet a change as much or more in the questions which are being asked as in the responses which are being supplied, it is still noteworthy. We are after all now systematically once again asking just those questions to which Aristotelian and Thomistic moral philosophy provides answers.

Bibliographical Note

The best introduction to recent virtue ethics is an anthology, *The Virtues: Contemporary Essays on Moral Character* edited by Robert B. Kruschwitz and Robert C. Roberts (Wadsworth: Belmont, California, 1987). It has an excellent bibliography. For examples of the earlier dominant view see R. M. Hare *Moral Thinking* (Clarendon Press: Oxford, 1981) and John Rawls *A Theory of Justice* (Harvard University Press: Cambridge, Massachusetts, 1971). The article by G. E. M. Anscombe cited in 'Modern Moral Philosophy' in Volume III of her *Collected Papers, Ethics, Religion and Politics* (University of Minnesota Press: Minneapolis, 1981). The passage quoted is on p. 30. For critics of the earlier view see Michael Sandel's critique of Rawls in *Liberalism and the Limits of Justice* and the essays collected in *Revisions* edited by Stanley Hauerwas and Alasdair MacIntyre (University of Notre Dame Press: Notre Dame, 1983). An an example of relevant recent writing on Aristotle see Norman O. Dahl *Practical Reason, Aristotle and Weakness of the Will* (University of Minnesota Press: Minneapolis, 1984). For a wide range of disagreements about topics in contemporary virtue ethics see *Ethical Theory: Character and Virtue* Volume XIII in Midwest Studies in Philosophy (University of Notre Dame Press: Notre Dame, 1988). Reference may also be made to Alasdair MacIntyre *After Virtue* Second Edition (University of Notre Dame Press: Notre Dame, 1984). On the relevance of Confucianism see David B. Wong *Moral Relativity* (University of California Press: Berkeley, 1984).

Chapter 16

PASTORAL CONCERNS
FAITH, NATURAL LAW AND VIRTUE

BISHOP: Either speaker could respond to this or, perhaps, both.

I was curious to know what direction you might give to the Church at this point and what advice would you give to us as bishops as to how we might pull morality together better in our country or give direction to what is taking place.

PROFESSOR FINNIS: The theological and philosophical work on a number of the matters which I touched on in my paper has now gone on as a kind of debate amongst theologians for twenty-five years or so. However, one of the important interesting features of the situation is that there hasn't been as much true debate as there would be in a healthy philosophical or theological community. Rather, there's been a certain concentration on expounding in as attractive a way as possible one view or another, and not enough really critical, close dialogue and debate between scholars.

The discussion has now gone on for twenty-five years and it seems to me that it's time for bishops to perform their proper office as bishops to make some judgment on some of the critical questions concerning the moral implications of the faith. And that, I think, would involve a rather more formal process of confrontation and debate amongst theologians, in the presence of the episcopate. After this debate the bishops would doubtless discuss the matter amongst themselves and make whatever judgment was the one that seemed right to the Holy Spirit and them.

DR. MacINTYRE: It is very important to think both of the needs of the Church and the needs of our society. In what Professor Finnis and I have talked about this morning, it is interesting that the case for affirming exceptionless moral norms and the case for affirming the relationship of moral rules to a determinate conception of the good have been shown to be more rationally defensible in secular philosophical debate than they have often been thought to be among theologians. And, therefore, I think it important that the bishops should listen enough, but not too much to theologians on these matters. I also think that this is a time when it is right for the bishops to address the larger society on just these matters and to bring to bear fundamental questions about moral norms and about the good, wrong answers to which are often presupposed in a public discussion but usually in a half-hearted, badly spelled out or not spelled out at all way. What the larger society is waiting for and needs is for the bishops to speak out with great clarity about certain simple and central issues.

BISHOP: In the deliberation taking place today and yesterday, the focus in terms of moral theology and moral philosophy has really been on a negative side focusing on evil more than the good. Isn't there a more positive approach based on the beatitudes and the positive directions that they would give? In terms of virtue ethics, could it be in terms of the project of Christ being focused on the fullness of life?

DR. MacINTYRE: Let me contrast three possible attitudes to moral rules.

The first is the view that such rules by themselves are self-sufficient and that, provided you know what the moral rules are and you conform to them, you will be adequately virtuous.

People who saw what was mistaken in that conception then made the mistake of going over to a second view, the view criticized so well by Professor Finnis, that of supposing that these rules are nothing more than generalizations of a rough and ready kind, and that there are no highly determinate exceptionless moral rules.

But this was the wrong way to go.

The right way to go is to have learned that part of the point of being educated into and through obedience to exceptionless moral rules is to move beyond that initial learning into the kind of creativity which makes our obedience to moral rules creative in a variety of positive ways. The need for such creativity emerges very clearly as a theme in contemporary virtue ethics.

And here what was just said to us about responding concretely to what Jesus Christ demands in particular situations is what is crucial. This is not something about which philosophers are able to say very much. But what they can point to is how one must move to the point at which one understands obedience to rules has to be related to what goes beyond rules, that is, to Charity and to the other theological virtues. The objections to legalism which have infected so much bad moral theology, were right insofar as they saw that legal requirements are always by themselves insufficient. But they wrongly construed this as meaning that they were not necessary.

PROFESSOR FINNIS: The intense philosophical and theological work on the foundations of moral philosophy and theology over the last thirty years is an attempt to respond to the call of Vatican II for a moral theology which would more adequately relate principles of moral life to the human "earthly-heavenly" calling. This was not just a response to the Council, but a response to the situation which, in its felt character, the Council was calling attention to the situation that can be summed up by saying that moral theology was in need of some foundational theological work. It's a very important feature of that work that it has in a way rediscovered or reappropriated but also developed the orientation of St. Thomas' work in ethics, in moral philosophy and moral theology. The results are importantly different from those of the neoscholastic revival in the later 16th Century and early 17th Century which formed the classic moral theological manual as we knew it in the first two thirds of the present century. Where the neoscholastics saw obligation as a kind of subjection to rule (rational rule, yes, conformity to human nature, yes, but ultimately, a matter of response to a divine decree), St. Thomas and the authentic revival

252

(but also development and extension) of his work in the last twenty or thirty years understand the whole of moral life in terms of a response to the attraction of the *good* which in more concrete terms is the attraction of the basic human *goods.*

It's very significant that St. Thomas again (in a decisive passage greatly misrepresented in the neoscholastic tradition) discusses the first principles of natural law as (plural) principles, first principle*s*.

Where the Neoscholastic revival translated, mistranslated, his identification of the very first principle of practical reason in terms of an imperative, do good and avoid evil, St. Thomas' own formulation is "the good is to be done and pursued—bonum est faciendum *et prosequendum-* and bad to be avoided." (S.T. I-II q.94 a.2) And "prosequendum", the response to the *attraction* of the good, is dropped out in the neoscholastic manuals. In the very same article, he identifies the goods of life and of procreation (or the procreative community) and of knowledge and of society, friendship between human persons and with God. One starts to see the outlines of an ethic which is an ethic of the goods, and is a response to the goods rather than a conformity to orders. Now, into that philosophical development there needs to be integrated a conception of the beatitudes which doesn't shuffle them to one side as counsels which are not truly obligatory, but rather portrays them in their true role as parts of the identification of one's vocation as a follower of the Lord, and sees them as part of the fundamental shaping of a Christian moral life which is very much in terms of the response to the affirmative responsibility of finding one's vocation, shaping it and pursuing it.

Now, the positive role of the negative specific moral norms in that life is, I think, very interesting.

Take the Lord's example of the specific moral negative absolute against adultery. It's as negative, exclusory as can be. It holds, as the old manuals rightly said, "semper et pro semper", whereas, affirmative norms holds "semper sed non pro semper." So it bites in every situation. One must never commit adultery.

Now, our Lord, in a certain sense, if you look at the text, *defines marriage* in negative terms, in terms of not committing adultery. Of course, there's a great deal more to a marriage than avoiding adultery, but what more? There is the good, the complex good of children, fidelity, friendship, mutual love and so forth (very beautifully expressed in a masterly sentence in *Humanae Vitae*). But if one attempts to define marriage in terms of a concrete, specific *objective* then you find the sort of modern, secularist conception of marriage in which there's a kind of technological goal of the partners developing each other, engaging in successful sexual experiences with each other and so forth; so that a marriage can be accounted a success or failure in terms of its relationship to those quite concrete, positive goals.

But that is not the way that the faith presents marriage to us. It presents marriage to us primarily in terms of the exclusory force of that negative, leaving in a certain sense to the spouses (to take up the term that Professor MacIntyre rightly pointed us towards) the creative development of their marriage, of their union, of their communion, in the unforeseeable contingencies of life, responding to all the relevant goods in a way which can't be specified normatively in advance.

So the role of the negative moral norm is simply to make possible, by excluding from deliberation, a certain response to difficulties. Within that, the positive affirmation attraction of the various goods can be creatively responded to. And that, I think, is a model for thinking of all the relevant norms.

BISHOP: Dr. Finnis, I think I have a problem, possibly, in understanding what you have in your outline. It says that revelation does not propose moral principles inaccessible to unaided reason but, by locating human nature within salvation history, revelation discloses some new specifically christian norms. Now, I may not understand the distinction between principles and norms or I might not understand the implications of inaccessible, but I've often thought that there are many things that we learned in natural theology or ethics which could not be established as absolutes without revelation. For example, it is said that one can put together an argument for the indissolubility of marriage on a natural basis. But to insist that it has to apply even to the very painful cases where, apparently, from the human point of view there'd be an advantage to dissolving the marriage, I don't think, myself, that that has ever been conclusive.

Further, we obviously can put together an argument against contraception from a natural point of view, but if that had come through strongly and clearly to everybody we wouldn't have wound up with the dispute that we had in the 1960s. I think the same thing applies to abortion in the conflict situations where there's a gigantic harm. It comes up in terms of rape or incest, those kinds of things in our own country. I'm inclined to think the same thing could occur at times from a natural point of view with regard to the morality of suicide, of some people being better off dead than staying around, that is, if we're operating without revelation.

I think you could apply the same thing almost to the question of martyrdom on whether or not it's a good way or a smart way to go rather than throwing a little bit of incense in and surviving to do a whole lot of good in the future.

It seems to me that the point is a little bit like the dispute between Gilson and Maritain over whether or not there is a Christian philosophy or not. Maritain said if it's philosophy it shouldn't be Christian and Gilson said if you look at it historically there are many things that wouldn't be in our philosophy if we hadn't learned them from revelation.

PROFESSOR FINNIS: I think that, interesting as it is, the question of the precise boundary line between what's specifically Christian and what's not is really of relatively secondary importance. It's a debate amongst academics, to some extent like the debate you alluded to between Maritain and Gilson, on the analogous question of Christian philosophy—to some extent a secondary question.

When I spoke of new, specifically Christian moral norms which are inaccessible to unaided reason, I certainly wasn't thinking of the norms you mentioned, for example, concerning contraception or abortion or suicide. The confusion that *de facto* exists concerning such specific norms of natural law can, I think, be quite readily explained by a philosophical account of, or on the basis of a philosophical account of, morality. Contrary to what was said by many of the moral theologians in the first half of the 20th Century (including some of those who later abandoned the old moral and took up a new proportionalist one), such norms as the norm about marriage or contraception or abortion are not primary intuitions or primary principles of the natural law grasped by a kind of direct intuition. The neo-scholastic manuals tend to propose such norms

255

as if they corresponded to what St. Thomas said are the first principles of the natural law, principles which, he says, are really held by everyone —principles which anyone who's capable of reasoning grasps.

Now, that tendency was unfaithful to St. Thomas who makes it quite clear that a norm like "robbery is always wrong" is a *conclusion* from further higher principles and is *not* held universally. St. Thomas points the finger at the Germans, amongst whom robbery is accounted no wrong. (I don't know the truth of that; St. Thomas is alluding to Julius Caesar's rather dim view of the Germans.) St. Thomas clearly doesn't hold that norms such as "no killing of the innocent", "no contraception," etc., are very first principles which are known to everyone who is of the age of reason. He thinks of them as conclusions.

Now, Aquinas doesn't fully satisfactorily set out, explicitly, the *process of inference* from the very first principles which identify certain basic human goods as to be done and pursued and what's contrary to them as to be avoided. And a lot of the work has had to be done in reviving, expounding and developing his work in the last thirty or forty years has been to identify the principles which are *intermediate,* i.e., between the very first principles and specific moral norms. I think some success has been had in the philosophical work on that question.

Now, part of that inference will be not only the identification of intermediate principles such as the Golden Rule (which is an intermediate principle) which start to shape specific moral norms, but also another critical part of the work is in reaching an exact analysis of action of the shape of a human choice, an analysis of action which will distinguish between that aspect of a choice which is its point or end, and that aspect which is of means, and that aspect which involves the disposition of the will to accept or permit side effects which while foreseen are none the less caused and yet not part of the proposal adopted by the choice.

It's very easy to see that many people are confused about the distinction between side effects and means. There's a great deal of simple philosophical and common-sense confusion about that, although common sense readily grasps that distinction once it is clearly put. And much of the confusion about abortion, contraception, hard cases, borderline cases, what isn't or what is sterilization or contraception, what is or isn't homicide in terminating a pregnancy, is a matter of simple, straightforward, philosophical or common sense confusions about what is *within* a proposal and what is not within a proposal but only *permitted.* Once one sees that this is *complex* but a matter of *truth,* one can see *both* how there can be true moral norms on this matter—norms which are true in a sense that is accessible to reason—*and* why there are so many mistakes about it.

It's complex. There's a lot of opportunity for the emotions to capitalize on difficult and fine distinctions, to shift reason towards the "convenient." The norms of natural law are accessible to natural reason, but that doesn't mean they are easily accessible. St. Thomas says that they are "evident to the wise," not to everyone.

DR. MacINTYRE: As a matter of autobiographical fact, I came to the conclusion that there were exceptionless and binding norms prior to and quite independently of any faith in Divine Revelation. We must not ignore that there is an issue here for the purely secular world and that it is in the end corrupting to suggest to that world that the only adequate grounds they can have for certain norms is that there is a revelation which declares there to be such. If that were so, people who did not accept revelation, who did not have the gift of faith, would be fully justified in not accepting those norms.

Let me add one remark to supplement what Professor Finnis has said. People who adopt a norm about marriage, about suicide, about truthtelling, which allows for exceptions are not only adopting a different norm. They are also adopting a different attitude to the norm and to norms as such. They are saying, "I am going to be bound by this most of the time, but I leave open the possibility that I may abandon my commitment at certain points." And it is rarely possible for such persons to specify with adequate precision in advance just where this will take defection to be justified. And so what happens is that a generally uncommitted or half-committed attitude to norms follows from this.

So the difference between a morality which allows for exceptions and a morality of exceptionless norms is not only a difference over the content and formulation of norms. It is a difference about what kind of commitment morality requires from us. It is important that morality requires in unconditional commitment by which we bind ourselves so that we then have to deal with particular situations in terms of that commitment. We have not left ourselves free.

Somebody who is thinking about marriage, and who considers marriage dissoluble, is not thinking about marriage in the same sense as someone who holds it to be indissoluable. Each of these envisages a different kind of possibility, one in which there is and one in which there is not an unconditional commitment. So different attitudes to norms involve a further difference about the way in which one relates to the institutions in whose life one participates and about the way in which one defines one's relationships to other people. All these issues arise just as much about the moral issue of truthtelling and lying which is one very little discussed in our public life as they do over abortion or over marriage.

BISHOP: It was suggested yesterday and today that there be some kind of a forum, that there be a discussion back and forth of various viewpoints and then the bishops would come to a judgment. With this judgment, it seems to me there would be two possible alternatives that wouldn't really be totally exclusive but one would be the conclusion that judgments that would be made would be a series of exceptionless rules. It would be sort of a disciplinary thing. The opposite of that would be based upon what we've heard this morning about morality involving the good as understood in revelation, the common good, what is good for all people. What is virtue? Who are heroes and saints? Would it be possible that while these two things would not be mutually exclusive, the conclusion, the judgment might be that we need better education as to the meaning of good as revealed to us and the common good.

DR. MacINTYRE: If I understand the question, the attempt to contrast a morality of exceptionless rules on the one hand and one which relies upon an adequate conception of human good on the other, as though these were rival alternatives is precisely the contrast which both I and Professor Finnis have been attacking. I do not see these as alternatives. An adequate conception of the human good will be given content by an account of what different types of human life exemplify that good. I say "different types of human life" because different occupations, different familiar commitments, different situations in the world always affect the way in which the good is realized in a particular life.

But what the exceptionless rules do is to specify the kind of commitments without which one cannot bring into being and sustain the kind of communal relationships through which alone the good can be achieved by anyone. So the exceptionless rules specify necessary conditions for the achievement of the good. I take it that it is the task of the bishops and, indeed, of no one else to speak to us in an authoritative voice about what revelation says on these matters. They characteristically have to take the advice of other people on how in particular types of cases, on particular policy questions, in the lives of particular communities, the relationship between goods and rules is worked out. Very often, the important work here will be done by theologians, by sociologists who have the relevant kind of commitment and even, occasionally, by philosophers. So what the bishops have to do for the rest of us is to produce the authoritative judgments which provide the context for this other work and only they can do that.

PROFESSSOR FINNIS: I think it's very important to see that the question of proposing to the faithful exceptionless moral norms is not in the first instance and fundamentally a matter of disciplinary norms. If they are proposed in the tradition, the tradition which has come into dispute in the last thirty years, they are proposed in the tradition *as truths about human good,* about the content and the requirements of human flourishing, *in the real human context* of human nature created, fallen, redeemed called to glory. The Church has proposed these exceptionless moral norms as truths not only in the clear (over long periods) teaching of the ordinary magisterium, universal and unanimous throughout the world, but also in the way that Professor MacIntyre was putting before us: by proposing to us heroes and saints.

A good number of the saints whom the Church has canonized are presented to us, in that formal act of canonization, precisely as models, as persons whose fidelity to the good took the form of unconditional adherence to exceptionless moral norms. If you'll pardon me mentioning an English saint, take St. Thomas More. He lost all his worldly goods and possessions and was imprisoned for life, *not* on account of his fidelity to the Papacy, but simply for one reason: he was unwilling to tell a lie, to swear an oath, not on a matter of theological doctrine but on a matter of fact: an oath that he thought that the marriage of Henry and Catherine had a character which, as a matter of fact, he thought it didn't have. So, here we have an example of someone held before us as a model, for his adherence not to a matter of discipline but to a truth, a truth about the exceptionless moral norm excluding lying on oath.

BISHOP: I would like to make some remarks regarding the paper of Dr. Finnis. First, it seems to me that a large amount of the confusion in the discussion of natural law is due to a certain shift of understanding of the notion of natural law.

St. Thomas understood, I think, by natural law the natural law in its strictest sense, that is, referring to the first principles which he referred to as "naturally known principles." Then subsequent theologians included in this notion the conclusions derived from the first principles and the eventual result in these conclusions which were derived from the first principles and were given the same necessity.

The second remark has to do with your outline referring to the Christian moral and social teaching grounded on natural law. I remember an article by Cardinal Ratzinger in 1968 when he proposed that the social teaching of the Church, the Christian social teaching, should not be grounded on the consideration of natural law but instead the social data, the social empirical data.

And the third remark is a question, maybe a restatement of the key thesis of your paper: How does revealed morality differ from natural morality?

DR. FINNIS: Well, we might have to recall the classic teaching that the Ten Commandments, or the second table of the Ten Commandments, in their specified content are all of natural law. This is not a late Neoscholastic development, but something even more clearly taught by St. Thomas, already being proposed by Fathers of the second century.

The natural law is, of course, a matter of first principles, but it's also a matter of the rational, reasonable, valid conclusions from first principles. St. Thomas is very clear that a valid process of inference from principles to conclusions is possible. And it's natural law all the way down, as far as this inference is valid. It goes down, so to speak, so far as quite specific moral norms such as: the innocent are never to be intentionally killed, killed as an end or as a means, and so forth.

So I don't, myself, agree that there was a late, questionable, dubious shift of understanding that extravagantly included conclusions where in truth it should have only accepted, first principles as matters of natural law.

As to Joseph Ratzinger's 1968 thoughts about Catholic social teaching, I wouldn't like to venture any opinion since I haven't seen or don't recall what he said. I would venture this, though: any sharp distinction, or any sort of potent distinction, between social teaching and moral teaching is open to very serious question. There is, of course, something which is conventionally referred to as Catholic social teaching which is commonly not thought of as including, for example, the Church's teaching on marriage or on sexuality or on abortion. But this is clearly no more than a rather questionable textbook convention which I think needs to be subject to pretty severe criticism.

The Church's social teaching, rather like the teaching on marriage which I expounded in terms of negative norms which make available a creativity of virtue towards the good—the Church's social teaching itself has a whole range of those classical moral norms as its fundamental principles.

In response to the third question, I think the primary function, the primary role of revelation is to clarify and make more accessible what in principle is already accessible but which is obscured because our situation is obscured. Our situation, our nature is not easily understood by us unless we see it in the true situation. That situation includes a supernatural destiny—not simply as some sort of extrinsic reward, summoned up by divine decree without an intrinsic relationship to our service of human goods, but, rather (given the gratuity of Gods promises and grace) as a matter involving some sort of intrinsic relation between that service of human goods and the shaping of the Kingdom which begins in this world. (See *Gaudium et spes* 39.) Now, once that situation is disclosed to us, then the rational force of many of the norms of the natural law takes on a clarity which it doesn't have especially in the flux of emotional and conventionally shaped life into which each one of us is born. So revelation clarifies principles, but introduces nothing new in the way of *principles*. There are, I think, specific Christian *norms* but they are specific conclusions from the naturally known or knowable principles, conclusions which are drawn precisely in the light of what our Lord's life and teachings disclose to us. So my example was a norm which gives the priority and shape that mercy has in Christian life.

That norm really only becomes rationally acceptable if human possibilities are seen in a way that is disclosed to us by revelation.

Chapter 17

THE CHURCH AND PUBLIC POLICY

Carl A. Anderson, J.D.

By "public policy" I understand, of course, that process in which laws are enacted within the legislative forum, agency rule-making is administered, and litigation proceeds within the judiciary. And by public policy I understand something more: the ideal or the expectation, sometimes unarticulated, which defines the context of public policy-making, which determines the environment in which certain questions may be asked and, perhaps more importantly, which questions may not be asked at all. In short, I include as part of the concept of public policy that ideal in the hearts and minds of the citizens against which the actions of those of us in the policy-making arena are measured.

During my professional life I have had the privilege of participating in the formulation of public policy from many perspectives:

that of the Congress, that of a cabinet-level department, and that of the chief executive office of government during my years at the White House. Having said this, let me say as well that during this time I have never met a Catholic participating in the public policy process who has sought to establish Catholic doctrine or Catholic moral teaching as such in law. I have seen only men and women who, upon reflecting on their own experiences and the experiences of others as well as the lessons of history, have sought to propose rules of reason for the common good to which all members of the larger society could be expected to assent.

Let me begin my remarks with three examples of the context in which the formation of public policy today takes place. First, let me relate an incident which occurred while I was working as a legal advisor to the Secretary of Health and Human Services. In April, 1982, in Bloomington, Indiana, the parents of a newborn infant with Down's Syndrome and suffering from a life-threatening, yet surgically correctable congenital defect, was allowed to die when his parents refused permission for the surgery to be performed. The Department of Health and Human Services responded to this case and others like it through the exercise of its rule-making power.[1]

While this rule-making process was underway, the Surgeon General of the United States, Dr. C. Everett Koop, and myself were asked by the Secretary to serve as co-chairmen of a series of meetings between representatives of medical, disability, and health care organizations, including among others the American Academy of Pediatrics, the American Medical Association, the American Hospital Association, and the Catholic Health Association. At these meetings health care representatives discussed the treatment that was afforded such infants and how treatment decisions were made in the best interest of the child. During this time the journal of the American Academy of Pediatrics published a two-page guest editorial by Peter Singer. In the editorial entitled, "Sanctity or Quality of Life?" Singer concluded as follows,

Whatever the future holds, it is likely to prove impossible to restore in full the sanctity-of-life view. The philosophical foundations of this view have been knocked asunder. We can no longer base our ethics on the idea that human beings are a special form of creation, made in the image of God, singled out from all other animals, and alone possessing an immortal soul. Our better understanding of our own nature has bridged the gulf that was once thought to lie between ourselves and other species, so why should we believe that the mere fact that a being is a member of the species *Homo sapiens* endows its life with some unique, almost infinite, value?

Once the religious mumbo-jumbo surrounding the term "human" has been stripped away, we may continue to see normal members of our species as possessing greater capacities of rationality, self-consciousness, communication, and so on, than members of any other species; but we will not regard as sacrosanct the life of each.... If we compare a severely defective human infant with a non-human animal, a dog or a pig, for example, we will often find the nonhuman to have superior capacities, both actual and potential, for rationality, self-consciousness, communication, and anything else that can plausibly be considered morally significant. Only the fact that the defective infant is a member of the species *Homo sapiens* leads it to be treated differently from the dog or pig. Species membership alone, however, is not morally relevant.[2]

My second example comes from the recent congressional debate involving the Hyde Amendment restriction on federal funding of abortion. As we know, last year for the first time in nearly a decade, the House of Representatives voted down the Hyde Amendment and replaced it with language providing for abortions in case of rape and incest. This defeat was made possible by the switch of 21 congressmen who had previously supported the amendment, 11 of whom were Roman Catholic. During congressional debate on abortion last year, perhaps the most outspoken advocate of abortion funding was a Congressman from California and a Roman Catholic. As Chairman of the House Select Committee on Children, Youth, and Families, this Congressman is one of the most influential members of the congressional leadership regarding laws affecting American families. He concluded his remarks on the floor of the House of Representatives urging the defeat of the Hyde Amendment by saying "Let us not turn the disgusting, violent, solitary act of rape into a gang rape by the Congress of the United States."[3]

From 1976 through 1981, I had the privilege of working closely with the prolife congressional leadership in both Houses in defending the Hyde Amendment in the Congress and as an attorney representing Senator James Buckley, Senator Jesse Helms, and Congressman Henry Hyde in their effort to defend the constitutionality of the Hyde Amendment before the United States Supreme Court. Two aspects of the current debate were made very clear even at that early date. First, that the Hyde Amendment always permitted prompt medical treatment (which, of course, excludes abortion) for victims of rape and that for those victims who have been so treated the incidence of pregnancy is virtually non-existent. Second, that many congressmen and especially some Catholic congressmen justified their votes against the Hyde Amendment with the explanation that the amendment must certainly be held unconstitutional and that therefore they could not in our pluralistic society impose their private morality upon our constitutional system. Once, however, the Hyde Amendment was held to be constitutional their voting pattern did not change, merely their public rationale for supporting abortion. I predict we will find the same behavior pattern when *Roe v Wade* is finally overturned. In fact, we are already beginning to see it.

My third example involves the cultural conditioning of public policy making. During 1986, I had the privilege of assisting their Eminences, Joseph Cardinal Bernardin and John Cardinal O'Connor, along with a number of Protestant clergymen, in organizing the Religious Alliance Against Pornography. That organization has done much to enliven the religious community in the fight against pornography. I was pleased to have the opportunity to host a day-long briefing at the White House for leaders of this organization which included a meeting with President Reagan. Later, this organization, along with the Knights of Columbus, was instrumental in the enactment by Congress of the Child Pornography and Obscenity Amendments of 1987.

One of the most pressing problems confronted by the Religious Alliance Against Pornography is the relationship between pornography and violence. This is a severe problem in itself but a pervasive tragedy when related to the issues of family disintegration, low self-esteem, sexual assault, pregnancy and abortion rates among unmarried teenagers. Some of you may have read or heard about a recent Oprah Winfrey show which featured the rap singer Ice-T and a song in which he sings about using a flashlight to perform sexual acts with a woman in language which is not fit to repeat. More depressing still, were the comments of women who appeared on the program who said they did not mind being referred to in such terms, who said they thought it humorous, or who said they thought that as long as the singer made a profit, it did not matter what he sang about.[4]

These three examples, spanning all the levels of our society, touch on three crucial areas of the Church's concerns in public policy; namely, medical treatment of the poor and disabled, the right to life of the innocent unborn, and the exploitation of women and children. Moreover, these three cases touch on the very heart of what it means to be a human person. These examples, I submit, are not aberrations. They represent a way of thinking that has become, in fact, the dominant way of thinking, consciously or unconsciously, of a large number of people whose hands guide the cultural and political state of our society. In this paper I shall seek to describe this way of thinking and identify its deepest roots. Finally, I will conclude by suggesting to you ways in which you, as our Bishops, can lead us toward that "civilization of love" which has become the goal of the new evangelization called for by the Second Vatican Council.

As the three examples above suggest, contemporary society's vision of the human person is at the foundation of the most pressing problems of public policy today. Elsewhere I have had the opportunity to explore at greater length the anthropological foundation of legal rights.[5] Let me say here that

> every legal system rests, consciously or unconsciously, upon a theory of man... [sometimes] the underlying theory is apt to be present only implicitly. But this does not lessen its influence.... [6]

My starting point today is that the secular humanist vision of the human person is constitutive of the present context of public policy debate and that it is a singularly tragic threat to the dignity of the human person in the public arena. At times this vision is openly espoused as in my first example. Yet this vision has become so pervasive that it is no longer resisted and may even be held by many who consider themselves believers. The challenge of this atheist anthropology has been brilliantly described by some of the Church's outstanding theologians, including Henri Cardinal De Lubac, S.J., Joseph Cardinal Ratzinger, and Archbishop Walter Kasper. As early as 1950, Fr. De Lubac's, *The Drama of Atheist Humanism*, traced the philosophical ascent of modern atheism through the work of Feuerbach, Nietzsche, Marx, and Comte. De Lubac sees the following words of Feuerbach as best describing the underlying presupposition of atheism:

> It is the essence of man that is the supreme being.... The turning point of history will be the moment when man becomes aware that the only god of man is man himself. *Homo homini deus.*[7]

Therefore, the question at the heart of modern atheism is less the question of God's existence than it is the question of man's identity. Modern atheism is, above all, an athropological conviction. The work of Feuerbach and the other "founding fathers" of atheism was primarily "to reveal to mankind its own essence in order to give it faith in itself."[8]

Paul Ricoeur has referred to Marx, Nietzsche, and Freud as the "masters of suspicion,"[9] thereby underlining the tactic with which atheism confronts the Christian faith. Their tactic has been to cast suspicion on the convictions of the Christian as referring, not to the reality of God, but as merely ways of coping with human situations which inhibit human freedom. Religious faith is seen by them as a mechanism to project into another world the tension which men cannot resolve in the present world. The task of atheism is to express what the atheist considers to be the true anthropological nature of the problem and thereby to free man. For the atheist, the destruction of religion and, in particular, the destruction of Christianity becomes the *sine qua non* for the establishment of the dignity of the human person. Atheism cannot peacefully coexist with theism. Nietzsche argued that for the modern mind the death of God is not a fact but an act of the will. The problem is not one of simply reading the five proofs for the existence of God. As Nietzsche wrote, "it is our preference that decides against Christianity—not arguments."[10] As De Lubac observes, "Atheism is, at the very root of it, an anti-theism."[11]

In his book, *Introduction to Christianity*, Joseph Cardinal Ratzinger relates the rise of atheism to the modern way of viewing reality. He sees modern man as having rejected first the scholastic formula, "being is truth" (*verum est ens*) and in its place substituting the equation, "truth is what we have made ourselves" (*verum quia factum*).[12] This substitution was followed by still another. Truth is now not what has been made by man, but what *can* be made by man: '*verum quia faciendum*,' or, if you will technology."[13] The implications of this new way of thinking in bioethics, in such matters as *in vitro* fertilization, fetal research, and fetal organ transplantation have already proved morally devastating.

Walter Kasper, in *The God of Jesus Christ*, provides a succinct description of the rise and nature of modern atheism which is fully compatible with the analysis of Cardinals De Lubac and Ratzinger. For Archbishop Kasper, atheism "came into existence only in the modern age."[14] It is a worldview

which denies any and every divine or absolute that is not simply identical with man and with the world of our empirical experience and with its eminent principles.[15]

The modern denial of God, he argues,

sprang into existence as a reaction, in the name of freedom, against an absolutist image of God. It is inseparable from modern subjectivity,.... In this secularized world God becomes increasingly superfluous as a hypothesis for explaining within the world; he loses his function in regard to the world. We must live in the world as though there were no God.[16]

Kasper also underlines another extremely important point for our discussion. Today's atheism, he argues, pre-supposes Christianity and could only arise as a "post-Christian phenomenon."[17] The reason is that it is Christianity that has made, in Christ, an insepable connection between the mystery of God and the reality of man. It is Christianity that has made unbreakable the link between man's nature and destiny and the truth about God. For the Christian faith, man is defined as the creature made for a share in God's own life. The fullest revelation of the truth about God is, for Christianity, the *humanity* of Christ. Henceforth, after Christianity, if one wills to be an atheist, to deny God's existence, it is necessary to alter the Christian view about the nature of man. Thus man becomes the locus of confrontation between faith and unbelief.

It is for this reason, it seems to me, that the Second Vatican Council, in its *Pastoral Constitution on the Church in the Modern World,* confronted the question of atheism in its discussion on the dignity of the human person. The Council stated that:

> Modern atheism often takes on a systematic expression which, in addition to other causes, stretches the desire for human independence to such a point that it poses difficulties against any kind of dependence on God. Those who profess atheism of this sort maintain that it gives man freedom to be an end unto himself, the sole artisan and creator of his own history.... Favoring this doctrine can be the sense of power which modern technical progress generates in man.[18]

The Council recognized modern atheism as a deliberate rejection of Christian anthropology. And it responded to the challenge by asserting the reality of the Incarnation, declaring that in Christ, the realities of God and man are inseparable. Hence we read:

> The truth is that only in the mystery of the incarnate Word does the mystery of man take on light.... Christ, the final Adam, by the revelation of the mystery of the Father and His love, fully reveals man to man himself and makes his supreme calling clear.[19]

It is this struggle for the very nature of the human person that the Council willingly took up. During the last general meeting of the Second Vatican Council, Pope Paul VI clearly pointed out this basic orientation of the Council when he stated:

> Yes, the Church of the Council has been concerned, not just with herself and with her relationship of union with God, but with man—man as he really is today: living man, man all wrapped up in himself, man who makes himself not only the center of his every interest, but dares to claim that he is the principle and explanation of all reality....
>
> The religion of the God who became man has met the religion (for such it is) of man who makes himself God.... [W]e call upon those who term themselves modern humanists,... to recognize our own new type of humanism. We, too, in fact, we more than any others, honor mankind.[20]

John Paul II, in his very first encyclical letter, stated it succinctly: man is "the way for the Church."[21] And who can forget the challenge with which he began his public ministry: "Do not be afraid!" Pope John Paul II's message has been clear: Modern man should not be afraid of Christ; afraid that He will take away anything of his liberty and dignity. The construction of a civilization worthy of man requires the rejection of atheistic humanism's war against the link between man and God.[22]

In the "desert of atheism," as Ghandi called it, men and women are imprisoned by a dialectic of left versus right, liberal versus conservative, collectivism versus individualism which at times may constitute two separate sides of the same secularist coin. Consider the abortion issue as framed by this kind of thinking. On the one side is the individualistic, autonomous zone of private decision-making established by *Roe v. Wade*: "*I* decide what to do or not to do; consideration of the common good plays no part in my decision."[23] At the other extreme is the position that what matters *is* only the collectivity (in Marxist terminology, the "species being" into which one's individuality must be submerged). The personhood of the unborn child cannot be considered since this is a matter of private belief. This is the situation today in the People's Republic of China when abortion is enforced as a method of population control.[24] Increasingly, one has difficulty in distinguishing which of these is the "liberal" and which is the "conservative" position. Meanwhile, the massacre of the unborn goes on. ...

To paraphrase St. Paul: who can deliver us from this deadly contradiction? Only an authentic vision of the human person can rescue us. It is the Church's task to promote this anthropological vision in forming that ideal in the hearts and minds of our citizens by which public policy is measured. In so doing, the Church is often hampered by another claimed dialectic. The problem has been formulated as determining how much of the Church's moral doctrine derives from reason and how much from revelation. Only that coming from reason, it is said, can be expected to be considered by a pluralistic secular society such as ours, and that is true enough. It is also said that what comes from revelation can only be perceived by faith and therefore cannot be proposed for incorporation into our public agenda, and, again, that is true. This question, however, should not be allowed to hamper the Church's contribution in this area. I say this for two reasons.

First, what Jacques Maritain wrote in his *The Right of Man and Natural Law* still remains true:

> there is, by very virtue of human nature, an order or disposition which human reason can discover and according to which the human will must act in order to attune itself to the necessary ends of the human being.[25]

Thus, the natural law remains the indispensable bridge for dialogue between the believer and non-believer in the public arena.

The second reason is that this way of posing the relation between reason and revelation in the moral order may be another kind of enslaving dialectic. Surely, one who accepts the mystery of the Incarnation cannot be entirely comfortable with this dualism. In the Incarnation there is only *one reality:* both "one and the same," human and divine, or if you will, natural and supernatural. To cope with this *oneness* while respecting the integrity of the human and divine order, the Church Fathers began the long process of the transformation of Greek philosophy by introducing into the world the notion of *person*, the end product of which would be an understanding of man as the modern idea of someone who is a unique and unrepeatable *who*, a *who* that can never be collapsed into any *what*. It is this notion of human personhood, of what came to be called personal rights and dignity, which comes from this encounter between faith and reason. It is this notion of personhood which formed the basis for our constitutional and legal system and which is disappearing today as the informing principle of public policy.

As I read the message of the Second Vatican Council it is that ultimately, only the mystery of the Incarnation discloses the fullness of the reality of human personhood; yet at the same time the Council is confident that all human beings will find within their own experience of personhood an echo of that Truth (whose name the Church knows). It seems to me the Council is confident too, that the anthropological vision which it proposes is the only one that fully corresponds to the reality of all human beings and will ultimately be seen by them as such. Thus this vision is far from a narrow sectarian creed, nor can it even be said to be limited to the broader Judeo-Christian tradition. It is, rather, an appeal to all persons of good will. The natural law tradition observes that a free society must be "personalist."[26] It must be a society which recognizes itself to be constituted by persons whose dignity is anterior to itself and who seek, in the words of Maritain, "a perfect spiritual liberty." But the assault on this tradition has been so oppressive that the Church must once again bear witness to the most fundamental perception and experience of human personhood.

Contemporary observers increasingly recognize that the foundational question confronting modern culture is the relation between human liberty and transcendence. This is perhaps seen most clearly in issues which deal with the very nature of human life and liberty, issues such as abortion, use of human fetuses for research, and euthanasia. Others, such as the bioethical issues raised in the instruction *Donum vitae*, can be added. Under the influence of the atheist mentality outlined above, society seems increasingly incapable of dealing with these issues. Public policy finds it increasingly difficult to do justice to the human person. The temptation grows daily to deal with human life issues by purely technical and utilitarian considerations. As a result, the needs of the powerless, the most vulnerable, the weakest, and the least visible are increasingly ignored, their rights and their dignity increasingly violated, and their very existence denied or extinguished.

Having abandoned "an order... which reason can discover," the atheist mentality responds to technological and utilitarian considerations with "good feelings" and "good intentions," and with a "tenderness" which, as Walker Percy has recognized, leads inevitably to the *destruction* of those whose "quality of life" does not measure up to contemporary standards; a tenderness which, in his words, "leads to the gas chamber."[27] This is the true drama of modern atheism: the destruction of man in the name of man as the inevitable result of the "death of God" in the modern consciousness. This, I submit to you, is the deepest challenge to the Church in our society today: to respond to what Cardinal Ratzinger called in a speech last month at the John Paul II Institute in Washington "the successful campaign of death's anti-culture."[28] At its core lies the definition of human personhood. Perhaps I should say the *perception* of personhood because public policy regarding the "human-life issues" is suffering from the loss of the ability to perceive the reality of human personhood and the character of a "personalist" society.

Why is it, ultimately, that some cannot perceive that the child in the womb is *someone,* a person unique and unrepeatable? Why is it that a patient in an irreversible coma, or dying slowly of an incurable disease is not perceived to be as much a human being as someone enjoying health and engaged in activities? Why is it that a frozen embryo is not perceived as a human being technologically impeded from his or her normal development? No, it is not true that only with the eyes of faith we may see these things. Reason alone is sufficient to teach us these lessons. Certainly in each case the individual in question is of the genus "human being." But why is it, that for so many, the lessons of reason do not resonate to evoke an affirmative response? Why is it, that during the national debate on the withholding of medical care from handicapped infants the American Academy of Pediatrics promotes the view that we must "strip away" the "religious mumbo-jumbo" surrounding the term "human," saying that simple membership in the species *Homo sapiens* is morally irrelevant? Why is it that in the national debate on abortion, Catholic public officials find it more important, on moral grounds, to embrace principles of equality or personal choice rather than to end the destruction of human life on this appallingly massive scale?

The answer was suggested two decades ago in an editorial in the journal of the California Medical Association. It stated, in part, the following:

> The traditional Western ethic has always placed great emphasis on the intrinsic worth and equal value of every human life regardless of its stage or condition. This ethic has had the blessing of our Judeo-Christian heritage and has been the basis for most of our laws and much of our social policy . . . [29]

The editorial went on to state that this traditional ethic was being eroded by scientific and technological developments empowering man to control the quality of life. As a result, the old ethic's insistence upon the absolute value of life was being replaced with a relative value. The editorial concluded:

> The process of eroding the old ethic and substituting the new has already begun. It may be seen most clearly in changing attitudes toward human abortion. . . . It is worth nothing that this shift in public attitude has affected the churches, the laws, and public policy rather than the reverse.[30]

How then can we restore the recognition of the absolute value of the human person? It can only be done through the honest confrontation by each person of the basic fact of his or her existence—the fact that each of us is a contingent being. The stark and honest confrontation of this fact makes possible the perception of one's personhood in its irreducible mystery. This may happen when one is placed in a situation requiring a decision where one's own identity is at stake. I think of my patron—the patron of lawyers—Thomas More, incarcerated in the Tower, and being urged to give in to the King's demands so that no further suffering would come to his wife and daughters. Appeals to his citizenship had not worked; threats to his own survival had not worked. An appeal was

275

now made to his most intimate relationships as husband and father. More was asked to measure the value of his duties as husband and father against the value of adhering to what his Catholic faith taught was the usurpation by the king of spiritual authority. Confronted by a situation in which his consent to God's sovereignty was at stake, More understood that his own identity was also at stake. If he compromised and withheld absolute consent to God's sovereignty, he would have measured the value of his existence by realities that were earthly and temporal. Such a compromise would indeed compromise himself since it did not correspond to what he knew to be the transcendent dimension of his own experience of "self-hood." He understood that to withhold absolute consent to God's sovereignty would destroy his own personhood. He would no longer be the same husband to his wife, the same father to his daughters. His wife and daughters did not simply want *a* husband and *a* father. They loved *him* who was *the* husband and *the* father. In attempting to save his life in this way he would indeed have lost it.

More's perception of his personhood was provoked by the demand that he swear to the Act of Supremacy, a situation which placed him standing before God's sovereignty. When one is placed in such a situation, one recognizes that finite calculations and utilitarian considerations fail to account for what the human conscience experiences. It is the refusal to undergo this experience which lies at the heart of the modern failure to perceive human personhood and its absolute value. This failure comes when one accepts the atheist position that man is God to man: *homo homini deus;* that the fullest expression of one's dignity and liberty requires the extinction of the awareness of the presence of God in our lives. No longer able to perceive personhood in ourselves we are blind to considerations of personhood in others, especially the "least of our brethren" whose only "activity" possible may be in being themselves. It is to this situation that modern atheism has brought us.

In his speech exploring the consequences of the rejection of the Church's teaching on *Humanae Vitae,* Msgr. Carlo Caffarra, president of the John Paul II Institute for the Study of Marriage and Family, summarized this situation as the "progressive dimming of the splendor of the glory of God" in our culture. There are certain moments, he stated, when human "free will is called to its supreme act: to acknowledge that God is the Creator of every person or to acknowledge that man is the creator of man. That is: either that man, in the very act of his being, is entrusted to a freedom that transcends him, or that man is entrusted exclusively to himself." The decision for atheism is a decision embracing the latter option. When this denial of the glory of God takes place, man is left at the mercy of his own misery, falling victim to what Caffarra called "the mutability of non-being,... the meaninglessness of error,... the desert of egoism." St. Paul taught this clearly:

> "they exchanged the glory of the immortal God for a worthless imitation... that is why God left them to... practices with which they dishonor their own bodies, since they have given up divine truth for a lie and have worshipped and served creatures instead of the Creator.... Since they refused to see it was rational to acknowledge God, God has left them to their own irrational ideas and to their monstrous behavior." (Rom. 1:23–28)

Coming to the end of my presentation, I wish first of all and above all to thank you, our bishops, for transmitting faithfully this "divine truth," what Walter Kasper has called "the prophetic interpretation of reality." This is absolutely the most important task you perform in promoting a society that respects the dignity of the human person. In this respect nothing is more important than to never call the light darkness or the darkness light. Please accept from me a word of encouragement: bear witness to the truth about the human person confidently and courageously in season and out of season. May I say that in this regard, the heroic example of John Cardinal O'Connor at St. Patrick's Cathedral after the recent desecration of the Mass comes immediately to mind. We must equally have confidence in man, created in the image of God. May I say that in this regard the thousands of Catholics who have warmly greeted Cardinal O'Connor in recent days at St. Patrick's Cathedral and elsewhere also come to mind. Confidence in man is *not* shown when the truth is compromised or hidden because of accusations that it is unrealistic or demanding or unpopular. These accusations will be made; but let us hope, as Pope Paul VI said at the end of the Council, that in the end it will be recognized that it was

277

confidence in man that motivated us and that in this way we have truly honored man.

I must say that many in the public arena are confused and disappointed when, especially in issues so directly touching the dignity of the human person, Catholic public officials often make the difference in defeating policies which promote this dignity. We saw this most recently in the turn-around of many Catholic legislators who made possible the defeat of the Hyde Amendment in the House of Representatives. What confuses many is not how because of weakness the truth may be compromised for political gain. What is so disturbing is why in the 17 years since *Roe v Wade* Catholic politicians have come to believe that they can repudiate the clear teaching of the natural law and the word of God without fear of the terrible spiritual implications. There is a sense here of what psychologists term "cognitive dissonance," of that disharmony between speech and affect that is so characteristic of the schizophrenic. If I may employ psychiatric terminology for a moment: How will this inconsistency in the informational interaction between the organism and environmental circumstances be reduced? Recently, Cardinal O'Connor stated that he believed that the "demon" of legalized abortion could only be driven out be prayer and fasting. It seems to me that the use of all spiritual resources and weapons (to use St. Paul's terminology) at your disposal in communicating this teaching is an inseparable part of the demonstration of confidence in man.

Let me conclude with the following observation. Most public opinion experts say that Catholics will be the most important political constituency in the United States in the coming decade. This was already evident in the last presidential campaign. I am told by members of the President's campaign staff that as early as April, 1988, they recognized that the Catholic vote would determine the outcome of the election. Both political parties know that no Democrat has won the White House in recent history with less than 60% of the Catholic vote, and both parties know as well that no Republican has won without carrying heavily Catholic states such as Illinois, New Jersey, and Ohio.

My point is this: consider the issue of abortion. If Catholics in America define themselves as a constituency for which abortion is an issue of decisive importance, they will not only be largely responsible for the success of the prolife cause but perhaps even more importantly, the Catholic people will decisively inform the political process during the coming decade. But if we do not do this; if we instead define ourselves as a constituency for which the sanctity of life issue is of no decisive importance, or is just one of many other social concerns; if, in other words, the Catholic people fail to bear witness to the prophetic interpretation of reality, then Catholics in America as a political constituency will be reduced to the typical matrix of education, wealth, age, and race. Their opportunity to frame the political agenda in any area in the coming decade will be dissipated and lost.

I believe that the abortion issue puts Catholics in America in a situation similar to that of St. Thomas More. Abortion is an issue of ultimate self-definition. When confronted with this decision, individuals are called to consent or to withhold consent to the glory of God as the only Creator of human persons. This decision will define *who* they are in the light of their relation to the one who sustains their very being and identity as persons. I submit that the issue of abortion has placed the Catholic church in our country in an analogous situation where its identity and future is also at stake. And this, I propose to you, is the real nature of the Catholic moment.

Notes

1. The Department's regulations were, for the most part, successfully challenged in federal court during 1983. Congress responded by enacting the Child Abuse Amendments of 1984. Most recently, the U.S. Commission on Civil Rights issued a report in September, 1989, on the topic of medical discrimination against children with disabilities which examined the nature and extent of the practice of withholding medical treatment or nourishment from infants born with disabilities. The report recommended that greater enforcement be undertaken by federal and state officials. For a comprehensive analysis see, U.S. Commission on Civil Rights, *Medical Discrimination Against Children with Disabilities* (Sept., 1989).

2. *Pediatrics*, Vol. 72, No. 1, pp. 128–29, July, 1983.

3. *Congressional Record*, October 11, 1989, p. H6909.

4. Tipper Gore, "Hate, Rape and Rap," *Washington Post*, January 8, 1990. Such lyrics are not limited to a particular racial or ethnic group as the music of rock groups such as Rigor Mortis, 2 Live Crew, Guns N' Roses, and Ozzy Osbourne make clear.

5. Carl Anderson, "Moral Norms and Social Consensus: Toward the Anthropological Foundations of Human Rights," in *Persona Verita e Morale* (Rome: Citta Nuova Editrice, 1987), p. 373.

6. I. Jenkins, *Social Order and the Limits of the Law* (1980), p. 314.

7. Henri De Lubac, *The Drama of Atheist Humanism* (1950) p. 10.

8. *Id*, p. 11.

9. Paul Ricoeur, *The Conflict of Interpretations: Essays in Hermeneutics* (1974), p. 148.

10. *Supra* note 7 at p. 22.

11. *Id*, p. 19.

12. Joseph Ratzinger, *Introduction to Christianity* (1970), p. 31.

13. *Id*, p. 35. Ratzinger continues: "The truth with which man is concerned is neither the truth of being, nor even in the last resort that of his accomplished deeds, but the truth of changing the world, molding the world—a truth centered on future and action....

... The combination of mathematical thinking and factual thinking has produced the science-oriented intellectual standpoint of modern man, which signifies devotion to reality insofar as it is capable of being shaped. The fact has set free the *faciendum*, the 'made' has set free the 'makeable', the repeatable, the provable, and only exists for the sake of the latter. It comes to the primacy of the 'makeable' over the 'made'....

... *techne* has become the real strength and obligation of man. What was previously at the bottom is now on top... : at first in ancient and medieval times, man has concentrated on the eternal, then, during the short-lived predominance of the historical approach, of the past; but now the *faciendum*, the 'makeable' aspect of things directs its attention to the future of what he himself can create." *Id*, pp. 35–36.

14. Walter Kasper, *The God of Jesus Christ* (1989), p. 16.

15. *Id*

16. *Id*, p. 10.

17. *Id*, p. 17.

18. Second Vatican Council *Pastoral Constitution on the Church in the Modern World, Gaudium et Spes,* 24:AAS 58 (1965), no. 20.

19. *Id*, no. 22.

20. Pope Paul VI, "Address to the Last General Meeting of Vatican Council II," reprinted in *Catholic Mind* (April, 1966) pp. 60–61. See also, Walter Kasper, *Theology and Church* (1989), pp. 32–53.

21. Pope John Paul II, encyclical letter *Redemptor Hominis,* 14:AAS 71 (1979), no. 14.

22. See, for example, Andre Frossard and Pope John Paul II, *Be Not Afraid* (1982), p. 97.

23. Roe v. Wade, 420 U.S. 113 (1973); see especially, George Grant, *English-Speaking Justice* (1985), p. 16.

24. Karen Hardee-Cleaveland and Judith Bannister, *Family Planning in China: Recent Trends,* U.S. Bureau of the Census (CIR Staff Paper no. 40) (May, 1988). For a brief outline of Marxist human rights theory see Jerome Shestack, "The Jurisprudence of Human Rights," in *Human Rights in International Law: Legal and Policy Issues* (T. Meron, editor 1984), p. 83.

25. Jacques Maritain, *The Rights of Man and Natural Law* (1986), p. 141.

26. *Id*, p. 104.

27. Walker Percy, *The Thanatos Syndrome* (1987), p. 128.

28. Joseph Ratzinger, "God and Freedom: Jesus, the Way, the Truth and the Life," reprinted in *Origins: CNS Documentary Service,* vol. 19, no. 36 (Feb. 8. 1990), p. 595.

29. *California Medicine,* vol. 113, no. 3 (Sept., 1970) reprinted in *The Human Life Review,* vol. 1, no. 1 (Winter, 1975), p. 103.

30. *Id*

Chapter 18

PASTORAL CONCERNS
THE CHURCH AND PUBLIC POLICY

BISHOP: Dr. Anderson, I'm very excited about the Catholic moment now being possible and the Protestant moment having past. Would you please develop that point.

DR. ANDERSON: I don't mean here a Protestant moment of the type that might be involved with Reinholt Niebuhr and his influence earlier in the century. I was thinking more in terms of the evangelicals and fundamentalists during the 1980's. It seems to me that the problem that Protestantism has in public policy is that it goes from one of two extremes as a result of not having a natural law tradition to guide it. It presents itself as either very secularized (in which it becomes indistinguishable from non-Christian participation in public policy) to, at the other extreme, very pietistic, that is, unable to relate to non-Christians. When you look at the fundamentalist preachers who were getting involved in politics and public policy during the 80's—Pat Robertson and Jerry Falwell—it is clear that they were not able to appeal beyond their constituency.

They had a very biblically-centered teaching which was good in terms of mobilizing their constituency but had a way of turning off many others. Therefore, they didn't have a bridge to move outside of their constituency. So while it was good for activating their people, it did not allow them to expand their base of support on public policy issues.

The Moral Majority has now disbanded and Pat Robertson's involvement in politics has come to an end at least for the time being. There was no internal dynamic within that movement that would allow it to expand and move beyond its own group of believers. That is why I think that the Protestant moment, such as it was, was limited by its own internal dynamic although it enjoyed a certain amount of success in the beginning.

I think the reason that there can be a Catholic moment is that the Church in its tradition offers a natural law "bridge" that can reach out to nonbelievers and at the same time be compatible with that other truth, the revealed truth.

BISHOP: Since Vatican II we have done a lot to prepare the laity in the Church. How can the laity confront in North America the points that you've addressed?

DR. ANDERSON: I would say two things. The first is that I believe that often the fundamental issues are not debated in many of these questions. It's rather clear in the question of abortion, but if you look at the issue of divorce during the late 1960's, there was really very little public discussion about what that kind of legislation was really all about. It changed not just the nature of divorce but the whole nature of marriage. There was almost no discussion of the anthropology that is behind a view of marriage that permits a no-fault divorce legal system as opposed to one that is structured to preserve marriage as an institution. I think there's a whole philosophical and anthropological level to many of these issues that has not been discussed.

The other point that I think needs to be developed further is the need to rethink what it means to be a Catholic citizen, and especially a Catholic public official in a pluralistic society. If we look at what some of the Catholic public officials who support legalized abortion are saying it doesn't have as much to do with abortion as it has to do with their self-identity as a Catholic citizen in a pluralistic society. We need to approach the issue at that level.

What is the responsibility of a public official and a Catholic in a secularized and pluralistic society? John F. Kennedy had an answer to that in 1960. It's been, to a large extent, the working model for thirty years. But it seems to me that it needs to be rethought to a certain extent.

BISHOP: I would like to know what are the means at your disposal to rally the forces of the sixty million Catholics to have them participate actively and respond to these issues. As you pointed out, if you don't do something within the next ten years, chances are that you will have lost the opportunity for some effective political impact on legislation.

Now, my second question would be do you sometimes work together with non-Catholic Christians, the Anglicans, the Lutherans, the others of that tradition who possibly have the same fundamental vision. Have you done that in the past or is it possible to envision that in the future?

In Canada, oftentimes, the bishops will go together before the government with the other Christian churches so that we can have a greater impact on the policies that may be decided.

DR. ANDERSON: In terms of the first question, the beginning of that direction was taken in November, when the bishops met in Baltimore and issued the statement on abortion. I think that the bishops in unity must take a leadership role in this whole area, and that is being done. It's certainly been done in the past, but I think it's being done with greater effect now and that needs to continue. It is too easy to trivialize this issue as a personal conflict or a "personal" fight between a bishop and a legislator in California or a cardinal and a governor in New York. It then devolves into a contest of personality and it shouldn't be that. I think it has to be a unified effort among the episcopacy. A pastoral statement on abortion might be considered as a first step. That statement could also involve a discussion of the responsibility of Catholics in public service in terms of the moral order and the formation of their own conscience and the relationship of their conscience to their public service.

I think that's a general first step. I think there are a lot of practical things that can be done in terms of increased education. More pastoral letters from bishops being read and things like that certainly need to be done.

It needs to be said that the Church's position is certainly clear on the issue of abortion. But a good number of people fail to appreciate the seriousness of the commitment. This situation worsens when the Church's teaching is not discussed from the pulpit or is not discussed in parish activities or there are no parish activities that reflect either a concern for pro-life education or promote alternatives to abortion, such as adoption. So there needs to be a much stronger emphasis in the parish life of the Church.

Now, as far as the second part of that question, coalitions with other Christians groups: to the extent that the pro-life movement has been successful in the United States, it seems to me it's been successful as a result of doing precisely that. There is a lot of fertile ground to be developed in an ecumenical sense of working with Evangelical or Protestant religious groups. Perhaps the biggest change in the pro-life demographics was the change during the early 1980's when the Southern Baptist Convention, the largest Protestant denomination in the U.S. switched its position from supporting the Supreme Court's decision in *Roe v Wade* to strongly opposing it. And they've been very active. They don't have the hierarchical system that we do. In fact, it's the opposite, but still they've been very active in southern states, quietly contacting legislators and actually turning some legislators around and certainly mobilizing their people.

BISHOP: I wonder how we as bishops could prevent the secular humanists from using the argument of pluralism to say you cannot impose your religious values while they're really imposing their own instead.

DR. ANDERSON: Well, that's really one of those difficult questions. I don't know if I have the best answer except I would think that you don't have to play by their rules. And in a sense, I wouldn't be bothered by that kind of a criticism and I would continue to be preaching what many would call a "prophetic interpretation" of reality.

That is, it seems to me that people who are public officials have a responsibility to employ natural law argument when entering into public debate. But pastors and Church leaders should not, because of any kind of claims of pluralism, be silenced, because they're imposing their views on the rest of us. I mean, that's what evangelization is really about. So I think, to be candid, at one level, we're respecting pluralism and at the other level, I assume we're out trying to convince everyone, so we are building a civilization that is based on Christian principles and the understanding of divinely revealed truths about the nature of the human person.

BISHOP: What does a bishop do vis-a-vis a very highly organized and dedicated if not fanatic single issue Catholic coalition when it comes time for elections in which there are also on the table issues of health, of environment and of taxation touching the entire economy: single issue, pro-life or pro-abortion.

DR. ANDERSON: Well, let me put it this way. We had in the recent gubernatorial election in Virginia a campaign highlighting a very, very clear-cut issue: Pro-life versus pro-abortion. The pro-abortion candidate was not a "personally-opposed-but" candidate. He was somebody who campaigned publicly that this was a public good, a public right. He put hundreds of thousands of dollars into media advertising attacking his opponent for being pro-life. That candidate was elected by less than 1 percent of the vote and he was elected with 44 percent of the Catholic vote.

Now, it seems to me that if somebody who champions public funding and legalization of abortion can obtain 44 percent of the Catholic vote, we have very little chance of really influencing the electoral outcome of a campaign.

Now, every campaign has particular specifics to make these kinds of things difficult. In the Virginia campaign it was the first time a Black candidate was running for governor and it was the first time a Black candidate was elected governor. In other states, it may be the first time a woman is running or it will be the first time that somebody else is running.

That's why I think it's very important that the Conference take a position, a very clear position on this issue; and, therefore, the bishops when they speak as a body, can speak without being hemmed in by the specifics of a particular campaign. I, for one, think that we're never going to solve the abortion issue politically unless we make it that type of an issue that is a decisive issue for us.

BISHOP: The bishops from the other countries may not realize that we've gone through a cataclysmic shift in the United States in the last six months. Just to capsule summarize it, the National Conference of Catholic Bishops has had a pro-life program for almost twenty years now and that involves three dimensions. Education, pastoral care and dealing with government. They have developed different strategies for dealing with government both at the federal level and at the state level. Most of that effort was directed towards either reversing the decisions of the 1973 Supreme Court decisions in *Roe v Wade* and *Doe v Bolton* or restraining other kinds of legislation that would make abortion easy. Mr. Anderson referred to some of them when he talked about the Hyde Amendment which is an amendment that goes on the appropriations bill each year to hold back money from abortion services.

Now those efforts had developed over the years and probably the pro-lifers had become fairly confident and maybe a little complacent. And I think they had become especially complacent during the Reagan years because they thought they had friends in high places. In July of this year, the Supreme Court of the United States pulled back from the 1973 decisions and two things happened. They set the stage for eventual reversal of *Roe v Wade*. And secondly, they triggered off a massive reaction from the pro-abortion forces and mostly, the radical feminists who then began to pour money into legislative campaigns such as the one Mr. Anderson just described in Virginia, as well as one in New Jersey that I know fairly well.

However, that has left the pro-life forces in something of a state of disorganization if not disarray. In order to go forward now they have to crystalize a new political plan and a program and that has to be more comprehensive than just trying to do one thing. Just restraining funds and just trying to reverse the Supreme Court is not enough. We have to have a program with a list of objectives so that if we lose on one of our objectives, we're still alive on the others. We have to confront the press and the media which we have not done effectively and in which we're being overwhelmed enormously right now and which faces us with massive expenditures of funds if we're going to try to do it and we probably do not have that kind of funding. We have proposals to raise money to do that but to do full scale media programs to reverse the present attitudes in the media would cost millions and millions of dollars that we don't have and really can't locate.

Nonetheless, we do have something: We have pulpits; we have educational programs that are in place and will be used to a greater degree than they have been perhaps in the past. And I think we have a renewal of commitment amongst the bishops. Again, Mr. Anderson referred to that when he said that the bishops issued a statement in November. Well, as you well know, issuing a statement doesn't do very much unless you back it up with a willingness to fight. But I think that the bishops in November realized that we're in this for a much longer fight than we originally had thought and that we have to organize ourselves a little bit better.

The Bishops' Pro-Life Committee now under the leadership of Cardinal O'Connor is intent on that kind of massive organization of Church forces throughout the United States first to establish a consistent and systematic program and to follow it methodically so as to eventually reinstate some kind of restrictive laws in regard to abortion and increasingly in regard to euthanasia, and secondly, to try to confront the massive propaganda brainwash that we face in the media. This is going to be a longer range, tougher and not as promising eventuality as the legislative area.

BISHOP: What were the salient points that turned that campaign around in favor of the pro-abortionists in Virginia? Was there something in the media that really turned a lot of people on so that they switched, so to speak?

DR. ANDERSON: Well, I think there are two things that are happening: First, the Supreme Court's decision in *Webster* was not a very good case for us because the *Webster* decision only cut back slightly on the application of *Roe v Wade* and, therefore, made onl minor regulations of abortion possible.

While the decision didn't do very much for us, it certainly showed the other side that *Roe v Wade's* days were numbered. Therefore, it activated them without giving us anything concretely.

But realistically, *Roe v Wade* could very well be overturned in the next year or two and probably will be or cut back decisively. That's number one.

Number two, during 1988 and 1989, the pro-abortion organizations invested a good deal of money into Madison Avenue and media consultants, polling, and in other political advisors and consultants to try to discover the demographics of the pro-life issue in terms of which individuals can be influenced and how.

Then they went to some very good advertising agencies in New York, Washington, and San Francisco to develop advertising campaigns that evoke a highly positive response among Americans. For example, the themes of freedom of choice, and getting the government out of your personal decision-making, frankly, were very positive themes that President Reagan was pushing for eight years. So in a sense, the Reagan years helped lay the groundwork for the recent pro-abortion success. It established a certain conservatism, a *laissez-faire* attitude towards government regulation that I think has helped allow the pro-abortion slogans and themes to resonate better than they had in the past.

So I would list those three characteristics: first, a shift in political view of the role of government; second, a very sophisticated marketing campaign; and third, the fact that *Webster* really changed the landscape in terms of the political debate. Organizations such as Planned Parenthood, NARAL, and NOW spent about 8 to 9 million dollars last year alone in national advertising to change public attitudes on abortion. They're going to spend more money this year. National Right to Life spent a good deal of money but I don't think that we've been matching dollar for dollar the pro-abortionists. And after all, Planned Parenthood, for example, makes about 30 to 40 million dollars a year through their abortion centers so it's a big business to them and they've got money to contribute for it.

BISHOP: In other words, we have to find some way to get more media presentation done?

DR. ANDERSON: Yes.

BISHOP: I'm surprised that you didn't mention in your reasons just now for the outcome of the election in Virginia the waffling by the Republican candidate Coleman. In the last months of the campaign, he shifted considerably from an at least partially pro-life position to a pro-abortion position. You mentioned the figure of 1 percent difference in the outcome of the election and I've heard that that translated into something like three voters per precinct. It's conceivable to me that there must have been at least three pro-life voters throughout all of Virginia who may have stayed away from the polls in view of Coleman's waffling. Isn't it possible that that was even a more significant factor than the more remote ones you just mentioned?

DR. ANDERSON: Let me say this. First of all, the Coleman campaign was very stupid in the way it handled the pro-life issue.

Pro-life people who were advising him on how to handle the issue certainly advised him differently than the way he handled it. It's true that there was a retrenchment, I would say, by Coleman. There was a tremendous reversal by the Republican candidate in New Jersey and a significant retrenchment by the Republican candidate in New York. But I think that Coleman did much less in those terms than the two Republicans in the other campaigns. Every pro-life organization that I know of worked hard for Coleman in Virginia and most pro-life organizations, as I recall, did not work for Coulter in New Jersey or Giuliani in New York.

So could Coleman have handled the issue better? Yes. But I don't think he moved from a pro-life to a pro-abortion position in the way that the candidates in New Jersey and New York City did. That's my assessment of it.

BISHOP: Just a few short comments. One Bishop has mentioned that we had settled into a kind of complacency over a period of time because of a certain success in keeping public acceptance of abortion from extending. But the fact of the matter is that from 1974, the total number of abortions in the United States has never fallen under a million and a half. If anybody could afford to be complacent in the face of that, it's crazy. I think it may well be true that there was a complacency but it's totally and absolutely unjustified. The figures can keep going. The last figure issued by the Center for Disease Control in Atlanta was more than 1.6 million. So whatever the success, the success has not been measurable in terms of more babies' lives being saved. On the matter of education, I don't think that we have yet become serious about education on the parish level. We don't have a lot of money for the media. We don't have the media on our side, but we have a lot of schools, we have a lot of church buildings where we have a kind of a captive audience. I don't mean on a Sunday morning, but many of our people—if they're asked to come for one presentation about what abortion is and what it does—those people would go away profoundly affected. It seems to me that every parish in our country, maybe with a few exceptions, should be showing at least once a month the kind of films that are available now that weren't available in 1973 and inviting people to come. But we haven't done that on any kind of a large scale.

I get constant complaints from people that they never hear a sermon on abortion. The answer that is given is that it might be upsetting to women in the congregation who have had an abortion. I think that's unreal. Those who are working with women who have had abortions often mention the terrible trauma that they run into five years or ten years after and at that time, there's nobody around to help them. If we continue to bury it as a topic from the pulpit, it's going to engender the idea that there is nobody to help them, nobody to look after them at all. I don't think we're doing what's within reach and what we could. I don't think that our schools are generating any enthusiasm on this question and I think that with young people there's a real possibility of that.

But again, I hear complaints from people who are pro-lifers that they find it harder to get in to give talks in Catholic schools than they do in public schools. I'm not saying that's a universal situation but it certainly exists in some areas and if it's true then we're shooting ourselves in the foot. We don't have a whole lot of money and I'm not trying to underestimate that. I don't know anything about political strategies but I get more and more convinced on this as I do on all church affairs that money is less important than dedicated people. If we can get people on fire to do something about this, they'll get the money they need and what's not there, they'll do without and manage at all and I don't think that that should become a big issue for us at all.

The issue itself is critical. Somebody mentioned whether it should be a single issue. If we were in Germany in the 1940's and had a vote on the holocaust, should it have been a single issue? There's no possibility of any other answer in saying it would have to be. We have killed in the United States two and a half times as many people as died in the whole of the holocaust, twenty-six million. I've never seen a figure for the holocaust that went over eleven million. I don't think there's any doubt about that.

What made the deepest impression, impact on me are two phrases from people who were early leaders in Operation Rescue: One, Randy Terry who says if you really believe it's murder, why don't you do something about it; and Joan Andrews who spent two-and-a-half years in solitary confinement for a non-violent crime of trying to unsuccessfully detach an abortion suction machine. Her explanation of why she did it was, "They are murdering my brothers and sisters." She said, "If you knew that your blood brother or sister were inside of a building about to be torn limb from limb or burnt to death, would you stay outside because there is a law against trespassing? Would you stay outside because somebody stood in the door and told you you had no right to pass?"

That's really the issue that's at stake and I think that we have to begin to confront it with the seriousness that's there. And there's a dozen things that need to be done and can be done. We can encourage people to pray. Old ladies who can't do a whole lot else can pray much better than many of us can here and in the long run that's going to make a gigantic difference.

We can try to help those in need. Women who are pregnant and single parents. And single parents in my area certainly normally means a woman who has been abandoned by the father of her child and left with the responsibility to raise it with very little in terms of resources. We can help them. We can help women who have had abortions. We can respond to the media and take on the arguments.

There are a whole slew of arguments across the board. The talk earlier brought that out to a great extent and many of us here are better capable or suited to answering those arguments than many others in the pro-life movement. We're not as well suited to demonstrating as they are but on intellectual arguments, most of us could do a whole lot that would mean more. We really have let them get away with it now for almost twenty years and the net result is that things get worse. More and more politicians will spring to the position. "I'm personally opposed but." We should make them accountable for that.

I grew up in a neighborhood where the politics was all Democrat. Nobody in my neighborhood believed in the honesty of politicians but they accepted that as a fact of life and we voted for the politicians that were a little bit more on our side than the other party was. But there's a certain amount of truth in that. The politicians now are screaming because the wind is blowing in a different direction and it means we've got to do something to make the wind blow back because if it does, they'll jump as fast as they jumped over and even more so.

DR. ANDERSON: I think in the past that pro-life politics has been split along party lines rather dramatically and that the pro-abortion candidate often tended to be a Democrat. What's happening this year, though, is that there's a huge effort in the Republican Party to reconsider whether the party should continue to have a pro-life plank in its national platform and whether pro-abortion candidates will be welcomed or promoted. So that unlike years past, the real battle on abortion is going to be fought this year within the Republican Party.

Therefore, the question of politicians who switch their position on abortion is going to be a big issue in the Republican Party this year. I believe that we have got to, sadly from my Republican perspective, defeat a number of Republican candidates who on other issues I would agree with. That will be the primary way of stanching the flow of candidates flip-flopping on abortion.

Therefore, 1990 presents us with a wonderful opportunity to be tremendously bipartisan or nonpartisan, if you will, in the articulation of the abortion issue and our pro-life position.

BISHOP: Has there been any attempt to research the relationship between this issue as a social issue and a moral issue and other socioeconomic issues? For the purpose of educating people and supporting a political stand, can you imagine the number of jobs that would be created just for the diaper industry alone for a million and a half babies.

DR. ANDERSON: Well, yes. For example, Alan Carlson at the Rockford Institute, a Lutheran, has done some very good work on this. What is the consequence of losing twenty-five million people from the economy in terms of productivity, taxes, and the gross national product? Even if you assume, the worst scenario, that a large percentage of these people would be welfare dependent, there still is a dramatic, detrimental effect on the economy.

We hear a lot of talk lately and we have heard a lot of talk about Social Security. But Social Security will never remain solvent if we continue on the downward slant in terms of population.

When Social Security was put into effect in the 1930's, there were two important conditions: Number one, there was approximately sixteen people paying in for every person that was taking out of the system; and number two, the age sixty-five was picked because that happened to be the life expectancy of the average male industrial worker. Today, we have fewer than three workers paying in for each person taking out of the system and as the population continues downward, the solvency of the system is going to be dramatically imperiled as the ratio of payors to payees continues to shift. The situation is even more acute in terms of health care financing under Medicare. So there are a lot of other social connections to the abortion issue that should be brought out that haven't been brought out enough.

BISHOP: In your education program, do you really ask people why do so many women want abortion?

I think we can try to face the law, we can try to face the abortion clinic and so on, but is not the major problem a problem of mentality?

DR. ANDERSON: Yes, I think of the section from *Laborem exercens* in which the Holy Father writes that the true ethical measure of any economic system and society is the value that it places on motherhood. That doesn't mean Mother's Day once a year. That means something quite different. Since the 1960's, at least in the United States, there's been a tremendous shift in terms of employment, other economic indicators, tax structure, and persons' expectations away from valuing motherhood and supporting a family based upon marriage towards other kinds of values.

We have, for example, no-fault divorce in virtually every state. The implicit message in that system is that commitment to motherhood, commitment to children is not valued and will not be protected or will not be rewarded. If you doubt that, take a look at the *Divorce Revolution* by Lenore Weitzman, perhaps the most damning attack on no-fault divorce that's been written.

But I think we need to reopen the whole question of what the Holy Father makes central in *Laborem exercens*—the value of motherhood. We need to look at it in all of its ramifications and begin to defend it on social grounds, on economic grounds, on tax grounds and to be serious about it. If we do that, then I think, we will have gone a long way towards dismantling the social and economic infrastructure of abortion.

Chapter 19

ENDNOTE: PANEL DISCUSSION

CENTRAL QUESTION: IS THIS "THE CATHOLIC MOMENT" FOR THE FUTURE?

George Weigel
David L. Schindler, Ph.D.
The Reverend Avery Dulles, S.J., S.T.D.

I. George Weigel

Since I'm batting first, I think we should begin with some definitions. And because the phrase "the Catholic Moment" is his, we should begin with Richard John Neuhaus's definitions of what the "Catholic moment" is:

"This ... is the moment in which the Roman Catholic Church in the world can and should be the lead church in proclaiming and exemplifying the Gospel. This can and should also be the moment in which the Roman Catholic Church in the United States assumes its rightful role in the culture-forming task of constructing a religiously informed public philosophy for the American experiment in ordered liberty."[1]

By "Catholic moment," then, Pastor Neuhaus means two things: an evangelical opportunity, and an opportunity to help shape public moral argument over the right-ordering of American society. Neuhaus is clear, as we all should be, that the first of these—the evangelical opportunity—is far more important than the second. In fact, it is very unlikely that the Church will have much of significance to contribute to the debate over public policy unless and until it has grasped and internalized the evangelical opportunity that is the core of the "Catholic moment" proposition.

Why is this "the Catholic moment," in both senses of the term?

There are demographic reasons for making this claim. Religion remains, against all the confident predictions of the secularization theorists, a powerful force in American life. Moreover, we are now, indisputably, in the midst of a circulation of elites in American religion. The great churches of the Protestant mainline are in rapid, and probably irreversible, deliquescence. The "growing ends" of American religion—the likeliest successors to mainline Protestantism's traditional culture-forming role—are Roman Catholicism, and evangelical and fundamentalist Protestantism.[2] But, and here I am speaking of the "public" side of the "Catholic moment" proposition, American evangelicalism lacks a developed social ethic and a mediating language for making moral arguments in the public square. Catholicism, on the other hand, has—or should have—both. Thus the door is open to a more vigorous leadership role for Catholicism in shaping the contours of public moral argument in the United States.

(Seizing this public dimension of the "Catholic moment" requires, parenthetically, internalizing something that few of us seem to have come to grips with, *viz.,* that Roman Catholics are 25% of the American population. Roman Catholicism, in other words, is the largest single voluntary association in America. Moreover, American Catholicism is, in the main, a middle-middle and upper-middle class Church, which means that we are in a far more advantageous position to leverage American culture than we were a generation or two ago. Yet how often do we still think of ourselves as an embattled, marginalized, beset minority?)

So the demographics support the "Catholic moment" proposition, and particularly the public dimension of the proposition. But demographics are statistics, and we all know about lies, damned lies, and statistics. What other evidence might we cite for this being the "Catholic moment?"

If Christians have struggled throughout this past century with the question of the compatibility of classic Christian truth claims and modernity, then seizing the "Catholic moment" will necessarily involve the Church's developing a persuasive answer to that question. I believe that the approach to such an answer is personified, providentially, in Pope John Paul II: who, Father McBrien notwithstanding, powerfully incarnates the model of a modern intellectual who is not a modernist. The pope's ministry should be understood as completing, rather than cancelling, the famous image of John XXIII as the pope who opened the windows of the Church to the modern world. Contrary to the crabbed views of many in the current Catholic opinion establishment, John Paul II's project is not to slam the windows closed (and the fingers on the windowsill be damned). No, and as Pastor Neuhaus put it so well, "John Paul II has entered the modern world to help open the windows of the modern world to the worlds of which it is a part"[3]—which include, pre-eminently, the worlds of transcendent truth and love.

Such a position, *ahead* of the now sterile argument between "liberals" and "traditionalists", seems an appropriate one from which to seize both the evangelical and public dimensions of this "Catholic moment." It is now quite clear that the churches of cultural accommodation—the churches which have acquiesced most supinely to the modernist quest for the unencumbered, autonomous self—which are hemorrhaging congregants. Americans, and I dare say people around the world, see little point in belonging to an institution which cannot tell you, with any certitude, what puts you inside its boundaries, and what puts you out. Despite the confusions and distractions of the past twenty years or so, most Catholics, and indeed most Americans, understand that there is still *content* to being a Catholic, and that while there are many legitimate expressions of that content, there are both boundaries and bottom lines.[4]

In the Eighties, in other words, American Catholicism has slowly, painfully, incompletely, but inexorably moved beyond porousness. Which is to say, we have moved beyond the deconstructionist impulse that asks, "How little can I believe and do and remain a Catholic?", and on to the far more interesting question, "How much of this rich, complex tradition have I made my own?"

The real answer to porousness, I hasten to add, is not a kind of Catholic fundamentalism. To reject the Jacobinism of the *National Catholic Reporter* is not to embrace the a-historical souredness of *The Wanderer.* Seizing the "Catholic moment" requires Catholic leaders—laity, priests, and bishops—capable of articulating the ancient truths of the Gospel, the Creeds, and the Councils in language and imagery that grips that contemporary imagination and calls individuals to a decision for Christ.

I must confess, in all candor, that I find us short of such leaders today. But we don't lack for models, and in our own American Catholic experience. John Carroll, John England, James Gibbons, and Isaac Hecker were all exemplars of what we need today: leaders formed in the classic tradition of the Church, yet capable of developing its catechesis to meet the demands of new cultural and political circumstances. A Church which could produce such giants in the 19th century, and under less favorable economic and cultural circumstances, should not be without the wit and will to do so in the 21st.

But getting that kind of vigorous, virile leadership means getting our priorities straight, and keeping the attention of bishops, priests, and laity focused on the two great challenges in the "Catholic moment" proposition: the challenge of preaching the Gospel, and the challenge of shaping public moral argument over the nation's business.

The leadership we need will not emerge in a Church that is constantly beset with the kind of narcissistic crisis-talk we have suffered for twenty years.

The leadership we need will not emerge in a Church that is choking on bureaucracy at the parish, diocesan, and national levels.

The leadership we need will not emerge in a Church whose public witness is primarily defined in lobbying terms, a Church whose activist wing and whose social ministry agencies are careening down the path to marginality pioneered by the churches of the Protestant mainline and the National Council of Churches.

The leadership we need will not emerge in a Church that is afraid of the intellectual life, any more than it will emerge in a Church which defines "the intellectual life" in terms borrowed, at heavy interest, from Harvard and Brown and Stanford.

The "Catholic moment" proposition is a call to greatness, all the more striking for having been issued by a Lutheran pastor. It is a call to reclaim the Christian distinctiveness that marked the public ministry of Carroll and England and Gibbons and Hecker: men who knew that their primary task, and indeed their great glory, was to tell, in and out of season, about the person and message of Jesus Christ. For in that Person and that Gospel, they believed, were found the answers to those perennial questions of identity and purpose and meaning that stirred human hearts in Baltimore and Charleston and New York in the 19th century, as they had in first century Jerusalem, and as they surely will in 21st century Dallas.

This moment, this "Catholic moment" if you will, is a time of great possibility. The bishops of the Church need to communicate this, with enthusiasm and vigor. It is a great thing to be a Catholic in America in the last decade of the 20th century. This culture of ours, for better and for worse (and usually for both), will set the cultural agenda for the world in the 21st century, as indeed it has for much of the 20th. We are in a distinctive, and unprecedented, position to shape American culture, and to rebuild its casements on those classic Jewish and Christian understandings about the human person, human communities, human history, and human destiny which, we believe, are the keys to the creation of a society fit for men and women created in the image and likeness of God.

Will we do it? I don't know. The "Catholic moment" is a possibility, not a certainty. But the opportunity before us is greater than at any time since Leonard Calvert and Father Andrew White got off the *Ark* on St. Clement's Island on March 25, 1634.

Notes

1. Richard John Neuhaus, *The Catholic Moment: The Paradox of the Church in the Post-Modern World* (San Francisco: Harper & Row, 1988), p. 283.

2. Cf. Wade Clark Roof and William McKinney, *American Mainline Religion: Its Changing Shape and Future* (New Brunswick: Rutgers University Press, 1987).

3. Neuhaus, *op.cit.,* p. 284.

4. The bishops' pastoral firmness, at the 1989 Baltimore NCCB meeting, on the question of Catholic public officials and the abortion debate post-*Webster* was a welcome expression of a commitment to a distinctively Catholic presence in the public arena. Moreover, it reminded many who may have needed reminding that "pastoral" and "firmness" are not antinomies.

II. David L. Schindler, Ph.D.

An answer to the assigned question requires an accurate reading of Catholicism on the one hand and of the history and current state of American culture on the other.

I.1. For the present context, the meaning of Catholicism can be best gotten at in terms of Vatican II's "call to holiness": "It is therefore quite clear that all Christians in any state or walk of life are called to the fullness of Christian life and to the perfection of love . . . " (*Lumen gentium,* no. 40).

I.2. The nature of Christian life and its perfection in love are given their form in the trinitarian God as revealed in Jesus Christ (through the Church by the Holy Spirit). It is Jesus Christ who "fully reveals man to himself and brings to light his highest calling" (*Gaudium et spes,* no. 22). The Word of God reveals to us "that the fundamental law of human perfection, and consequently of the transformation of the world, is the new commandment of love" (*GS,* no. 38).

I.3. The proposal, then, is that Vatican II has affirmed what can justly be called a kind of Christocentrism ("Christ is the light of humanity [*Lumen gentium*]": *LG,* no. 1),—and indeed this Christocentrism has been emphasized and developed further during the pontificate of John Paul II.[1] *All* human beings are called, from the depths of their being, to the perfection of love, and this love is given its form (or "logic": *logos*) in Jesus Christ. The mission of Christians, given in baptism, is thus to assist each and every person toward the realization of this call (*LG,* nos. 17, 31).

I.4. For the present context, it will suffice to record three main features of this call to holiness as understood in the documents of Vatican II: transformation, eschatology, and prudence. (a) "Transformation" tells us that we must seek to integrate (incarnate) all that we are and do and make in terms of the form of love as revealed in Jesus Christ. (b) "Eschatology" tells us that, because of finitude and sin, this transformation and integration to which we are called will nonetheless be complete only in the next life; and that we must therefore also become prophetic critics who ever remind cultures that their human activity is not to be confused "with the final ordering that is the prerogative of Christ."[2] (c) *Dignitatis humanae* (no. 14) tells us that the dynamic for integration must

300

proceed in a way which is respectful of the dignity and freedom of other sojourners (*DH,* nos. 1, 2, 3), and thus in a way which is never premature or coercive. The methods by which Christians seek to order all things in and toward Jesus Christ must be methods consistent with the love that is revealed in Christ—and in this sense methods of prudence.

II.1. To assist us in moving toward a judgment about American culture, I offer three comments. To begin with, it seems to me important to distinguish the Enlightenment tradition as reflected in the revolutionary period in France from that characteristic of the revolutionary period in America. In contrast to the Jacobin animus against religion, and its fallout into viciousness, the disposition of the American Founding was favorable toward both religion and the development of civic virtue. Indeed, America's characteristic generosity is evident today in its continuing humanitarianism.

But there has nonetheless been a downside to all of this, which is reflected at the present time (for example) in the holocaust of abortion and in pervasive consumerism.

How, then, do we make sense of the ambiguity here, wherein a deep generosity and religiosity in America exists coincident with a virulent selfishness and secularism? The work of the Jewish philosopher of religion, Will Herberg, may be helpful in sorting through this ambiguity.

II.2. In the face of public opinion polls which then (1955) indicated—as they do again today—a resurgence of religion, Herberg argued that the very conditions making for this resurgence were also what accounted for secularism.[3] Herberg's argument, in other words, is that, in America, religion and secularism have a peculiar way of turning into each other (*PCJ,* p. 3). Simultaneous with a strong sense of religion identification, Americans nonetheless live and think "in terms of a framework of reality and value remote from the religious beliefs" they profess (*PCJ,* p. 2)—a framework of reality which is not so much an overt philosophy as "an underlying, often unconscious, orientation of life and thought" (*PCJ,* p. 1).

Herberg labeled this orientation the "American Way of Life," and suggested that it could "best be understood as a kind of secularized Puritanism" (p. 81). Some of the main terms he employs to describe this way of life are: democracy; free enterprise; pluralism; equalitarianism; optimism; humanitarianism; individualism;

301

pragmatism; judgment of worth by achievement; extroversion; activism; moralism; and so on. There is of course much ambiguity in these terms. Herberg's point is simply that the terms reflect goals and values which all Americans are expected to share, that is, *by virtue of being American.* The Christian and Jewish faiths, rather than really shaping these values, transforming them where necessary, have tended instead to do little more than provide for their "sanctification and dynamic" (*PCJ,* p. 271). Herberg is thus led to the conclusion that "secularization of religion could hardly go further" (*PCJ,* p. 83).[4]

II.3. Thirdly, then, as a way of making sense of what Herberg—rightly in my judgment—calls attention to here as the peculiar coincidence of religiosity and secularism in America, I propose that we distinguish the intention and good will of Americans on the one hand, from the deeper logic or order of American culture on the other. The innate good will of Americans, it seems to me, is what gets reflected in the humanitarianism and strong religious identification characteristic of much of our history. On the other hand, it is the deeper logic—what Herberg calls the unconscious "framework of reality"—which accounts for America's selfishness and secularism. This peculiar mix of moral generosity and a deeper logic of selfishness is the essence of the liberal tradition as carried in America.

I would single out for present purposes two salient features of this logic. (a) First, it is a logic of autonomy, in the sense that relation to God and to others is a matter of choice (or voluntary) before it is a matter of being (or ontological). I suggest that it is precisely this logic of autonomy, with its consequent self-centered conception of human rights, which has made America vulnerable to official acceptance of abortion. (b) Secondly, America's logic seems to me a logic rather of having and externality than of being and interiority. I suggest that it is precisely this underlying logic of having which has given rise to our present culture of pervasive consumerism, with its attendant trivialization and neglect of the contemplative and non-utilitarian dimensions of truth, beauty, and goodness.

I would emphasize that any intelligent appeal to the pluralism of religious beliefs and practices in America must take account of the unitary character of the logic of American culture as noted here.[5]

III.1. With this, then, I return to the assigned question about the state of America relative to Catholicism. My quarrel with the suggestion of a "Catholic moment" as made, for example, by Richard Neuhaus, George Weigel, and Michael Novak, is whether that notion as they understand it does not offer us what is merely an-other—Catholic—version of the American Way of Life as thematized by Herberg, that is, with the same mix of moral generosity coupled with a deeper logic of selfishness and secularization. If I may put the matter as sharply as possible—and its rhetorical form may serve in any case to stimulate our discussion—my question is whether their "Catholic moment" does not offer us what is merely a conservative version of yuppie culture—a yuppie culture with a moral conscience. On the one hand, these men urge an America which would, for example, restrict abortion and in general avoid moral relativism. On the other hand, the virtues which they tend disproportionately to extol, now in the name of Catholicism, are those which are consistent with and attendant upon the long-standing liberal tradition in America of democracy and capitalism (for example, entrepreneurship, tolerance, voluntarism, and the like). (Which of the terms proper to Herberg's "American Way of Life" undergoes significant revision in the work of these men?)

The concern here is not to deny the legitimacy in principle of such (liberal) virtues, but rather, with Herberg, to direct attention to their profound ambiguity. The concern is to point out how deep is the transformation required to give these virtues a form adequate to the Gospel perspective as carried in the Catholic tradition. We must recognize, for example, how important a disposition of contemplative prayer is for all human activity—precisely for its integrity as human; how deeply the Gospel reverses the consumerist and extroverted orientation of our culture; how profoundly the cruciform character of Christian love reverses America's prevalent self-centered logic of rights.

III.2. In sum, my criticism of Mr. Weigel and his Neo-Conservative colleagues is twofold. First, in terms of the call to holiness urged at Vatican II: I fear that the "Catholic moment" proposed by these men continues to give support, however unwittingly, to the two-tiered approach to holiness characteristic of much of post-Tridentine and pre-Vatican II spirituality, and thereby to the dualism of nature and grace implied by the spirituality.[6] That is—though these men make their claim now in the name of a prudential realism—there remains, in effect, the graced life of holiness to which the few are called, and an ethics of nature—what I would term a kind of bourgeois virtue and civility—for the rest of us.[7]

Secondly, to put the same point in terms of the main features of the call to holiness: I fear that these men emphasize prudence and eschatology to the neglect of transformation. The result—inevitably—is an all too worldly sense of this world and an all too external and distant sense of the world to come.

IV. What, then, is my own response to the question put to our panel? I believe that there is indeed a profound stirring in the religious soul of America. This stirring, manifest for example in the youth counterculture of the 60s and the evangelical revival of the mid-to-late 70s, is described in studies like those of Roof and McKinney.[8] But, to understand the deepest source and meaning of this religious stirring, we need only listen to the Gospel as interpreted in the memorable words of St. Augustine, who reminds us that our hearts—not just Christian hearts but all human hearts and therefore including also American hearts—are made for the infinite trinitarian God of Jesus Christ, and that their restlessness is therefore restlessness for him. In the light of all this, then, I do believe that the time may indeed be ripe for a Catholic moment in American history—perhaps now as never before. But this moment has a chance of occurring, and will be recognizably Catholic, only on the condition that we read and respond correctly—that is, sufficiently radically—to the religious restlessness of America.

Here, then, is my general proposal: that the key to any possibly Catholic moment lies above all in getting clear about the nature of religion or religiosity. The difficulties which face us in our present circumstances in America bear most fundamentally on the nature of the human being's relation to God, considered, that is, against the backdrop of the liberal and Englightenment tradition on the one hand, and the Catholic tradition on the other. The difficulties are spiritual and theological before they are political, economic, or legal (for example, matters of the church-state relation).

Religion or religiosity, on a truly Catholic understanding, is given its form in the agapic and kenotic—the radically other-centered, self-emptying—love revealed by God in Jesus Christ. The first and basic question for a Catholic, therefore, concerns the sense in which this agapic love should inform the religion to which one would give witness in one's public life and thought. Further and more specifically, the question for a Catholic concerns the ways in which this agapic love should give form to what one means by "natural law," "rights," "openness to transcendence," "public philosophy," "religiously-grounded values," "common human experience," "civic virtue" and all the other terms which are so central in the present debate.[9] Working through the answers to these questions will of course not yet resolve all the difficult prudential and legal-juridical issues regarding religion in relation to public life. But it will nonetheless help us, as we turn to take up these further issues, to avoid, at least in principle, confusing a liberal form of religion with a Catholic form of religion. Avoiding such confusion is the necessary condition for judging truly what suffices as clothing for America's currently naked public square and culture.

Notes

1. For but one important example, see *Redemptor hominis.*

2. Edward Goerner, *Peter and Caesar* (New York: Herder and Herder, 1965), p. 270.

3. Will Herberg, *Protestant—Catholic—Jew* (Chicago: University of Chicago Press, 1983), p. 3.

4. That is, because America's secularization, unlike that often characteristic of European and indeed Eastern cultures, is "found within the churches themselves and is expressed through men and women who are sincerely devoted to religion" (p. 271).

5. In connection with this suggestion of a kind of unitary logic in America, it is interesting to reflect on Tocqueville's statement that America was more Cartesian than any nation he knew (*Democracy in America,* vol. II, pt. 1, ch. 1), as well as on his justly famous claim: "I know no country in which, speaking generally, there is less independence of mind and true freedom of discussion as in America" (vol. I, pt. 2, ch. 7). Or again, see Alasdair MacIntyre's statement that "the contemporary debates within modern political systems are almost exclusively between conservative liberals, liberal liberals, and radical liberals" (*Whose Justice, Which Rationality?* [Notre Dame: University of Notre Dame Press, 1988], p. 392). The question of the logic of American culture has been treated at length in my "Grace and the Form of Nature and Culture," *Catholicism and Secularization in America: Essays on Nature, Grace, and Culture,* ed. by David L. Schindler (Notre Dame: Communio Books/OSV Press, 1990).

6. There are, it seems to me, differences between Neuhaus, Weigel, and Novak relative to the point suggested here—differences which, not surprisingly, are reflective of the Lutheran (Neuhaus) and Catholic (Weigel and Novak) traditions in which they respectively stand. To generalize, although they all—in my judgment—leave intact a modern dualism of grace and nature, Neuhaus has tended to develop his arguments more in the language of "paradox," Weigel and Novak in the language of "natural law." Nonetheless, these three have made a point of presenting a united front publicly; and I think they are right to do so, for

their projects converge on major issues. For further discussions pertinent to my criticism of Neuhaus, Weigel, and Novak as outlined in the present lecture, see my articles in *Communio*, Vol. XIV, No. 3 (Fall, 1987) and Vol. XV, No. 1 (Spring, 1988) (the latter issue includes a response by Weigel); in *The Thomist*, Vol. 53, No. 1 (January, 1989) (on Neuhaus); and in *30 Days* (May, 1989 and June, 1989) (the latter issue includes a response by Novak, Neuhaus, and Weigel).

7. My point here is not at all to suggest that natural law no longer has a place in the discussion of Catholicism and American culture. Quite to the contrary: the main Catholic tradition holds that nature—and hence by implication some sense of natural law—is never eliminated or replaced, either by sin or by grace. My intention is merely to suggest that recognition of this should serve not as the ending point but as the starting point of discussion. For the pertinent question is how the one final end given (de facto) by grace reaches into nature and thus in fact already orders nature from within. To put it more concretely, the question is how Jesus Christ, that is, the agapic and kenotic love revealed in Jesus Christ, gives form to nature, from the beginning of nature's existence. (Cf. *Gaudium et spes*, no. 22: Jesus Christ "fully reveals man to himself.") To what extent is that love necessary for the form and content of any legitimate appeal to natural law?

If I might offer a pertinent rule of thumb, I would say that any appeal to a natural law argument which does not cost a transformation or conversion in one's being is likely, given the context of contemporary America, to be liberal, which is to say too pale or minimalistic.

The work of Alasdair MacIntyre, Stanley Hauerwas, and Vigen Guroian is generally helpful for the line of argument intended here. The work of Hans Urs von Balthasar, Henri de Lubac, and Joseph Ratzinger sets the theological context for that line of argument.

8. Wade Clark Roof and William McKinney, *American Mainline Religion* (New Brunswick, NJ: Rutgers University Press, 1987).

9. It seems to me useful to ponder here how classical American liberals such as Madison, Jefferson, or Franklin might answer this question, that is, in contrast to Catholic Christians such as Balthasar, Ratzinger, de Lubac, or Pope John Paul II.

III. Father Dulles

The proposition that ours is the "Catholic moment" could be true or false, probable or improbable, according to how one understands the key term. It can best be understood, I submit, according to the mind of those who have coined it. Richard John Neuhaus in his 1987 book, *The Catholic Moment*, seems to have originated the term. A Catholic interpretation has been provided by George Weigel in his *Catholicism and the Renewal of American Democracy* (1989). Neither of these authors is saying that we are about to witness a mass of conversions to the Catholic Church, nor does either predict that the Catholic moment, as they define it, will be successfully realized. Their central contention is that the Roman Catholic Church is today called to take the lead in the culture-forming task of constructing a religiously informed public philosophy for the American experiment in ordered liberty. For their conception of the American experiment both these thinkers rely heavily on the work of John Courtney Murray.

I personally agree with Neuhaus and Weigel that the Catholic Church is uniquely qualified to raise public discourse in this country to a more substantive level by drawing on the twin sources of biblical revelation and classical wisdom. Roman Catholicism has a number of resources that equip it for this task. These include, first of all, its traditional recognition of the dignity of the human person as having been created in the image of God and as still retaining that image notwithstanding the effects of original sin. Secondly, the Catholic Church is heir to a rich fund of biblical and liturgical symbolism, empowering it to effect conversion and to maintain the loyalty of its own membership. Thirdly, the Church's natural law approach to moral reasoning enables it to engage in dialogue with nonbelievers. And finally, it has built up a valuable heritage of social ethics sustained by the principles of personalism, the common good, solidarity, and subsidiarity.

All of these resources are much needed in our time when individualistic utilitarianism, pragmatism, positivism, and emotivism have taken a heavy toll on the kind of ethical and political reasoning that was familiar to the authors of the Declaration of Independence, the Constitution, and the Bill of Rights. In many respects

Catholics are today, as Murray contended, the legitimate heirs to the propositions on which our republic was founded.

Neither Neuhaus nor Weigel is unaware of the debilitating influences of anti-authoritarian liberalism and neurotic restorationism. In place of the modernity of the left and the anti-modernity of the right they propose a post-modernity that draws creatively on authoritative sources to nurture a greater fidelity to the gospel and a fuller human life. Pope John Paul II and Cardinal Ratzinger, in their opinion, are seeking to reestablish continuity with a long-standing tradition that is today threatened by libertarianism on the one hand and authoritarianism on the other. Both authors recognize the need for a new self-discipline in the Catholic theological community, a new ecumenism that reaches out to evangelical Protestants, and a style of public discourse based on confidence of universal human reason.

The Neuhaus-Weigel project is sometimes understood as an effort to commit the Church to political neoconservativism philosophy, embroiling the Church in secular issues. I prefer to understand them in a different way. I hear them as asserting that the Church makes its greatest contribution to the political order when it insists on the primacy of the inner life of faith. The Church, they believe, best serves the world by being unabashedly the Church. They deny that it is the hierarchy's business to solve all political, social, and economic problems. Instead of becoming one political agent among others, the Church, they hold, must strive to keep all political proposals under moral judgment.

If we define the Catholic moment as Neuhaus and Weigel do, with the many cautions and reservations they provide, we may agree that this is indeed the Catholic moment. These authors can help to arouse in Catholics the sense of tradition, the self-confidence, and the openness to dialogue that are needed to meet the challenges they describe.

In their books Neuhaus and Weigel concentrate almost entirely on the task of constructing "a religiously informed public philosophy." Yet they admit, even insist, that the principal task of the Church is to proclaim and exemplify the gospel, and that the maintenance of this priority is essential for their program. By not developing this latter point, Neuhaus and Weigel may seem to define the Catholic moment too narrowly.

To spell out what needs to be made more explicit in the Neuhaus-Weigel proposal, I would suggest that the Catholic Church should deliberately adopt a two-track program. In matters of public policy it may promote an ethics based on reason or natural law and a political philosophy that stands in the classical American tradition. But for the religious formation, guidance, and motivation of its members the Church must insist on the primacy of biblical revelation and the symbols of the Catholic tradition. A successful dialogue with contemporary culture requires that American attitudes and projects be tested and scrutinized in the light of the gospel. The impression must not be given that reason can supplant the need for faith or that some generalized civil religion can take the place of Christ and the Church. Only when paired with a renewed attention to the specifics of Catholic Christianity can the neoconservative program hope to reap the full potential of the "Catholic moment."

Index

313